# Lobbying the Corporation

# LOBBYING THE CORPORATION

## Citizen Challenges to Business Authority

---

DAVID VOGEL

Basic Books, Inc., Publishers    New York

Portions of this book have appeared in a different form in the following articles by the author.

"The Politicization of the Corporation." *Social Policy*, May–June 1974, pp. 57–63.

"The Corporation as Government: Challenges and Dilemmas." *Polity* 8, no. 1 (1975): 5–37.

"The Corporate Board: Membership and Public Pressure." *Executive*, spring, 1977, pp. 8–11.

Library of Congress Cataloging in Publication Data

Vogel, David, 1947–
   Lobbying the corporation.

   Bibliography: p. 229
   Includes index.
   1.   Industry—Social aspects—United States.
2.   Corporations—United States.  I.  Title.
HD60.5.U5V627     301.5'1     78–54496
ISBN: 0–465–04157–4

TO VIRGINIA

*With Love and Respect*

# Contents

# Preface

THE IDEA for this book first occurred to me when I was a graduate student in the Department of Politics at Princeton University. In the course of writing a dissertation on the political and economic significance of contemporary changes in public attitudes toward the large corporation, I was struck by the novel form in which many public criticisms of the corporation had come to be expressed. Those seeking to change the policies and challenge the prerogatives of management were not confining their efforts to pressuring the government: they were taking many of their grievances directly to the firm. I documented and briefly analyzed this development, first in a chapter of my thesis and subsequently in a lengthy paper entitled "Contemporary Criticism of Business: The Publicization of the Corporation," presented at the 1973 Convention of the American Political Science Association. This book is an outgrowth of that essay.

The completion of this project was delayed two years, primarily by the researching and writing of *Ethics and Profits: The Crisis of Confidence in American Business*, which I coauthored with Leonard Silk. The delay proved fortuitous. By the mid-seventies, the impact of direct challenges to business had significantly increased from when I first identified them as a distinctive political phenomenon. This not only meant that far more material was available, but the persistence and steady expansion of citizen demands on business between 1973 and 1977 confirmed my earlier appraisal of their political significance. In the interval, I also had the invaluable experience of working closely with Leonard Silk, whose writing style provides a model of clarity and economy that I have tried to emulate.

In the course of researching the history of citizen challenges to business I frequently found myself my own subject. I recall, as a teen-ager, picketing the local branch of Woolworth's in New York City in order to show support for the sit-ins in the South, and as a graduate student, picketing recruiters for the Dow Chemical Corporation. Like a good many of my contemporaries, I refrained from buying Saran Wrap and went without eating grapes for several years. I also dimly recollect voting my three shares of General Motors stock in favor of the proxy proposals offered by "Campaign GM" in 1970 and 1971. I was not at the time aware that I was engaging in a new form of political expression; that awaited my role as a scholar.

# Preface

This book, however, is not a brief for citizen challenges to business; it is an analysis of them. It is a study of the emergence of an arena of political conflict, not a study of vice and virtue. My extensive personal interaction with corporate executives, both during and since the researching of *Ethics and Profits*, has given me an invaluable understanding of their concerns. I have tried to describe both their perspectives and that of their critics as fairly and as accurately as possible. Nevertheless, I want to make my bias explicit: I find myself on the whole sympathetic to the efforts of corporate activists. While I neither support all their demands nor uncritically accept their vision of corporate accountability, I think their overall impact has been a positive one. Debate over the social and moral implications of corporate decisions is too important to be confined to the governmental process; it needs to be conducted in as many forums as possible.

This book owes much to the assistance and encouragement of several people, and I am pleased to acknowledge their contributions. My research was greatly facilitated by the willingness of Timothy Smith of the Inter-Faith Center on Corporate Responsibility, Jamie Heard of the Investor Responsibility Research Council, Alice Tepper Marlin of the Council on Economic Priorities, and Mike Phillips of the Glide Foundation to make their publications and files available to me. The secretaries of the School of Business Administration and the staff of the Institute of Business and Economic Research at the University of California, Berkeley, typed various drafts of the manuscript. The greater part of the burden of the task of translating my scrawls into intelligible prose fell to Marcy McGaugh, who performed the task with her usual good cheer and efficiency. Stephanie Lenway, my research assistant, helped gather and organize research materials, and Paul Tiffany assisted me in the preparation of the footnotes; their cooperation and diligence is deeply appreciated.

This book could not have been written without the four years of generous financial assistance provided by the Institute for Business and Economic Research. Writing was also facilitated by the summer support made available by the School of Business Administration.

Dow Votaw and Joseph Pratt, my colleagues at the School of Business Administration, Michael Rogin of the Department of Political Science at Berkeley, Phillip Brenner of the Department of Political Science of the University of Maryland, Phillip Blumberg, dean of the Law School at the University of Connecticut, Theodore Lowi of the Department of Government at Cornell, Karen Orren of the Department of Political Science at UCLA, Lynn Eden of the University of Michigan, and David Langsam of the Chase Manhattan Bank were kind enough to read over various drafts of the manuscript. Their perceptive comments and criticisms made a significant contribution to the tone, style, and content of this study; its remaining shortcomings reflect my stubbornness.

In addition, Timothy Smith, Alice Tepper Marlin, Jamie Heard, my colleague Edwin Epstein, William Maslow of the American Jewish Congress, John Holcomb of the Foundation for Public Affairs, Howard Schomer of the United Church of Christ, and Fred Smith of the Center for Urban Encounter checked various sections of the book for accuracy. None of these individuals bears responsibility for the final product; that burden rests entirely in my hands.

Two names are missing from the above list: Raymond Bauer of the Harvard Business School and H. H. Wilson of the Department of Politics at Princeton University. Both died shortly before the first draft of the manuscript was completed. The material prepared by the Corporate Responsiveness Research Group at Harvard under Bauer's direction provided much of the data on which this study is based, and I deeply regret that he was not able to critically evaluate my use of it. H. H. Wilson helped inspire and sustain my interest in the corporation during the years before business again become a fashionable subject of academic inquiry. His influence has been far greater than he knew.

A particular debt of gratitude is owed to my editor at Basic Books, Martin Kessler, both for encouraging me to pursue this project and for insisting that a book can be both scholarly and intelligible.

I can never adequately acknowledge the contributions of my parents, Charlotte and Harry, for instilling in me both a dedication to learning and a fascination with politics. I also want to thank my children, Philip and Barbara, for the interest they have shown in my work and for putting up with all the hours I've had to spend at the typewriter. My deepest appreciation is to my wife, Virginia, who encouraged my effort over the seemingly endless period of time that it took to complete this study; her faith in me helped sustain my own.

Oakland, California
May 1978

# CHAPTER

# I

*Politicizing
the Corporation*

**O**VER the past fifteen years, a new way has been found to influence the decisions of corporations in the United States. No longer are public demands for change in corporate behavior addressed exclusively through government. Instead, a growing number of groups and individuals are taking their criticisms of corporate conduct directly to the firm: they are lobbying the corporation as well as the government. Just as the trade union movement has sought to advance its interests both directly at the workplace and indirectly through the political process, so now have those concerned with the social aspects of corporate performance begun to participate in two distinctive political arenas.[1]

Many of the most controversial issues affecting business in the sixties and seventies—the treatment of blacks and women, the conduct of the war in Vietnam, the role of American-owned corporations in Angola, Namibia, and the Republic of South Africa, and the compliance of American-owned corporations with the Arab boycott of Israel—have come directly before decision-making bodies in both the private and public sectors. The whole process of involvement has become institutionalized: citizen pressures have become a permanent feature of the political, social, and legal environment of the corporation. Moreover, the terms of citizen access to the corporation have themselves become an important issue of public policy, particularly before the Securities and Exchange Commission and the federal courts.

The business corporation has been subject to periodic hostility since its emergence in the United States in the first decades of the nineteenth century. What is new—and significant—is the form in which some public criticisms of business are now being made. In addition to political pressures from the state and the trade unions, the corporation today must also deal increasingly with direct pressures from organized citizen groups. The emergence of citizen challenges to business represents one of the most distinctive features of the current period of relatively widespread mistrust of the large corporation. What this rather novel and still developing political phenomenon means both for the corporation and for our political system is the subject of this book.

The new public lobbying against business originated with the civil rights and antiwar movements and, indeed, constitutes one of their most important political legacies. Between 1966 and 1973, Eastman Kodak, Dow Chemical, Honeywell, and the Bank of America were all confronted with direct—and sometimes violent—challenges to their employment and investment policies from civil rights and antiwar groups.

However, direct pressures on business did not decline with the atrophy of the civil rights and anti-Vietnam movements of the sixties; rather, they became more legally oriented. Thus, in 1970, a small group of individuals inspired by Ralph Nader formed an organization called the Project on Corporate Responsibility and succeeded in convincing the Securities and Exchange Commission to force General Motors to include two socially oriented shareholder resolutions in the proxy statement mailed to the corporation's 1.3 million owners. Their tactic was rapidly adopted by others, including a coalition of major Protestant denominations, who saw in the proxy resolution a means of influencing corporate policies. As of 1977, nearly 600 public interest resolutions have been submitted to the shareholders of more than 150 corporations. The issues raised by these resolutions touch on virtually every political and social issue affecting business that has become an object of public attention over the last seven years.

Most dramatically, the corporate annual meeting has itself become politicized. Professional shareholders such as the Gilbert brothers no longer find themselves virtually alone in questioning management judgments and prerogatives at annual meetings. Since 1967, the annual meetings of the nation's largest and most visible corporations have come to resemble more closely the spirit and tone of the New England town meetings on which they were modeled originally. As a result, the public has become an important part of the dialogue between shareholders and management. Corporate officials are increasingly under pressures to defend their decisions in terms of their general impact on society and not simply on the welfare of their shareholders.

The consumer has also become more politicized. Allowing political or moral preferences to influence one's purchase of products is not, of course, an idea that was invented in the sixties.[2] Consumer boycotts played an important role in the American colonists' prerevolutionary struggle against England and have been used periodically both by and against various economic and ethnic groups throughout American history. And the American trade union movement has frequently encouraged the boycott of various products as a way to apply pressure on recalcitrant employers. But over the last fifteen years, such consumer boycotts have become more frequent, better organized, and identified with a much broader range of issues. Scarcely a month now passes without the public being asked to boycott a particular product or company in order to express disagreement with some decision of the private sector. These decisions include bank lending practices in declining neighborhoods, popularly known as "redlining"; the employment policies of several local and national firms; the marketing of gold coins from South Africa; and the manufacture of various products held to be detrimental to the environment.

## The Emergence of Citizen Pressure on Business

The development of direct citizen protests reflects the influence of a large body of legal, academic, and popular opinion that regards the modern corporation as a private government, enjoying a substantial immunity from the constraints of both the market and the state. This perception is, in turn, related to a decline in public confidence in the official government, especially among those critical of business.

Ever since Berle and Means's *The Modern Corporation and Private Property* first publicized the formal separation of ownership and control, nearly fifty years ago, the belief that the corporation can be usefully understood as a political system or a private government has become virtually a commonplace among students of business.[3] Writers as diverse as Robert Gordon, Walton Hamilton, James March, Richard Eells, Peter Bachrach, Robert Dahl, and Wolfgang Friedmann—have all made this point repeatedly in their writings.[4] Some suggested that describing the corporation in political terms would, in the words of Richard Eells, "contribute toward a better public understanding of business politics; their special requirements for authority concentrations and distributions within the corporate structure."[5] Or, as Dow Votaw put it in one of the standard texts on the modern corporation:

The modern corporation is a private governmental system. Traditional economic and legal theories do not adequately explain the total role of the corporation or provide the workable concepts of legitimacy, accountability, and responsibility that will permit the corporation to continue as a major contributor to our entire social system.[6]

But beginning in the early sixties, another group of writers began to take a more critical tack. A handful of political scientists and lawyers explicitly challenged the double standard of political accountability applied to governmental and nongovernmental institutions. If the corporation is indeed a government, why, they wanted to know, should it be exempt from the constraints of democratic and republican rule which the American political tradition imposes on the "official" government? As Earl Latham argued,

The problem is . . . one of imposing on the corporation the same limitations that experience has shown must be laid upon the exercise of power in the public government, if the "welfare and rights of the entire mass of people are the main consideration, rather than the privileges of class or the will of a monarch," to recall the law dictionary definition.[7]

Note that this analysis of the corporation directly challenged the property rights of shareholders. Not only did there appear to be something about the shareholder role that deprived it of the legitimacy traditionally associated with private property rights—a phenomenon first noted by Marx and made popular by Berle and Means—but, more importantly, the pervasive social impact of the typical twentieth-century corporation appeared to make a mockery of its claim to be considered a private institution. The Securities and Exchange Act had given legal recognition to the rights of shareholders to participate in the governance of the corporation—even though these rights had rarely been exercised. But what about the accountability of management to the other constituencies affected by the large investor-owned firm? Was it reasonable to expect them to be content with speeches describing the sincerity of management's responsibility to them? In the words of the political scientist Robert Dahl:

Whatever may be the optimal way of governing the great corporation, surely it is a delusion to consider it a private enterprise. . . . Why should people who own shares be given the privileges of citizenship in the government of the firm when citizenship is denied to other people who also make vital contributions to the firm?[8]

The corporate accountability movement represents an attempt to realize in practice what scholars such as Latham, Dahl, and others have argued in theory—namely that corporations wield the power of governments and should, therefore, be treated like governments. The movement is accurately described as a movement for corporate *accountability* because its basic thrust is to make corporate officials as responsive to those affected by their decisions as are elected officials. By reviving the symbols and mechanisms of corporate governance—the annual meeting, the annual report, the proxy resolutions, the board of directors—the advocates of corporate accountability are attempting to make the relationship between the officials of the private sector and the public resemble more closely that between government officials and their constituencies. Activist shareholders regard themselves as a surrogate for society; their basic intent is to make management accountable to all those affected by their policies—a notion that goes far beyond the letter and spirit of the securities laws.

Traditionally, in liberal political thought and practice, only one institution was thought to be responsible for looking after the public welfare—the state. To the extent that the public had common interests and shared common values, it was the responsibility of government officials to articulate and represent them. For in their *political* roles, as public officials or citizens, individuals were presumed in principle to be motivated by the interests of the commonweal. Lincoln Steffens vividly captured the contrast in the standards of conduct for officials of the private and public sectors when he noted in his *Autobiography* that public officials are considered corrupt when they act as businessmen normally behave.[9] These principles were, of course, routinely breached, as Steffens himself exhaustively documented, but they did establish a division of labor that was widely accepted—at least as an ideal. However, during the last fifteen years the corporate accountability movement has challenged them in a number of respects.

First, as this book demonstrates, individuals and organizations who disapprove of particular corporate policies are now as likely to address their grievances to the firm as they are to use the formal political system.[10] While this has always been true of corporate policies affecting workers, it now holds for virtually every political issue in which business is implicated.

Secondly, private consumption and investment decisions have increasingly acquired political as well as economic significance. In *On the Jewish Question*, Karl Marx gave his well-known criticism of the double standard of bourgeois society:

Where the political state has attained to its full development, man leads, not only in thought, in consciousness, but in *reality*, in *life*, a double existence—celestial and terrestrial. He lives in the political community, where he regards himself as a *communal being*, and in *civil society* where he acts simply as a *private individual*, treats other men as means, and becomes the plaything of alien powers.[11]

The contrast between our behavior with respect to voting on one hand and consuming and investing on the other clearly illustrates Marx's point: when we vote, we try, at least in principle, to advance our perception of the general good. Consuming and investing, which are "economic" decisions, are legitimately guided by only self-interest. The "politicization" of the corporation has blurred this contrast by forcing consideration of social factors in both investment and consumption decisions.

Thirdly, the public's expectations of corporate officers have come to resemble increasingly those it holds of governmental officials. Thus, business executives are challenged to make decisions that are in the best interests of society as a whole and not just of their shareholders. Profit maximization has become significantly less acceptable as a public justification for corporate actions. At shareholder meetings, chief executive officers are now often subject to the same kind of intense and irreverent questioning—conducted in full public view—that has traditionally been reserved for politicians.

With the collapse of the double standard, higher expectations of the state have also been applied to the corporation. Thus, the contemporary concern with corporate accountability is part of a broader preoccupation with the accountability of all institutions, private and public. (Similarly, the protection of "whistle blowers" from the ire of their superiors has been advocated for both private and public officials.)[12] Opponents of the Vietnam War sought to apply the principles of individual responsibility developed at Nuremberg to officials in both sectors. Most recently, the Carter Administration's public emphasis on the promotion of human rights as an important goal for U.S. foreign policy has prompted various ethical investors to demand that multinational corporations make their investments abroad on the basis of similar principles. Those who challenge foreign investments argue that all of our relations with foreign nations—whether made through private or public institutions—should be subject to the same moral and political criteria.

The corporation is currently being subjected to the same democratic pressures experienced by the American State 150 years ago: just as property holders were forced then to share the franchise with other members of the political community, so now are shareholders being pressured to accept the participation of the corporation's other less affluent constituencies. In both cases, claims to participation based on property ownership have been eroded—though the formal exercise of the shareholder's franchise still carries with it a property qualification. Thus, like the democratic State, the contemporary corporation must now continually adjust to a series of competing and conflicting demands on its limited resources: if political leaders must continually balance the needs of corporations with a variety of other political pressures, so the corporate executives now are forced to weigh the demands of their profit-oriented shareholders with their need to appear responsive to the political and social demands made on them by their other constituencies. The tension between accumulation and legitimacy is no longer confined to the state; at least in the United States, it now also affects the corporation.[13]

### THE DECLINE OF PUBLIC AUTHORITY

The challenges to corporations growing out of the social movements of the sixties were part of a more general crisis of authority that affected all the major institutions of American life. The state, the university, the corporation, and the church were all subject to demands for increased accountability and participation; the race and sex of the members of their respective governing bodies, for example, became an issue for each of them. And, as this book illustrates, the political pressures on each of these institutions were, in fact, frequently interrelated. In effect, the social movements of the sixties stood the postindustrial society literature on its head: if postindustrial society was characterized by the interdependency of major bureaucracies, then each constituent element of the "establishment" was equally responsible for society's shortcomings and subject to similar standards of accountability.[14] Given this perspective, it was beside the point to argue that neither Columbia University nor General Motors was responsible for the mistreatment of blacks; each was part of an interrelated political "system." Their division of labor could be regarded as a matter of administrative convenience, not of principle.

This explanation, however, is insufficient, for it does not explain why demands on the corporation persisted even after the mass movements that had inspired them atrophied. Why do so many of the controversies of the seventies—"Corporate Watergate," the Arab boycott, feminism, and ecology—continue to come before the corporation directly instead of going exclusively to the state?

I believe that the development and persistence of these citizen challenges is in part a reflection of the declining legitimacy of the state in U.S. society. The reason many organizations and individuals have sought novel avenues of access to corporate decision making is that they do not trust their government to represent adequately all of the public's interests. The notion of the corporation as a private government or public institution takes on political urgency when the public government is no longer regarded as

9

sufficiently accountable. And today citizens of all political views are much less likely to regard the government as responsive to their interests than was the case in the early sixties.[15] The public's expectations of business and government leaders have thus become increasingly similar in a perverse way: politicians are now commonly assumed to be motivated by the same self-serving incentives that inspire bureaucrats in the private sector. A distinctive and characteristic aspect of the contemporary period of American reform is that citizen challenges to business reflect the lack of legitimacy of *both* business and government. During the Progressive Era and the New Deal even those who were critical of the corporation retained considerable faith in public authority. It is an important difference. Public disappointment with corporate behavior would not of itself have produced direct pressures on the corporation. That disappointment had to be joined to a belief that government by itself could not or would not adequately counterbalance the goals of the investor-owned enterprise.

This concern emerges most clearly in those challenges that seek to supplement the state's law enforcement mechanism: here the government is simply not trusted to adequately enforce its own laws. It also emerges, although more indirectly, in those demands that are addressed predominantly to corporations; in these instances the corporation, rather than the state, is viewed as the major locus of authority. And it is also a factor in those citizen pressures that seek to influence government policy—usually in the direction of increased regulation. In all of these instances, corporations are criticized directly, largely because they are seen as an important— usually too important—source of influence on the state. Note that the corporate critics' distrust of government has not led them to cease pressing for additional intervention by the state. On the contrary, pressuring the firm is seen as a means of increasing the effectiveness and scope of government regulation of business.

The corporation thus tends to be viewed as a "public" institution by those who regard corporations as insufficiently accountable to the public. But when the ideologists of the corporate accountability movement talk about the "public" status of the corporation, they may mean one of two things. Some, like Galbraith, view the corporation as public because of its dependence on and close links with the government.[16] Others, like Dahl, consider the corporation public by virtue of its extraordinary size and pervasive social impact—regardless of the extent of its particular ties with the state.[17] A favorite example of the former is Lockheed; that of the latter, General Motors.

Both of these conceptions assume that those who manage corporations enjoy substantial immunity from the discipline of both the marketplace and the democratic political process. But there is an important distinction between them. If corporations were as closely integrated with the government as many activists assume, it is unlikely that citizen challenges would have developed in the United States. Direct challenges to corporations are a distinctively American phenomenon, and what distinguishes the American pattern of business-government relations from that of Europe is precisely the relative independence of the American corporate sector from public authority. In other democratic capitalist nations, corporations are rarely the focus of political challenges from consumers and investors, precisely because they are, in fact, already closely linked to the state. That is why political challenges to business in these nations focus directly on the state and pay little attention to the firm. Paradoxically, it is the relative "privateness" of the American business corporations that accounts for the pressures that their contemporary critics place upon it.[18]

## The Significance of the Citizen Protests

### IMPACT ON CORPORATE BEHAVIOR

Measuring the effectiveness of citizen lobbies is difficult if for no other reason than that the political processes of the private sector remain relatively closed, and firms are often reluctant to acknowledge that public protests influenced their business judgments. Nevertheless, citizen protests have had a discernible impact. Polaroid's decision to terminate its sales in South Africa, Whirlpool's cessation of its production of antipersonnel weapons, and several banks' announced restrictions on their loans in South Africa can all be largely attributed to nongovernmental political challenges.

There have been other less dramatic but equally significant responses. Persistent pressures by religious organizations have resulted in a measurable upgrading in the working conditions of black employees in a number of American-owned firms in the Republic of South Africa and Namibia. And actual and threatened consumer boycotts resulted in a marked increase in the number of blacks employed by several firms in northern cities throughout the sixties. The organizing efforts of the United Farm Workers and the Amalgamated Clothing Workers have also been noticeably helped by organized consumer pressures. Shareholder suits filed by a number of public interest organizations have succeeded in forcing the executives of several corporations convicted of illegal political participation to personally assume a larger share of the financial consequences of their generosity. Two firms, Northrop and Phillips Petroleum, were required to make radical, and unprecedented, changes in their boards of directors as a result of such suits.

Yet these substantive changes in corporate policies are exceptional; relatively few citizen challenges have had such direct and measurable impact. More typical is the behavior of Gulf Oil and Honeywell, which were subjected to more kinds of citizen pressures for a longer period of time than any other firms over the last decade. Neither company yielded on the fundamental issue that mobilized their critics: Honeywell continues to produce antipersonnel weapons for the U.S. government and Gulf remained in Angola throughout the entire military conflict in what is now an independent African nation. More generally, no American-owned firm has withdrawn its investments from any nation primarily as a result of moral and political criticisms, though a few have deferred additional investments, in part due to such pressures.

Indeed, much of the effect of private political pressures on business has been procedural rather than substantive. One of the most visible of these procedural changes has been in the composition of some of the corporate boards of directors. These boards are no longer a virtually exclusive white male institution. A 1976 survey of the boards of 370 major companies reported the percentage of boards with women members at 21.3 percent—up from 11.4 percent just two years before; 13.1 percent had at least one minority member—up from 10.7 percent in 1974, but slightly below the 1975 total of 15.1 percent.[19] This change has resulted almost exclusively from citizen pressures, since in the United States neither trade unions nor the state has shown much interest in the social composition of the corporate board. True, the addition of these new members has not resulted in any substantive change in corporate policies, but they are nevertheless important symbols of management's recognition of the legitimacy of a broadened constituency.

In addition to broadening their boards of directors, some companies—including the Bank of America, General Motors, and Dow Chemical—have responded to citizen protests by establishing high-level management committees responsible for monitoring the firm's relationship with its social environment; a total of thirty-five companies now have such committees.[20] Many corporations have also increased the amount of information they are willing to make public, while others have publicly agreed to change their policies. Thus, more than fifty corporations have made public their Equal

Employment Opportunity reports in response to shareholder resolutions. And over twenty-five have formally reported to their shareholders, and thus the public, about various aspects of their operations in Africa and Asia, while the American Jewish Congress has persuaded forty corporations to go on record as refusing to participate in the Arab boycott of Israel. Of course, whether these stances and disclosures have resulted in any actual changes in corporate behavior is more difficult to assess.

Of more far-reaching significance is that corporate reformers seem to have set in motion some rather fundamental changes in the relationship of institutional investors to corporate managers. The "Wall Street Rule," which mandates that the selling of securities is the only appropriate way for institutional investors to express their disagreement with management performance, has been significantly modified since 1970. Institutional investors are slowly beginning to use some of the power they have accumulated since the early fifties. Even profit-seeking institutional investors, such as banks, insurance companies, and mutual funds, have begun to scrutinize management policies more carefully, not only financially, but also socially. While institutions continue to vote with management most of the time, their decision to do so has become less automatic.

Liberalization of rules governing access to the proxy machinery, politicization of shareholder suits, growth in the number and importance of outside directors, and greater willingness of both individual shareholders and institutions to vote against the recommendations of management—all these developments point to a historically important decrease in the autonomy and authority of those who manage corporations. The power of management over shareholders increased steadily from the 1940s; the 1970s thus appear to represent a historic turning point in the distribution of power within the corporation.

CITIZEN CHALLENGES AND THE POLITICAL SYSTEM

Still, if the significance of the corporate accountability lobbies were confined to their direct impact on corporate priorities, they would hardly merit a book. Compared to either the government or trade unions, citizen challenges still provide relatively few constraints on corporate decision makers. Their importance lies elsewhere.

Where counter-corporate pressures have come to play a more important role is in setting the agenda of the governmental process. Through the filing of proxy resolutions, the questioning of corporate executives at annual shareholder meetings, and the release of various research studies, corporations have become forums for injecting new issues onto the political process and for discussing and reviving old ones.

The extent to which demands addressed to the corporation anticipate the substance of subsequent government regulations of business is indeed striking. Issues that were brought directly to the attention of corporate executives before they became subjects of public policy include: equal access to public facilities (the sit-ins), preferential hiring of minorities (*CORE* versus *Bank of America*, *FIGHT* versus *Kodak*), the morality of weaponry used in the conduct of the war in Vietnam (Dow campus demonstrations), the continuation of the air war in Indochina (Honeywell Project), the composition and role of the board of directors ("Campaign GM"), the participation of the corporation in domestic electoral politics (Project on Corporate Responsibility shareholder resolutions, 1973), the role of the United States in Angola (Gulf Boycott Project, 1970), the social impact of bank lending policies (the Center for New Corporate Priorities, 1971), the political consequences of American investment in South Africa (the protests against the loan policies of American banks, 1966), corporate compliance with the embargo against Rhodesia (the People's Bicentennial Commission versus Mobil, 1976), the marketing of infant formulas abroad (*Sisters of Mercy* versus *Bristol Myers*, 1976), and, most recently, the decision of the Department of Commerce to restrict the sale of technology to the South African government (the *Interfaith Center on Corporate Responsibility* versus *IBM*, 1974). And the disclosure requirements associated with illegal domestic campaign contributions and payments abroad are perhaps the most obvious example of a more politically aggressive pattern of securities regulation that began with the commission's recognition of the public interest proxy resolution in 1970.

Of course, in only a minority of these instances have direct challenges to business been the primary reason why these issues came to the attention of public officials. Still, the private sector has been relatively more accessible to groups with limited political resources; it is far easier to file a proxy resolution or announce a boycott than to have legislation debated in Congress.[21] While the number of participants in citizen challenges has often been rather small and their political constituencies at times unclear, the issues they identify do frequently echo concerns that are widely shared among the broader public. Thus, the private sector essentially provides a convenient initial arena.

It is a critical limitation to the effectiveness of citizen challenges that they are rarely capable of resolving the issues they raise. For one thing, they generally lack the political power and the legal authority of, say, trade unions in their negotiations with management. Their constituencies are often ill-defined and their tactics are primarily *ad hoc*. Moreover, many of the issues with which these direct challenges are concerned—the economic conditions of blacks and employment opportunities for women, the protection of the environment, the conduct and continuation of the war in Vietnam, the relationship of the United States to Chile, the Soviet Union, and South Africa—cannot be adequately dealt with by any one firm or large group of firms, even if the firms were so motivated. In the final analysis they are matters of public policy and are most importantly affected by the decisions of government. Ironically, while citizen challenges are based on the premise that corporations are an independent source of power in American society—exercising authority that dominates or at least parallels that of the state—whatever eventual success they have had in changing corporate decisions is due almost entirely to the exercise of public authority.

## THE PRINCIPLES OF CORPORATE CONDUCT

But there is another reason why these challenges are important: they have raised in a particularly stark and dramatic form the whole question of the corporation's power and how that power is used in the American political economy.

What divides corporate activists from the executives they challenge is not *whether* privately owned enterprises have a social impact, but rather: for *what* is a corporation responsible? Traditionally, the issue of corporate social responsibility has most often been phrased affirmatively, that is, should the corporation rebuild the central cities, hire minorities, clean up the environment, and so forth? But the politically more significant issue raised by participants in the corporate accountability movement concerns the extent to which corporations should be held responsible for the social and political impact of their "normal" business decisions. Critics contend that those who run the modern corporation do, in fact, wield considerable authority: the power of a privately owned corporation is comparable to that of a government.

It is on this question of corporate power that the issue is most clearly joined. Thus, the position of Honeywell with respect to its investments in Angola, or the Bank of America with respect to its loans to Chile, or that of several scores of corporations with respect to their compliance with the Arab boycott or their presence in South Africa—all hinge on the identical argument: we, the corporations, are being unfairly held responsible for presumed injustices that it is not in our power to correct. Political or economic constraints make it impossible for us to accede to your requests, and even if we did what you want, the abuse that upsets you would remain.

The variety of business responses to activist demands hinges in large part precisely on this issue. Corporate executives are at times willing to correct abuses that they believe are in their power to affect. But their perception of what they can do differs markedly from that of their critics. Indeed, this perspective provides a useful litmus test of the political orientation of both executives and their critics. The more liberal or "enlightened" the corporation, the more social ills or injustices for which its managers are willing to hold themselves responsible. Alternatively, the more radical the critic, the more expansive his or her view of the public consequence of corporate decisions.

What direct citizen pressures on business have done is to convert the idea of corporate social responsibility from a philosophy of management into a justification for the right of all those affected by the corporation—or their representatives—to help shape the goals of the firm. In effect, the corporate accountability movement has forced the business community to confront the practical implications of its own legitimizing ideology. Executives often contend that social responsibility in the private sector is an alternative to increased government regulation: many citizen challenges provide an opportunity to test the willingness of business to respond voluntarily to social pressures before they become reflected in public policy.

Few executives would deny that political factors routinely enter into corporate decisions. But they tend to see them as constraints on economic accumulation, not as objectives; as means, not ends. To suggest that executives should take into consideration the social effect of how they pursue their profits raises a series of extremely complex political and moral issues. In defending their refusal to integrate restaurants in the South prior to 1964, their investments in South Africa or their trade with the Soviet Union, corporate executives argue that they are not responsible for making political judgments, to which the critics respond that this distinction between economics and politics is illusionary: the issue is not whether the corporation should make political judgments, but in whose interests it should make them. It is a debate that informs many of the controversies explored in this book.

There is also a moral dimension to this issue. Citizen pressures have become an important mechanism for raising moral issues both in the board room and throughout the society. Under what circumstances, if any, should a firm refuse to produce a product because the conditions under which it is produced or the ends for which it is to be used are morally wrong? Under what circumstances, if any, is it right for a commercial enterprise to benefit from a political system that is obnoxious to the moral sensibilities of the American public? In short, who is to determine the dictates of the "corporate conscience"?[22] Few executives scrutinize the decisions of the companies they manage in these terms. But the unwillingness of at least some shareholders to remain morally indifferent to the sources of their dividends and capital gains has prompted an intense, and at times quite sophisticated, debate about the moral responsibilities of the modern corporation. In the course of personifying "society," the movement for corporate accountability has also helped to personify the corporation, forcing executives to justify their own behavior as well as that of their company.

## THE DIRECTION OF PUBLIC POLICY

Finally, the citizen challenge movement deserves scrutiny because it illustrates an important contemporary dimension of federal regulatory policy. Much of the contemporary debate over the appropriate structure of the American corporate system has been cast in terms of government control versus market competition. But a more fundamental issue is: what is the impact of various public policies on the locus of power within civil society? Do they encourage the centralization of authority—whether in the hands of the state or the large firm—or do they promote pluralism—both within the private and the public sectors?

Posing the issue in these terms allows us to distinguish two distinct kinds of public intervention in the economy. One set of policies tends toward bureaucratic statism. Regulatory policy, government contracting, and most direct and indirect subsidies to business fall into this category; so do most programs associated with the welfare state. These policies usually involve large state expenditures and/or major expansions of the public bureaucratic apparatus. But there is another type of public policy that attempts to increase the number of political and economic actors in society by making both the political and economic systems more heterogeneous and competitive. Apart from the common law system, antitrust law is the most notable example of this kind of intervention, although regulations enforced by the National Labor Relations Board and the Securities and Exchange Commission also tend to fall into this category. These public policies require neither large outlays of public funds nor significant increases in public bureaucracy. Rather, their purpose is to establish ground rules through which private actors can define and advance their own interests vis-à-vis the large corporation. Ideally, they, like the marketplace model to which they are related, are largely self-regulating and self-enforcing.

Most contemporary discussions of public policy confine their analysis to policy issues associated with the first kind of policy. Thus, virtually all the left-liberal critiques of public policy written during the sixties contend that public control of the corporation has been inadequate because the state has remained too weak.[23] These writers identify progressive policies with a strong state: only "big government" is capable of serving as an adequate counterweight to the power of "big business." More recent criticisms of the pattern of government regulation, written from a conservative perspective, simply turn these authors upside down: public policy is deemed counterproductive precisely because it allegedly puts excessively centralized economic decision making in the hands of the government.[24]

There is no doubt that this debate remains a highly relevant one, particularly with respect to macroeconomic policy issues. Much of the contemporary populist and socialist political agenda contains proposals whose effect would clearly be to strengthen state authority—presumably to the applause of writers such as Lowi, McConnell, Reagan, and Engler and the chagrin of writers for the editorial pages of the *Wall Street Journal*, *Fortune*, and the *Public Interest*. Wage-price controls, national health insurance, and national economic planning are the most prominent examples.

The contemporary public interest movement, however, rejects the terms of this debate, for it does not equate increased public control of business with the centralization of authority in the state. What distinguishes the public interest movement from the mainstream of the New Deal left-liberal tradition is its relative lack of confidence in either public or private bureaucracies. An important objective of many of the movement's policy initiatives has been to decentralize the formulation and implementation of regulatory policy; activists have placed major emphasis on the development of a wide variety of private enforcement mechanisms. Their solution to the problem of corporate power is not simply to make the public sector stronger, but to make both sectors more public.

The development of the corporate accountability movement reflects this policy thrust; it has also been a major beneficiary of it. The judiciary has greatly helped through the liberalization of standing requirements and, for a time, its tolerance of class action suits. (It was a judicial decision, moreover, that made possible the submission of public interest proxy resolutions.) A number of laws enacted by the federal government since the mid-sixties can also be seen as a part of this tradition. These include the funding of poverty law firms—most of whose energies are devoted to suing the government—as well as the Freedom of Information Act Amendments of 1972. Furthermore, the provisions of the Civil Rights Act of 1964 and Clean Air Act of 1970 allow citizens, acting in the capacity of "private attorneys general," to be compensated for court costs and attorneys' fees by the offending parties, usually a corporation. And increasingly, government regulations are permitting and subsidizing public participation in the proceedings of regulatory commissions. Citizen challenges to business are thus linked to a wide range of policies and decisions that attempt to provide expanded opportunities for public participation in both corporate and public decisions. These statutory and judicial recognitions of citizens' rights of participation represent one of the most important policy developments of the last decade and one whose evolution and future significance will be re-examined at the conclusion of this study.[25] Citizen pressures on business thus represent a "tip of the iceberg" whose full significance may emerge during the next decade.

## The Organization of the Book

This discussion of the politics of corporate accountability is selective rather than definitive: it attempts to strike a balance between a series of in-depth case studies and a historical narrative that would provide a complete picture of the range of participants and the diversity of issues with which they have been concerned. The former approach would not make sufficiently clear the ideological, tactical, and organizational connections among contemporary critics of business, while the latter method would not permit the kind of detailed treatment that is required to do justice to the more significant citizen challenges. This book is thus more a study in political analysis than in contemporary history. It explores one particular aspect of the contemporary political and legal environment of the business corporation.

Chapter 2 is primarily historical. It deals with the treatment of blacks and the war in Vietnam, linked by their relationship to the social movements of the sixties. Chapters 3 and 4 each focus on the development of a particular political strategy. Chapter 3 examines challenges based on the politicization of the shareholder role. It begins with a detailed study of "Campaign GM," followed by an analysis of the effort of a coalition of community groups in Minneapolis to use the proxy mechanism to elect a public interest representative to the board of directors of Northern States Power Company. It also discusses the seven-year history of the public interest proxy proposal, the changing role of institutional investors, and the impact of "the Corporate Watergate." Chapter 4 explores citizen pressures for increased disclosure. It discusses the strategies of citizen research organizations, the history of ethical investment, and the interest in corporate disclosure on the part of the women's movement. Chapter 5 introduces the most important participant in citizen challenges: the Protestant and Catholic churches. It examines their role, along with that of the American Jewish Congress, in protests over the political and moral implications of the foreign investments and trade policies of U.S. corporations, with particular emphasis on southern Africa, the marketing of infant formulas, and the Arab boycott. The last chapter offers an overall assessment of the corporate accountability movement, tracing the response of business to it and its significance for the future of public control of the corporation.

# CHAPTER

# II

---

*Origins:*
*Civil Rights and*
*Antiwar Protests*

FROM the mid-fifties through the early seventies, many of the most important and widely publicized confrontations—over the rights of black Americans and over the U.S. presence in Vietnam—directly affected institutions in the profit sector, most notably the Bank of America, Kodak, Dow Chemical, and Honeywell. These challenges to business were unique in that they were integral parts of broader social movements; subsequent corporate challenges have not usually involved such large numbers of people. On the other hand, there is a clear continuity between the protest movements of the sixties and the more legalistic approach to the problem of corporate accountability that has evolved in the seventies. Much of the underlying ideology, organizational structure and tactics, and personnel of the contemporary corporate accountability movement originated in the conflicts and confrontations described in this chapter.

Both of the two critical events that sparked the civil rights struggle involved the efforts of black citizens to pressure businesses—one public and one privately owned—to end their policy of providing separate facilities for black and white consumers. On December 1, 1955, Mrs. Rosa Parks was arrested for refusing to give up her seat on a Montgomery City Line bus to a white passenger. Following her arrest a friend casually suggested that "every Negro in town should stay off the buses for one day in protest."[1] The subsequent boycott lasted a year, costing the bus company more than $7,000 a day in lost revenue and severely undermining the economy of the downtown business district. It also mobilized the black community of Alabama's capital city and within six months "had become the most popular cause in the United States."[2] More importantly, it marked the national debut of the civil rights movement's most influential national leader, the Reverend Martin Luther King, Jr., and his strategy of nonviolent resistance.

Economic pressures proved to work both ways. White insurance companies began canceling the insurance on station wagons used in the alternative car pool. The city of Montgomery also sought to obtain an injunction against the car pool, charging that it was a "public nuisance."[3] The bus company, which was on the verge of bankruptcy after four months of the nearly total loss of black patronage, was quite willing to comply with the April 23, 1956, decision of the Supreme Court declaring segregation on intrastate buses unconstitutional. The city's officials, however, refused to recognize the applicability of the court's ruling and forbade the bus company from changing its policy and thus "getting off the hook."[4] At the same time, they attempted to seek economic damages from the black community for the financial inconveniences caused by their pressures. It finally took a specific order of the Supreme Court before Martin Luther King, Jr., on the morning of December 22, 1956, dramatically ended the boycott by boarding a bus and sitting in the front section. The main significance of King's victory was that it suggested a vehicle by which masses of individual blacks could directly challenge segregation. Within a month, the Southern Regional Council announced that bus segregation had been ended in twenty-five southern cities as a result of various kinds of direct public pressure.

Four years later, an investor-owned corporation provided the setting for a political activity that ignited a second major wave of protest throughout the South. Like the boycott, the "sit-in" was a tactic particularly oriented to pressuring businesses. Although the Congress of Racial Equality (CORE) had successfully used sit-ins to desegregate public accommodations in Chicago, St. Louis, and Baltimore between 1943 and 1959, it was the spontaneous decision of four black college students to sit in the "whites only" section of a Woolworth lunch counter in Greensboro, North Carolina, on February 1, 1960, that had major political ramifications. Within two months, sit-ins had taken place in seventy-eight southern communities, resulting in 2,000 arrests. Within twenty months, approximately 70,000 people in both the North and the South had either marched, sat-in, or picketed various business establishments. As a result, public accommodations in 110 cities and towns in southern and border states were desegregated. "The movement managed to shake the foundations of Southern white society as it had not been shaken since Reconstruction. . . ."[5]

The fact that many of the early sit-ins took place at the southern outlets of national retail establishments was fortuitous: it provided the opportunity for both white and black sympathizers in the North to express their support for the southern students. When executives of Woolworth's and Kress, meeting with CORE officials in New York, refused to desegregate their southern lunch counters, the recently revived civil rights group called for a nationwide boycott. Support rallies and picketing of dime stores took place in a number of northern cities, including Chicago, San Francisco, Philadelphia, and New York. In Los Angeles, the NAACP, ILGWU, United Auto Workers, and American Jewish Congress helped organize picketing. The most extensive pressure occurred in New York City. On April 4, picket lines were established at thirty-five stores; three Saturdays later, sixty-nine stores were picketed. The picketing made the boycott relatively effective. One observer commented, "In some stores there weren't a dozen customers all afternoon."[6] Woolworth officially reported an 8.9 percent decline in sales during March of 1960 from that of the previous year, for which CORE claimed credit.[7]

In spite of the apparent vulnerability of national retail enterprises to the consumer boycott and widespread public pressure generated in the North, the stores' central management refused to interfere with the policies of their regional managers. In time, public support in the North began to wane without the drama of the southern sit-ins to sustain them. As a CORE official acknowledged, "After all, it is difficult to expect the same people to picket week in and week out for a very long period of time."[8] The actual degree of integration of lunch counters was largely a function of local political pressures and social conditions. Thus, nearly all of the 140 cities in which dime store lunch counters were desegregated were located on the periphery of the South. Store policies were changed in much of the Southwest and in parts of North Carolina, Virginia, Tennessee, Kentucky, and southern Florida. In the Deep South, on the other hand, where white attitudes were more intransigent, most public accommodations remained firmly segregated until passage of the Civil Rights Act of 1964. Even the Freedom Rides were unable to desegregate railway and bus terminals, although the Supreme Court had earlier held segregation of these facilities to be illegal. *De facto* segregation did not end until 1962, after three years of persistent direct pressures.[9]

The sit-ins and boycotts of the fifties and early sixties were directed at changing both corporate and governmental policies. Corporations became an important target not because they themselves were held responsible for the second-class status blacks endured. Rather, it was in their economic roles that blacks experienced the indignities of segregation on a daily basis, and challenging corporations provided one of the few available mechanisms through which blacks could become involved in political life. Much of the effectiveness of the protests can clearly be traced to the wide degree of public participation they were able to encourage and the even more widespread acknowledgment of the legitimacy of their demands—at least outside white communities in the South. Aside from igniting a major political and social movement, the most important accomplishment of the sit-ins was to place the issue of segregation of public accommodations on the national political agenda. Seen from this perspective, the sit-ins' concrete impact on business policies was secondary.

## Black Employment in the North

As the setting of civil rights conflicts moved North in the early sixties, attention shifted to the employment opportunities of blacks. Between 1960 and 1964, hundreds of businesses in the North were pressured to increase their number of black employees.[10] In addition to picketing, demonstrations, and selective boycotts, more disruptive tactics were also used. These included "shop-ins," many individuals filling their shopping carts with groceries then leaving the groceries at the cash register without paying; "cross filing," taking products from one part of a store and placing them on other shelves; and "phone-ins," tying up telephone lines by frequent calls. Retail banks were at times disrupted by individuals alternatively waiting on a cashier line to convert their change into a large denomination and then asking that their larger bill be changed.[11]

Because of their vulnerability to boycotts, activists decided to concentrate on consumer goods manufacturers and retail establishments. In St. Louis, a successful attempt was made to mobilize the enthusiasm generated by the dime store sympathy boycotts into pressure on the same stores' local employment policies. In Detroit, 300 ministers asked their congregations to refuse to buy Tip Top bread and Borden's milk; pamphlets were distributed that read, "Lock the Gate. Elsie Won't Cooperate." A Seattle NAACP-CORE boycott of the Bon Marche department stores resulted in the hiring of forty blacks. In Berkeley, fourteen local retail businesses signed employment agreements with CORE; under pressure from Berkeley CORE, Montgomery Ward agreed to hire a total of eighty-five minority members. In New York, National CORE, along with support from local chapters of NAACP, CORE, and Puerto Rican groups, won a preferential agreement from A&P: the supermarket chain agreed to employ 400 blacks and Puerto Ricans within two years without even forcing civil rights activists to resort to direct action. New York also provided the setting for one of CORE's most impressive concessions from the consumer goods sectors.

A "TV Image Campaign" threatened several major companies with a consumer boycott unless they sponsored integrated commercials. By October 1963, more than a dozen companies were using blacks in their commercials.

## THE ISSUE OF PREFERENTIAL HIRING: THE BANK OF AMERICA

Between 1960 and 1964, the nature of the demands of civil rights activists shifted in a way that foreshadowed the course of federal equal employment policy over the forthcoming decade. At the end of 1962, CORE began to deemphasize the signing of pledges of nondiscrimination and insist that firms adopt preferential employment policies. CORE's national council issued a set of guidelines for local chapters on the issue which noted that many chapters had taken a "soft" approach to management and urged that instead "very specific demands [be made] which far exceed tokenism."[12] Reversing their previous policy of supplying a list of qualified blacks to prospective employees, the civil rights group now contended that "it is management's responsibility to locate, select, train—if necessary—and hire non-white employees." A national CORE leader wrote:

Heretofore, we used to talk simply of merit employment, i.e., hiring the best qualified person for the job regardless of race. Now, National CORE is talking in terms of "compensatory" hiring. We are approaching employers with the proposition that they have effectively excluded Negroes from their work force for a long time and that they now have a responsibility and obligation to make up for their past sins.[13]

A number of firms, including Sealtest Dairy Company, the Meadowbrook National Bank in New York, Lucky Markets, and A&P supermarkets, did agree to engage in preferential hiring programs. Others, however, proved more reluctant.

The confrontation between CORE and the Bank of America, the world's largest bank, was one of the most prolonged and bitter of this period.[14] It provides a useful illustration of some of the dynamics of the disputes between civil rights groups and the large corporation. In January of 1964, CORE, NAACP, and a third organization—the Ad Hoc Committee to End Discrimination—attempted to change the hiring practices of selected firms in the San Francisco Bay area. They chose to confront three kinds of firms with high consumer and public visibility: hotels, auto dealerships, and banks. The hotels yielded relatively easily. Following a weekend of rather boisterous demonstrations in front of and in the Sheraton-Palace Hotel—involving 1500 people and resulting in 167 arrests—the San Francisco

Hotel Employees Association signed an agreement that established specific hiring quotas and allowed the Ad Hoc Committee to monitor compliance. After mass sit-ins at three automobile showrooms—one from each of the major manufacturers—the NAACP concluded a similar preferential hiring agreement covering the major showrooms in the city. Both agreements had been arranged with the cooperation of the mayor's office. Flushed with their local success, San Francisco CORE decided to choose a considerably more ambitious target: the Bank of America, with its 900 branches and 29,000 employees scattered throughout California.

The bank decided not to follow the pattern of the previous settlements. After a press conference at which CORE's national program director, Norman Hill, accused the bank of employing only "1.9 Negroes out of every hundred employees," bank officials announced that they would "refuse to sign any agreement giving a private group authority to police our personnel policies" and that, furthermore, they would not "accede to arbitrary quota systems which disregard qualification."[15] The bank's president, R. A. Peterson, reiterated the position of his institution in an open letter to the Fair Employment Practices Commission. He wrote:

In common with all good Americans we are anxious to do all we can to end the ugly specter of racial prejudice. . . . But also, as good Americans, we will not now or in the future capitulate to illegal pressures of the type prominent in San Francisco over the past few weeks. . . . [We will] not sign any agreement or furnish any reports on the racial characteristics of [our] employees to any nongovernment agency.[16]

The nature of CORE's demands signified an important development in the sophistication of citizen challenges to business. The issue was not whether the Bank of America was committed to equal opportunity employment. Not only did the bank acknowledge a particular social commitment to this area, but, more importantly, a governmental mechanism did, in fact, exist that established a legal standard of responsibility: the California State Fair Employment Practices Commission (FEPC). At no point did CORE or the FEPC specifically accuse the bank of noncompliance with the law. What was in contention was whether or not the bank should officially recognize the legitimacy of a "nongoverment" agency's jurisdiction over its hiring practices. Specifically, should the bank release to CORE its turnover statistics, the names and addresses of minority personnel, and a detailed statistical accounting of job applicants by race, job classification, and location? The crux of the issue for the bank was the preservation of its organizational autonomy: to comply with CORE's demands would mean to "surrender personnel promotion power to an outside organization."[17]

The civil rights group, on the other hand, was not satisfied that the FECP was adequately monitoring the bank's performance: its leaders felt that CORE could do a better job. As CORE's national director, James Farmer, told the *U.S. News and World Report*, "Laws . . . provide a tool with which you can work. You can work to secure enforcement and implementation of the law."[18] For CORE, the establishment of the FEPC clearly was necessary, but not sufficient: the purpose of demanding public disclosure of the bank's employment practices was precisely to enable a private organization to supplement the government's efforts. As the bank accurately understood the significance of the issue, CORE was, in fact, attempting to encourage a new "form of pressure tactics."[19]

As a result of extended negotiations with CORE leaders, the Bank of America did become the first major employer in California to sign a voluntary "memorandum of understanding" with the State Fair Employment Practices Commission. The bank also made public some of the employment data that it submitted to the FEPC. In addition, it agreed to establish the post of human relations coordinator in order to supervise efforts to place more blacks on the payroll. CORE's Bank of America negotiating committee deemed these concessions insufficient, and on May 22 picketing began in front of several branches of the bank throughout the state. At the same time CORE added another demand: that the bank hire between 300 and 800 minority group applicants within the month and 3600 over the next year.

Notwithstanding all the press attention that the controversy received, the direct action effort itself was rather anticlimactic. CORE was simply unable to generate popular enthusiasm for another corporate campaign while the mass arrests stemming from their previous efforts in San Francisco were still being adjudicated by the courts. At the outset, the picket lines typically consisted of less than fifty people, and within a few weeks they had virtually disappeared altogether. CORE's previous disruptive tactics, while effective in the short run, in the long run had cost them valuable public support. On the other hand, the bank defined and presented its position very ably and clearly. Its firm stand received the support of the local press and much of the public whose support for civil rights did not extend to an endorsement of either CORE's new aims or its tactics. In the late summer, chairman of San Francisco CORE, William Bradley, announced that the project would be suspended, conceding that although 240 blacks had been hired in white-collar positions between May and July, CORE's demands had not been met.

The CORE–Bank of America conflict underscores an important dynamic of direct citizen challenges. Challenges tend to be more successful in influencing corporate policies when a substantial public consensus exists that supports their legitimacy. Demands that ask corporations to make "socially responsible" decisions that go beyond the requirements of the law are most likely to be complied with when the law appears to be lagging behind what Adolf Berle characterized in the *Twentieth-Century Capitalist Revolution* as the "frame of surrounding conceptions" around the corporation.[20] In these circumstances, nongovernmental groups become the keepers of the corporation's conscience. On the other hand, this gap cannot be too wide. The Bank of America, like many other businesses in the North, appeared willing to comply with the essential provisions of the yet to be enacted 1964 Civil Rights Act. It was not, however, willing to accede to demands for public disclosure of employment data that, fifteen years later, still remain a point of legal and political contention.[21]

The demand for the Bank of America's "recognition" of CORE, as well as the bitterness that surrounded the disputes over corporate employment practices in the Bay Area, also symbolized a shift in the nature of the civil rights struggle toward more militant confrontations. This shift was reflected in a remark that the chairman of CORE in St. Louis, Robert Curtis, made in 1963. He argued that the job struggle with local banks was "a war that's to be fought in terms of power. I believe," he concluded, "we have to fight with the same type of weapons as the man with his foot on our neck."[22] The ghetto riots that were so prominent in the headlines over the next three years both reflected and reinforced this atmosphere of confrontation between blacks and business: businesses became the target not only of picketing and boycotts, but also of arsonists and looters. Corporations, to use the slogan that Eldridge Cleaver made popular during this period, were increasingly seen as part of the problem, not its solution. Business was viewed less as an institution which had the responsibility for immediately improving the economic condition of blacks, and more as an integral part of the national and local structures of power that oppressed them. In other words, as the sixties progressed, the challenges civil rights activists posed to business became less tactical and more ideological. The stage was set for the confrontation that would climax the interaction of the civil rights movement with business in the North following the Civil Rights Act. It would also permanently transform the nature of the politics of corporate accountability.

### KODAK AND FIGHT

In July of 1964, race riots occurred in Rochester, New York, a city whose economy was dominated by high technology corporations with relatively liberal and enlightened positions in race relations.[23] While unemployment in the metropolitan area was only 1.8 percent, the city's 60,000 blacks had benefited only very minimally from the prosperity brought to Rochester by the presence of such corporations as Eastman Kodak, Xerox, Bausch and Lomb, General Dynamics, and General Motors. Following the riots, a group of local black and white church organizations decided that the city's minorities needed a political organization capable of articulating and representing the needs of the black poor. They invited Saul Alinsky, the "middle-aged *deus ex machina* of American slum agitation,"[24] to come to Rochester to organize the city's black community; $100,000 was raised, largely by local and national church groups, to pay for a two-year contract with Alinsky's Industrial Areas Foundation. In the spring of 1965, 134 local black organizations joined together to form FIGHT (Freedom-Integration-God-Honor-Today). During its first year and a half, FIGHT followed a pattern similar to that of other antipoverty organizations around the country that were attempting to mobilize the poor. It concentrated on securing federal antipoverty funds and on participating in the city's urban renewal program. In addition, it picketed landlords in order to encourage them to make repairs on their buildings and organized a small recruitment and training program in cooperation with Xerox.

At its June 1966 convention, FIGHT resolved that "Eastman Kodak be singled out for special investigation this year."[25] Why Kodak? If anything, Kodak had behaved like a model corporate citizen: it had publicly cooperated with President Kennedy's Committee on Equal Opportunity Plan for Progress, supported the United Negro College Fund, and generally gone out of its way to comply with both the letter and the spirit of the equal employment provisions of the Civil Rights Act. FIGHT's motivations appear to have been twofold. First, Kodak's pivotal position in the Rochester economy—employing 13 percent of the area's labor force—made it a logical target for any group concerned with the economic condition of the community's residents. Anticipating the Equal Employment Opportunity Commission's (EEOC's) affirmative action guidelines, Bernard Gillford, president of FIGHT between 1969 and 1971 and currently associated with the Russell Sage Foundation, remarked:

The real question is: What were the results of Kodak's hiring policy on its work force composition? Issuing great policy papers on equal employment opportunities without supplying back-up muscle . . . is like feeding a hungry man the sizzle rather than the sausage. . . . We knew that Kodak did not plan on bombing the ghetto, but if it did not provide jobs for people who lived in the ghetto, then maybe it would have been more merciful if it in fact did bomb the ghetto.[26]

Kodak's economic importance thus made it an ideal example for Alinsky to use in expanding the boundaries of a corporation's responsibility for the welfare of the community in which it was located. One of Alinsky's major objectives, in the words of Ed Chambers, his chief organizer, was "to force corporate America to live up to its previous statements about corporate social responsibilities." Alinsky told *Business Week*:

American industry had better recognize—and some do—that they have a special obligation. . . . the Kodak situation dramatically reveals that today's ghettobound, militant urban Negro may generate even more problems for business than the civil rights struggle in the South created.[27]

The idea was to create a domino effect: ". . . we knew that if we could get Kodak in line every other business would follow."[28]

Secondly, Kodak was also a major political force in Rochester; Alinsky contended that it was the most powerful institution in the city, controlling the banks, local university, hospitals, and charitable organizations. "Had its management agreed to work with FIGHT," Alinsky predicted, "it would have been a substantial step toward bringing Negroes into the mainstream of Rochester."[29] Drawing on the analogy of the racial struggles in the South, Alinsky compared Rochester to a southern plantation: what was needed was not paternalism, but democratic participation. As FIGHT's first president, the Reverend Franklin Florence, remarked, "Taking on Kodak was something else. That just wasn't done in Rochester."[30]

At a meeting of FIGHT officials with Kodak's top executives, the organization's demands were put in writing. They were simple: Kodak should hire and train 600 minority group members—to be selected and referred by FIGHT—over an eighteen-month period. FIGHT's request was roughly similar in kind to that made by CORE two years before in San Francisco, and Kodak's reply paralleled that of the Bank of America:

We [cannot] enter into an arrangement exclusively with any organization to recruit candidates for employment and still be fair to the thousands of people who apply on their own initiative or are referred by others. We [cannot] agree to a program which would commit Kodak to hire and train a specific and substantial number of people which would extend so far into the future.[31]

As in San Francisco, the conflict generated considerable ill will on both sides. *Business Week* commented:

No business would find it easy to keep pace with Alinsky's fast moving, bareknuckles style of civil rights campaign. . . . Kodak's dealings with FIGHT, in fact, starkly dramatize the clash of modern, radical Negro tactics with wellmeaning but traditionalist business attitudes.[32]

But unlike San Francisco, the relative importance of the two contestants in their respective communities considerably increased the level of tension. Kodak was concerned not simply about the challenge to its autonomy, but about the effect an agreement would have on the power of FIGHT within the black community. They did not want to give FIGHT "patronage power in the ghetto areas— . . . power which would render Kodak more vulnerable to future demands . . . and undermine more moderate influences."[33] FIGHT, in turn, wanted official recognition for precisely these reasons; it would help FIGHT mobilize the black community.

After extended negotiations, an agreement was signed between Reverend Florence and John Mulder, the assistant general manager of Kodak Park Works and a company assistant vice-president. The corporation agreed to recruit 600 unemployed people over the next two years and FIGHT agreed, at its own expense, to provide counseling for the employees selected by Kodak. Despite its vagueness, FIGHT regarded the agreement as a major victory.

Kodak's senior management also saw it as a major victory for FIGHT. Louis Eilers, the company's president, was outraged when he learned of the agreement, and the next day the company's executive committee unanimously repudiated it. Kodak apologized for the misunderstanding, but stated that it could not "discriminate by having an exclusive recruiting arrangement with any organization."[34] Kodak's decision totally transformed the nature of the conflict: its arena shifted from the local to the national level, and its debate shifted from the nature of Kodak's social responsibilities to a discussion of its integrity. Florence noted:

When they tore up that agreement they tore up the hopes of the poor people of Rochester. The issue is, have they signed an agreement with us—are they honorable men? Do their signatures mean one thing to white men, another to black?[35]

One public relations counselor observed:

[It] fell like a bombshell into the pro-civil rights milieu of contemporary America. A company dependent on good will went against all the current social mores and folkways. It was a colossal public relations blunder that will go down in history.[36]

The very factor that led Kodak officials to become so upset by the signing of the agreement was also the factor that caused them to handle the controversy so ineptly. Kodak was a nonunion company with little experience in bargaining with nongovernmental organizations. Chambers subsequently noted, "Had they had labor experience, Kodak never would have its top management agree to direct meetings in the first place. They simply had no experience with negotiations." The phrase in the agreement that referred to the discussion of job openings and hourly rates "agreed upon by the joint group" led one executive to "detect the faint odor of a labor contract."[37] Having successfully resisted sharing authority over employment policies with a union—forty years after such arrangements had become commonplace—Kodak was hardly about to enter into a roughly comparable arrangement with a citizens' organization. Indeed, Eilers's charge that "unemployment is only an issue or device being used to screen what FIGHT is really doing—making a drive for power in the community,"[38] echoed similar accusations made by corporate executives against unions a generation before. The Kodak-FIGHT conflict is the citizen challenge movement's closest parallel to the labor-management struggles of the thirties.

As Benjamin Phelosof, acting president of Friends of FIGHT, a white liberal support group, told a reporter, "If I were Alinsky, I would have bribed Eilers to repudiate the agreement."[39] FIGHT's response was to increase the number of participants in the conflict. Having been held to a standoff in Rochester, it sought to mobilize its allies to bring pressure on a national basis. What strategy could FIGHT employ? Demonstrations in Rochester were dismissed as ineffective, and an economic boycott was ruled out because of Kodak's domination of its primary market. Alinsky decided to confront Kodak at its annual shareholders meeting which was to be held in April in Flemington, New Jersey. FIGHT bought ten shares of Kodak stock and sent 700 letters to clergymen and civil rights groups asking them to encourage their members who owned Kodak stock to attend.

The use of annual meetings as a forum to protest company social policies did not originate with Alinsky, though he certainly popularized it. What made Alinsky's strategy novel was that FIGHT asked its supporters to withhold their proxies from management—an act that was unprecedented in the absence of a contest for financial control. In response, various church organizations and a score of investors announced that the power to vote a total of approximately 40,000 shares would not be surrendered to management, but would instead be used to protest symbolically Kodak's treatment of FIGHT. This marked the origin of a tactic that subsequently developed into one of the most important nongovernmental mechanisms to protest corporate policies over the next decade. Writing in *Rules for Radicals*, four years later, Alinsky recalled:

Like any new political program, the proxy tactic was not the result of reason and logic—it was part accident, part necessity, part response to reaction, and part imagination, and each part affected the other.

The proxy idea first came up as a way to gain entrance to the annual stockholders' meeting for harassment and publicity. . . . The first real breakthrough followed my address to the National Unitarian Convention . . . in which I asked for and received the passage of a resolution that the proxies of their organization would be given to FIGHT.

Proxies were now seen as proof of political intent if they came from large membership organizations. . . . It meant publicity and publicity meant pressure on political candidates and incumbents. We . . . set sail into the sea of churches. I couldn't help noting the irony that churches, having sold their spiritual birthright in exchange for donations of stock, could now go straight again by giving their proxies to the poor.[40]

The Kodak-FIGHT conflict climaxed at the annual meeting. Seven hundred demonstrators marched through Flemington carrying signs that read "Kodak is Out of Focus," and "Kodak Snaps Its Shutter on the Ghetto."[41] At the meeting itself, Florence, one of the firm's more recent shareholders, angrily confronted Kodak's chairman William Vaughn and then led FIGHT's supporters out of the meeting. The *New York Times* reporter commented, "It was the biggest event here since the trial of Bruno Richard Hauptmann for the Lindberg kidnapping, in 1935, which is still a topic of conversation."[42]

The meeting, however, was not disrupted, and there were no arrests. Two months later, the dispute was settled through the mediation efforts of Daniel P. Moynihan. Both sides claimed victory: Kodak recognized that FIGHT "speaks in behalf of the basic needs and aspirations of the Black poor in the Rochester area,"[43] and agreed to send interviewers into the city's slums, accompanied by representatives of FIGHT. On the other hand, Kodak's management prerogatives were left intact: it did not commit itself to any specific hiring quota. FIGHT's efforts did result in the securing of between 200 and 600 jobs for Rochester's black unemployed with Kodak. It also, as its organizers had hoped, had a limited snowball effect; following the settlement with Kodak, Xerox agreed to become partners with FIGHT in a community-owned electronics subcontracting plant called FIGHTON. When asked to reflect on his corporation's behavior during the long, widely publicized dispute, Eilers remarked, "I think we used too much patience."[44]

### SOUTH AFRICAN LOANS AND AMERICAN BANKS

The same year that FIGHT began organizing, direct pressures on business emerged from another direction.[45] Earlier, in 1960, a massacre of unarmed blacks by the South African police at Sharpsville focused world attention on that nation's apartheid system. An international conference was held in London to organize a worldwide boycott of South African products, but it was not until the mid-sixties that the issue began to generate momentum in the United States. In 1966, public attention became focused on the ten American banks that had six years earlier arranged a revolving loan to the South African government. The purpose of the loan was to provide a cushion for the government's foreign exchange reserves, which had become sharply reduced by international reaction to the massacre at Sharpsville.

George Houser, a founder of CORE and the director of the American Committee on Africa, a private group interested in African independence, played a major role in organizing the 1966 protests. He recalled:

It was easy to make the transition from the sit-ins to the defiance campaign in South Africa. To enforce the sanctions against South Africa, we had to go directly to business. We could not count on the government.[46]

Citizen pressures centered on the two banks with the largest loan commitments: Chase Manhattan and the First National City Bank. A broad cross section of the civil rights movement was mobilized, inspired by the parallels between the treatment of blacks in South Africa and in the United States. A. Phillip Randolph, Stokely Carmichael of SNCC, and Floyd McKissick of CORE all endorsed the *ad hoc* Committee of Conscience Against Apartheid, formed specifically to pressure Chase and City Bank to refuse to lend money to the South African government. In a rare display of unity, Randolph was the committee's chairman and CORE organized support demonstrations at the United Nations. Randolph noted:

It is, of course, our ultimate hope that these banks will decide to withdraw their support from South Africa, but if we are able to bring this issue to the public in a meaningful way and create public sentiment and support for American disengagement, then we will consider this effort a success.[47]

Several liberal groups, including Americans for Democratic Action and the American Civil Liberties Union, also supported the committee's demands.

The controversy over the loan decisions of the two New York banks also marked the debut of the New Left as a pressure group on business. One of SDS's first major demonstrations took place at Chase Manhattan Plaza in the spring of 1966. Ironically, when SDS planned its spring demonstrations for 1966, its leaders placed their major priority not on the April 17 march in Washington against the war in Vietnam, but on the protest at Chase

Manhattan. The latter, which included a sit-in at which fifty people were arrested, was seen as important in demonstrating the connection between corporate liberalism at home and racism and exploitation abroad. Recruiters on several college campuses were confronted, and Princeton and Cornell were successfully pressured into selling their stocks in the two companies. While the treasurers of the universities claimed "financial reasons" for the sale, President Goheen of Princeton did announce, after a lengthy student-faculty study of the university's investments, that no more stock would be bought in banks loaning money directly to the South African government.[48]

The contemporary interest of the church in the involvement of American corporations in southern Africa also dates from the 1966 conflict. In 1968, the United Methodist Church Board of Missions became one of the first institutions to use its financial resources to attempt to change directly a specific corporate policy. It withdrew its $10 million investment portfolio from the First National City Bank. In addition, representatives of the American Committee Church groups attended the annual meetings of Morgan Guaranty Trust, Chase Manhattan Bank, and First National City Bank in 1967 and 1968, in order to publicize their disagreements with the decisions of the banks' management; the meetings were also picketed. All told, a total of $23 million was withdrawn from Chase, First National City Bank, and other banks, by more than 200 groups and individuals to protest their financial support for the South African government—considerably more than the banks' exposure in the loan itself.

In November of 1969, the South African finance minister announced that since the credit had not been used for three years, "it was not deemed necessary to incur the expenses of extending it."[49] None of the ten banks admitted that political factors played a role in the termination of the long-term agreement. The withdrawal of the loan, however, was interpreted as a clear victory by those who had pressured for it. The American Committee on Africa concluded:

The original and limited aim of the bank campaign has been realized. . . . There is little doubt that the banks wanted a way out. The $40 million was not worth the trouble to the banks, and no given banks had very much invested.[50]

An official at Chase Manhattan privately admitted that the protests were an important factor in the bank's decision. Their more important effect, however, was to call public attention to the presence and role of American corporations in South Africa and their links with the South African government. As will be explored in more detail in chapter 5, this issue remains a focal point of citizen protests.

PUSH

Alinsky had hoped that the development of the proxy tactic would provide a mechanism for revitalizing the civil rights movement. His aspirations, however, were not to be realized. By 1968, the civil rights effort, divided internally by the growth of black separatism and increasingly overshadowed by the issue of the war in Vietnam, had once again become an issue rather than a cause. The effort to use community pressure to encourage corporations to employ more blacks did, however, persist into the seventies, though in a sharply attenuated form. It became the focus of "Operation Breadbasket" and later of a new organization called PUSH (People United to Save Humanity).[51] Both these groups, headed by Jesse Jackson, a black Chicago minister, were based on the principle of translating "Black Power" into economic terms.

In 1962, Operation Breadbasket was established as an official economic arm of the Southern Christian Leadership Conference. Its purpose, in the Reverend Abernathy's words, was "to bring bread, money and income into the baskets of black and poor people"[52] through the selective use of black consumer dollars. It drew its inspiration from a three-year drive on industry in Philadelphia that the Reverend Leon Sullivan had organized between 1959 and 1962. Using the organizational structure of the black church, Sullivan, working with 300 black ministers, was able to encourage a significant number of the city's black residents to discriminate against those firms that had discriminated against them. Boycotts of Pepsi-Cola, Gulf, Sun Oil, and Tastee Baking Company were particularly effective. Sullivan claimed that as a direct or indirect result of boycotts aimed at thirty companies, a total of 5,000 jobs had been created.

Jesse Jackson attempted to organize a similar effort in Chicago. In 1966, in order to encourage corporate compliance with the letter and spirit of the Civil Rights Act, three industries were chosen because of their heavy reliance on black patronage and particularly unresponsive hiring policies: milk bottling, soft drink companies, and supermarkets. As a result of threatened or actual boycotts, a small number of additional jobs for blacks were secured from firms in the first two categories. The supermarkets proved a far more difficult target. High-Low, a Chicago-based supermarket chain, did agree to sign a covenant after a month of picketing, but it provided only forty-four of the 183 jobs to which it was committed, and Operation Breadbasket was unable to continue to apply pressure. Chicago A&P, after eighteen months of intermittent negotiations, agreements, repeated noncompliance, and "the most intensive and exhaustive boycott of a major food chain in recent history," which cut heavily into A&P's Chicago sales, finally provided Jackson with an agreement.[53] A follow-up study undertaken four years after a final agreement was concluded revealed that A&P had significantly improved its employment record, going beyond the requirements that the Breadbasket ministers had negotiated.

Operation Breadbasket had been originally conceived by King as a national effort. But Jackson, who became Breadbasket's national director in 1967, was never able to involve the black community on a nationwide basis. Jackson's strategy sounded convincing on paper. He told a *Playboy* interviewer in 1969:

We have the power, nonviolently, just by controlling our appetites, to determine the direction of the American economy. If black people in thirty cities said simultaneously, "General Motors, you will not sell cars in the black community unless you guarantee us a franchise here next year and help us finance it," GM would have no choice but to comply.[54]

But in the aftermath of King's death, Operation Breadbasket was unable to realize its goal of organizing the $30 to 40 billion national black market. Its most sustained and ambitious effort was directed against A&P. In 1970 boycotts of A&P stores in twenty cities were organized to pressure the nation's oldest and largest supermarket chain into hiring more blacks and increasing its purchases of services and products produced by minority-owned enterprises. The company's president, William Kane, refused to meet with Breadbasket representatives. A company spokesman asserted, "We're not going to make a big to-do of this in public, because all it does is give [them] a boost. . . ."[55] This response prompted Huntington Hartford, an heir to the A&P fortune, to criticize the company's management: "A&P was a very human company when my uncles were alive. Today it's different . . . it's a closed shop."[56] In spite of a sit-in at the company's New York headquarters at which thirty-five clergymen were arrested, A&P's management held firm.

Jackson broke with the SCLC in 1971 to continue his efforts through a nationwide organization of black ministers called PUSH. Much of its efforts have been directed at encouraging major corporations to contract with black firms in order to promote entrepreneurship within the black community, particularly in Chicago. This campaign appears to have taken priority over the promotion of black employment and has prompted charges that Jackson is simply manipulating black consumer preferences in order to prompt the fortunes of favored black entrepreneurs—who, in turn, became financially indebted to Jackson. On the surface, PUSH's accomplishments since its founding in 1971 have been impressive, and it is often credited as one of the more viable organizational vestiges of the civil rights movement. PUSH has signed covenants (the biblical terminology is intentional) with five national major corporations—Avon Products, General Foods, the Miller and Joseph Schlitz Brewing companies, and Quaker Oats —reportedly worth $300 million in jobs and contracts to the black community, as well as with several local firms. What is questionable, however, is the actual worth of these agreements. PUSH simply does not command the resources or the mass following to monitor compliance. A reporter for the *Wall Street Journal* who interviewed several white businessmen who had recently signed agreements reported that

> Some white businessmen call Jackson the moral Mafia because he is so good at putting the pressure on. Others quickly identified his weakness of being publicity hungry. So they would quickly sign the covenants and hold a press conference with Jesse . . . it would emphasize their social consciousness. But from the publicity stages was about as far as some of the corporate leaders intended to go because they knew that was Jackson's first concern and he wouldn't double back on them to check on progress.[57]

Others have suggested that Jackson carefully picked companies that were already moving toward minority involvement. There is no doubt that PUSH has increased both the credibility and visibility of black companies within the white corporate world and this, rather than concessions allegedly made by major corporations under the threat of black boycotts, may represent its most tangible accomplishment.

## The Antiwar Movement

For all the innumerable points of conflict between the civil rights movement and business enterprises throughout the fifties and sixties, the movement itself can hardly be classified as "antibusiness." While obviously forcing managers and executives to face a variety of decisions they would have preferred to ignore, its concrete demands on business were relatively modest; in no instance did they involve any discernible financial sacrifice. Although the movement's origins lie in the mobilizing of the power of blacks as consumers, its most publicized confrontations and the major direction of its energies were focused on influencing the decisions of governments—including the city of Selma, Alabama, and the U.S. Congress. Moreover, most of the history of the movement itself took place within the context of a period of unusually high public approval of the large corporation; the period from the forties through the mid-sixties represents the longest sustained time span of relatively high public support for business in the twentieth century.[58] The civil rights movement neither reflected nor contributed to public disapproval of the corporation.

The result was that business's "baptism by fire" with direct citizen challenges took on an atmosphere of relative civility and goodwill. In the South, business policies were not alleged to be the cause of racial inequalities, only an example of them. While the demand for preferential hiring of blacks after 1964 clearly provoked more contention, it was the practices rather than the principles of corporate conduct that were at issue. By the time Alinsky suggested that one of his purposes in challenging Kodak was to force corporations to broaden their conception of their responsibility to society, the notion that corporations had a particular responsibility to ameliorate the conditions of cities in general and the plight of blacks in particular had acquired the status of a cliché within the business world.[59]

The antiwar movement's demands on business took place in a considerably different context. From its inception, the New Left was explicitly critical of business and the corporate system. In the Port Huron Statement, the founding document of Students for a Democratic Society, Tom Hayden wrote in a language and style that would be repeated by spokesmen for "Campaign GM" nearly a decade later:

Within existing arrangements, the American business community cannot be said to encourage a democratic process nationally. Economic minorities not responsible to a public in any democratic fashion make decisions of a more profound importance than even those made by Congress. . . .[60]

In a symposium entitled "Thoughts of the Young Radicals," published in *The New Republic* in 1965, Todd Gitlin suggested that "The dual engines of industrialization and war have created a tightly planned corporate complex that dominates the economy. . . . The great corporations should somehow be made responsible to workers and consumers. (Here we are in special need of free thinking and honest experimentation.)"[61] Throughout the sixties, radicals participated in challenges and published exposés of corporate policies in a number of areas, including environmental protection, investments in South Africa, and labor disputes, but their major direct interaction with the corporation focused on the issue of the production of war materials.

Underlying the direct political challenge to corporations such as AT&T, ITT, Bank of America, United Aircraft, Honeywell, General Electric, and Dow Chemical were three sets of factors. The first was political: corporations were seen as the most powerful and important part of the American political economy. Given this analysis, the involvement of particular enterprises in the war effort was merely fortuitous; their needs and priorities shaped the basic nature of American society at home and the direction of its policies abroad. Accordingly, corporations were as responsible for the direction of U.S. foreign policy as was the U.S. government—indeed, perhaps more so. Carl Oglesby, an early leader of SDS, explicitly linked domestic consumption with U.S. imperialism abroad, at one of the very earliest antiwar rallies. He stated:

All of us are born to the collessus of history, our American corporate system— in many ways, an awesome organism. There is one fact that describes it: with about 5 percent of the world's people, we consume about half the world's goods.[62]

Secondly, whatever the influence of this conception of America as a "corporate system," in point of fact each of the dozen corporations that were confronted had something more specific in common: they were financially involved in the war effort and thus identified with Eisenhower's "military-industrial complex." As such they appeared to profit from the distortion of national priorities associated with military spending in general and the Vietnam War in particular.

Thirdly and most importantly, the antiwar movement's challenges to business had a particularly strong moral dimension. Implicit in many of the criticisms of church groups as well as in the "draft resistance" was the Protestant conception of individual responsibility. In a sense, corporations were being asked, quite literally, to have a "soul" by not allowing the products of their capital and labor to be used for immoral purposes. It was for this reason that the corporations that were the subjects of the most widely publicized and sustained challenges—namely Dow Chemical and Honeywell—were those identified with a particularly objectionable weapon, one whose use personified the immoral conduct and continuation of the war itself.

The overall consequence of these factors was to invest challenges to corporations over the issue of the war in Vietnam with extremely serious political implications for business. What corporations were being asked to do was to divorce themselves from the official policy of the United States government. This, of course, was also true, on a local level, about the demands on southern businesses by the civil rights movement before 1964. Yet asking corporations to adopt policies inconsistent with those of local authorities on a domestic issue about whose legitimacy there existed a broader national consensus is quite different from the demands that were addressed to war contractors. They were being asked to refuse publicly to supply military material to the Defense Department while their nation was at war. Presumably, any corporation that resisted fulfilling its contractual obligations might well find itself facing considerable financial, political, and legal difficulties from the U.S. government not unlike, in severity, those experienced by draft resisters.

One of the antiwar movement's major purposes was to isolate the government from the major institutions of civil society and thus ultimately force it to conclude the war effort. While it was likely that napalm and antipersonnel weapons would continue to be used in Vietnam even if Dow and Honeywell had stopped producing them, the political repercussions of a public announcement by these corporations that they would no longer make various material for the Defense Department—perhaps accompanied by the resignations of their chief executive officers—would have been enormous. Although only the government could end the war—as corporate executives stressed repeatedly—it certainly required the cooperation of American business to continue it. Meanwhile, the repeated pressures on and denunciations of Dow and Honeywell served as a constant public reminder of the immorality of America's policy in Vietnam.

DOW CHEMICAL AND NAPALM

Dow Chemical Corporation enjoys the distinction of being directly challenged by more people using a greater variety of tactics than any other firm in the postwar period.[63] Between October 1966 and October 1969, a period that encompasses all but the last two years of popular antiwar pressures, the degree of visibility and attention that Dow experienced not only overshadowed that of any other nongovernmental institution; on many dimensions it rivaled that of any public one. From Dow Chemical's point of view, their company was singled out unfairly. Not only did its production of napalm represent less than 1 percent of the company's total sales (these were approximately $1.4 billion in 1967), but the corporation did not regard itself as an integral part of the nation's military production system; Dow's business with *all* branches of government accounted for less than 5 percent of its sales. From the point of view of those opposed to the war in Vietnam, these considerations were irrelevant. Challenging Dow Chemical, like resisting the draft or demonstrating at the Pentagon, essentially represented another way of expressing opposition to the American military presence in Indochina.

Dow, more than any other corporation, became a major focus of the student movement. On many campuses, the issue of whether or not Dow should be allowed to recruit became one of the most important and divisive controversies. Between 1966 and 1968, the chemical manufacturer was the object of 183 major campus demonstrations; in the fall of 1967, over one-third of all campus demonstrations protested Dow's presence on campus. During the 1967–68 academic year, Dow made 339 campus recruiting visits; it was demonstrated against or prevented from appearing at one-third of them. Dow's public relations director noted with mixed pride:

In frequency and consistency of attack this is a record unmatched over the past two years even by the recruiters for the U.S. armed forces. It is unmatched by CIA recruiters, unmatched by any other company.[64]

At the University of Wisconsin, 200 students sat in at the building where placement interviews were scheduled, producing one of the most violent campus incidents of the decade when police sought to remove them.[65] At Harvard, Dow's laboratory director was effectively held prisoner for seven hours.[66] (Subsequently, as insurance against similar eventualities, Dow's recruiters began to carry ham sandwiches in their briefcases as standard equipment.)[67] Dow received so much attention from students opposed to the war because, in part, its presence on campuses made it "handier, more tangible [and] more accessible" than the war itself.[68] Furthermore, its status as a business corporation made it an ideal target for a student movement also concerned about demonstrating the interdependence of the society's dominant institutions in order to challenge their legitimacy. In many cases Dow was simply the subject of a demonstration. The object was to demand that the university assert its autonomy from both business and government by denying the use of its facilities and resources to both those institutions for as long as the war continued. A leaflet passed out at the University of Wisconsin made this point clearly: "We pick this week to demonstrate against Dow, against the University as a corporation and against the war because *they are all one.*"[69]

Although it was the most important, the campus was not the only arena of confrontation between Dow and citizens. In Washington, D.C., a group of priests, nuns, and draft resisters subsequently known as the "D.C. 9" broke into the company's offices and poured blood over its files.[70] Its Midland, Michigan, headquarters were also vandalized. Many of the company's factories and sales offices in the United States, Canada, Asia, and Europe, including its international headquarters in Midland, were picketed. In 1969, Dow became the second corporation, after Eastman Kodak, to experience a major confrontation at its annual shareholders' meeting: 300 college students and clergymen wearing black armbands picketed the meeting and sent a small delegation inside to personally challenge its chairman. In addition, a consumer boycott of two of Dow's better-known products, Saran Wrap and Handi Wrap, was attempted. In New York City leaflets were distributed listing Dow's consumer products and informing shoppers: "If you buy Dow products, you help kill. *Do not* buy Dow products—buy substitutes as long as Dow makes napalm."[71] In some parts of the country, physicians ceased using drugs produced by Dow Chemical, and an effort was also made to encourage investors to sell their stock in the company.

Finally, Dow was subjected to a novel form of citizen pressure. In 1968, the Medical Committee for Human Rights, an antiwar organization of medical personnel, was given ten shares of Dow stock as a gift. Unlike Alinsky, however, Dr. Quentin Young, the committee's national chairman, was not interested in using the stock to gain entrance to the company's annual meeting. Nor was he interested simply in encouraging shareholders to withhold their proxies from management. Rather, Dr. Young decided to use his recently acquired role as a shareholder to propose an amendment to "his" company's charter of incorporation specifying that "napalm shall not be sold to any buyer unless that buyer gives reasonable assurance that the substance will not be used on or against human beings."[72] In support of his proposal Young noted that although his objections to napalm were "primarily based on the concerns for human life inherent in our organization's credo," he had been informed by "investment advisers" that the product was "also bad for our company's business."[73] He wrote to management:

It is now clear from company statements and press reports that it is increasingly hard to recruit the highly intelligent, well-motivated, young college men so important for company growth.[74]

After not hearing from the company for nine months, Young again wrote to Dow's management and requested the resolution be included in the company's 1969 proxy materials. Shortly afterward, Dow's corporate secretary formally denied the request.

Dow's argument rested on two somewhat contradictory contentions. On one hand, it reasoned that the Medical Committee's proposal was a matter of "ordinary business operations" and thus lay within the sphere of management's exclusive expertise. On the other, the company cited the large number of political protests that had been directed at them because of their manufacture of napalm. Dow concluded that the proposal was not a proper subject for shareholder consideration because it was submitted "primarily for the purpose of promoting general social or political causes."[75] Young responded by retaining counsel and asked the Securities and Exchange Commission to undertake a staff review of Dow's decision. On April 2, 1969, the SEC decided that Dow was within its rights in omitting the proposal. The commission's ruling was appealed to the District of Columbia Court of Appeals. In 1970, in a highly significant decision, the circuit court found the arguments of the counsel for the regulatory commission unpersuasive and instructed the SEC to reconsider the Medical Committee's request. The commission appealed to the Supreme Court, which dismissed the case as moot since Dow, while still contending it was within its rights to omit the proposal, in fact did agree to include it in the 1971 proxy statement that it submitted to shareholders. By this time, however, the controversy itself had become moot since Dow Chemical was no longer producing napalm.

### THE IMPACT OF THE PROTESTS

The boycott's financial impact is the easiest to measure: it appears to have been nil. According to a representative of the corporation's consumer marketing division, sales of Saran Wrap, the product most frequently singled out for attempted boycott, in 1967 ran 6.5 percent ahead of plan. He noted:

> Though it is true that we don't know how much better than this sales might have been had there not been the napalm problem, our sales forecasts aim for absolute realism and historically are very accurate. Six and one-half per cent is a substantial and unusual increase over plan.[76]

Not only was the boycott unsuccessful, but Dow's statement suggests that there is some evidence that it might have proved counterproductive: some individuals showed their disapproval of the protests and their support of the war and Dow's contribution to it by increasing their purchases of Saran Wrap. The purchase of Saran Wrap became, in effect, a referendum on the war. The impact of the protests on the price of Dow's stock is, of course, more difficult to measure. While the napalm issue had no observable effect on the stock price, in the first half of 1968 the number of shareholders did decline from 95,000 to 90,000—a development "the company feels . . . may in part be ascribed to the napalm situation."[77] The Union Theological Seminary of New York, for example, did sell its 6,000 shares of Dow Chemical stock as a "symbolic act" to protest the company's involvement in the war."[78] Dow's executives were more troubled by the long-range impact on the company's image from the publicity it received. The company's treasurer noted, "Whether our stock will develop a defense image or a defense stock orientation as a result of our close association with napalm is definitely a problem."[79]

An assessment of the impact of the campus protests on the company's recruiting efforts is also difficult to assess. Only a few interviews were canceled because of demonstrators, and a survey of student attitudes on fifteen campuses conducted by Dow's Consumer Products Marketing Research Section in 1968 reported that 90 percent felt that recruiters from Dow should be allowed on campus and that 75 percent were willing to go through a demonstration to complete a scheduled interview.[80] On the other hand, Dow's management and recruiting staff were worried about the effect of the protests on the quality of students being interviewed. One argued:

There is a good possibility that the really top-notch imaginative guy is leaning toward the demonstrators . . . out of a few thousand scientists involved in research I bet there aren't 25 who I'd call the really top ones. Of this group, I'd say maybe 80 per cent are liberal in politics.[81]

Its concrete impact on Dow's fortunes notwithstanding, there is no question that the length and bitterness of the protests were extremely troubling to Dow's senior management; they felt caught between the demands of the government and the protestors' cries of "Merchants of Death." It is one thing when nongovernmental political pressures attempt to force the firm to go beyond the regulatory requirements of the government, but quite another when they attempt to specifically and willfully contradict them. Dow's chairman, Doan, remarked that the whole controversy "is a stinking, lousy, goddam mess. None of us likes war. None of us likes to be called murderer."[82] The company's board of directors, which included both "hawks" and "doves," spent two full days discussing the issue of napalm production. After a reportedly troubled night's sleep, they unanimously concluded that the company should continue its current policy.

Doan's successor, Carl Gerstacker, later admitted, "We've been hurt by these demonstrations and there's no question that we've been hurt. The only question is how badly."[83] The company's concerned management was less upset by the immediate day-to-day difficulties of running a corporation practically under siege than by the long-range impact of the controversy on Dow's corporate image. While a company survey revealed that only an extremely small section of the public identified Dow with napalm production, its management was haunted by DuPont's experience as a result of World War I. One executive commented:

DuPont still has an image as a munitions maker for the government. This goes back to World War I. They have already spent millions of dollars fighting this image. We don't want this happening to us. We don't want to be a "merchant of death."[84]

At the company's annual meeting in 1969 held in Midland, Michigan, Gerstacker stated:

There's a rumor that we're going out of the napalm business. Let me say clearly, it's not true. We are producing napalm now. We expect to bid on other government contracts, and if successful [we] will continue to produce it.[85]

Yet within six months Dow Chemical was no longer producing napalm. Their contract had expired and was awarded to the American Electric Company, a California subsidiary of a New York investing company that had underbid them. Dow officially denied that it had deliberately bid too high; the company insisted its loss was just a normal business event. It also made the public announcement of its loss of the Air Force contract very casually, not revealing it for six months—during which time demonstrations against Dow continued. Dow's reluctance to acknowledge the link between the protests and its subsequent contractual relationship with the Defense Department is, of course, understandable. Having been thanked publicly for its contribution to the war effort by Secretary of Defense McNamara, it was hardly about to acknowledge its vulnerability to nongovernmental pressures on what had become one of the most controversial issues in the United States. An official from Dow remarked:

To deny that the protests had any impact on our bid would be to deny the facts. We were getting awfully tired of the protests and the people who prepared the bid were hoping that we wouldn't get it.

He added, however, that the corporation "did make an honest effort to continue our business of producing napalm" and did not intentionally seek to submit an uncompetitive bid. This version is disputed by some of Dow's critics, who believe their role was more influential.[86]

The protests against Dow were not simply designed to influence the government; they were also concerned with affecting public opinion. When examined from this perspective, their success appears considerable. The public furor over Dow Chemical had the effect, for a large cohort of college students, of linking business with the war in Vietnam and with the particular barbarity with which it was fought. For those who became more radicalized, Dow's overt cooperation with the U.S. government became an important vehicle through which they began to perceive the interdependence of business and government—a relationship that appeared to make a mockery of the idea of American pluralism. The ideologies of the New Left were both reflected and reinforced by the emergence and evident energy of nongovernmental pressures on Dow. For much of the broader public, increasingly turning against the war by 1968, Dow's production of napalm also became a symbol of the ethics of big business. At least some of the decline of the public's confidence in corporations that polls begin to reveal in 1966 and 1967 can be traced to the popular identification of decisions of a major chemical corporation with charred infants. For many students, Dow was the first corporation they began to view in political terms. This identification has probably become as indelibly planted in the consciousness of college graduates of the sixties as the relationship of DuPont with munitions manufactured for World War I was for their grandparents.

One of the most important long-term impacts of the antinapalm protests had less to do with the image of business *per se* than with a reformulation of the responsibility of management to the broader society. In its public defense of its production of napalm, Dow's management refused to take a stand on either the morality of napalm or the appropriateness of the war itself. Gerstacker argued: "Our position . . . is that we are a supplier of goods to the Defense Department and not a policy maker. We do not and should not try to decide military strategy."[87] He told the five protestors who attended Dow's annual meeting in 1968, "Companies don't start wars, and companies can't end them. You are talking to the wrong people; if you want to stop the war why aren't you talking to legislators?"[88]

On the other hand, Dow's management did not consider the manufacturing of napalm as simply a normal profit-seeking activity. On the contrary; Doan remarked that "there is principle involved. . . . Principle must take precedence over profit."[89] What was this principle that was at stake? It was that the U.S. government is essentially moral and, therefore, "simple good citizenship requires that we supply our government and our military with those goods which they feel they need."[90] Accepting the principle of the Nuremberg trials, but denying their acceptability in this particular historical situation, Doan stated:

We as a company have made a moral judgment on the long-range goals of our government and we support these. We may not agree as individuals with every decision of every military or government leader, but we regard these leaders as men trying honestly and relentlessly to find the best possible solutions to very, very complex international problems. As long as we so regard them, we would find it impossible not to support them. . . . Our company has the responsibility to act like a good citizen.[91]

Doan indicated that he understood and was prepared to accept the full implications of his position. If the American government ceased to be chosen democratically and "despotic leaders" succeeded in perverting America's "historic national purpose," then Dow "would cease to support the government." Alternatively, if through a radical change in the international balance of power, the present rulers of the United States became branded as war criminals, then Dow would be "willing to stand judgment for our choice to support our government."[92]

Few not already sympathetic to Dow were persuaded by this argument. It did, however, prove to have important legal and political implications. It became an important basis for the court of appeals' historic decision in *Medical Committee for Human Rights* v. *SEC* (432 F2d 659, DC Cir 1970). Although this decision had no substantive impact on the nature of citizen challenges to Dow Chemical, it played a decisive and critical role in establishing and creating a new arena for citizen participation in corporate decision making: the public interest proxy contest. In its decision, which represents the first and only judgment expressed by the judiciary on what has subsequently emerged as a rather critical arena of citizen pressure on business, the court held:

The management of Dow Chemical Company is repeatedly quoted in sources which include the company's own publications as proclaiming that the decision to continue manufacturing and marketing napalm was made not *because* of business considerations, but *in spite of* them; that management in essence decided to pursue a course of activity which generated little profit for the shareholders and actively impaired the company's public relations and recruitment activities because management considered this action morally and politically desirable. . . .

It concluded:

Management[s cannot] treat modern corporations with their vast resources of power as personal satrapies implementing personal political or moral predilections. It can scarcely be argued that management is more qualified or more entitled to make these kinds of decisions than the shareholders. . . .[93]

In essence, the student antiwar movement, by challenging Dow's management to formulate a coherent justification for what had previously been regarded as a routine business corporate decision, helped change the interpretation of one aspect of corporate law. The court came close to ratifying what Dow's critics had already argued: to the extent that corporate decisions become defined as political, they may well become objects of public —or in this case, shareholders'—deliberations. Dow's public relations director concluded an article on the corporation's handling of the protests by prophesying, quite accurately:

In becoming the symbol of student protest, Dow Chemical may also become the symbol of another trend: in today's society the responsible corporation must increasingly meet moral responsibilities that it did not even know it had.[94]

CORPORATIONS AND THE NEW LEFT

If Saul Alinsky became the leading theoretician of the civil rights movement's engagement with business, then the former Yale University historian Staughton Lynd played a roughly analogous role for the antiwar movement. In an article in the November 19, 1969, issue of the *Guardian* (at the time one of the most important radical newsweeklies) headlined "Attack War Contractors' Meetings," Lynd wrote:

Why . . . do we continue to demonstrate in Washington as if the core of the problem lay there? The small group of activists who have burnt . . . corporate records have pointed to the proper target. . . . We need to find ways to lay siege to corporations. . . . We need to invent anti-corporate actions which involve masses of people, not just a dedicated few.

After noting that most corporations hold their annual meetings during the spring season when antiwar activity is traditionally at its height, Lynd explained the political purpose behind direct challenges to business:

The fundamental purpose of this activity is to educate the peace movement and the public at large. The message is that Vietnam . . . [has its] basic cause in the business-as-usual of the American corporation. . . . by journeying, next time, not to the White House . . . but to the General Electric stockholders' meeting in Beverly Hills . . . we can most simply make clear the heart of our analysis.[95]

Lynd proceeded to list the annual meeting dates of twenty-one of the largest defense-related corporations. He predicted, "Our inevitable enemy in the coming year is the corporation." Shortly after the publication of Lynd's article, National Action/Research on the Military Industrial Complex (NARMIC), a project of the American Friends Service Committee that had been established in 1969 to call public attention to U.S. military production, published an eighteen-page "Movement Guide to Stockholders Meetings." The guide, which was updated in January 1971 and went through three editions, noted that, "to many in the peace movement, the workings of stockholders meetings are unfamiliar and somewhat mystifying." It sought to explain the securities laws as they affected public participation at stockholders' meetings and suggested a variety of "possible tactics for inside the meeting so that the most effective demonstrations and protests can be conceptualized."[96]

Both publications evidently had an impact. The New Mobilization Committee, a national coalition of antiwar groups, helped to coordinate demonstrations at the annual meetings of several corporations in the spring of 1970.[97] Its efforts coincided with the high point of the popular strength of both the New Left and the antiwar movement. At the meeting of the United Aircraft Corporation in Hartford, a local group called the Anti-Aircraft Conspiracy produced several hundred pickets. The six members who passed the scrutiny of United Aircraft's lawyers and were admitted to the meeting found themselves confronted by a security force they estimated at three hundred. Following the meeting, a rally was held in a downtown Hartford park. The next day, 4,000 individuals organized by the Student Mobilization Committee demonstrated in front of the annual meeting of AT&T; they were driven back by mounted police. The committee had obtained proxy shares admitting thirty of its members and proceeded to nominate three antiwar candidates for the company's board of directors.

The influence of the antiwar activists on the tone of AT&T's annual meeting may be suggested by the following dialogue between a young woman and Walter Romney, the corporation's chairman:

Young woman: Mr. Chairman, I dig this meeting and I would like to pose a question to . . . one of the management nominees for the board of directors. I would like to ask Mr. Gilmer if he would be willing to tell the Federal Government that A.T. and T. will accept no more military contracts, since military spending has gotten entirely out of hand. . . .

Chairman: No, you can't ask Mr. Gilmer, or any of the others that question.

Young woman: I certainly won't vote for them.

Chairman: Well, that's fine. That's all right.[98]

Later on in the meeting, an Oberlin College student shareholder shouted at the chairman, "You shouldn't need cops on horses outside this building to suppress legal demonstrations. If that's the kind of company this is, then screw it!"[99] All told, angry confrontations or disruptions occurred at the meetings of approximately one dozen corporations; over seven firms were the objects of assorted acts of violence.[100]

The Bank of America's meeting attracted particular attention from the antiwar movement because its branch in Isla Vista, near the University of California at Santa Barbara, had been burned to the ground by a group of students and community residents a few months previously. While the circumstances of the burning remain unclear, it appears at least in part to have been motivated by student and community dissatisfaction with the bank's social and political performance in two areas: environmental protection and the war in Vietnam. The bank responded by taking out a full-page ad in several newspapers and magazines around the country. Headlined "Violence in America, One Company's Position," the text applauded the right to dissent but emphatically condemned the use of violence. The bank informed the public that it planned to reopen the Isla Vista branch within two weeks. It declared:

We realize that there is danger in this course of action. But we believe the greater danger to ourselves and to all the people in this nation is to be intimidated by mob violence. We refused to be so intimidated. . . . We are but one bank but we have decided to take our stand in Isla Vista.[101]

The bank's decision to take a public stand on the incident made it into a national political symbol. An issue of *Ramparts*, then the most widely read radical magazine, subsequently featured a picture of the flames surrounding the bank's branch with the caption: "The students who burned the Bank of America accomplished more good than all the environmental teach-ins combined."[102]

Although the bank became the *bête noire* of the antiwar movement and the New Left, its chairman, Louis Lundborg, was personally opposed to the war. Shortly after the 1970 shareholders' meeting he testified before the Senate Foreign Relations Committee, calling the Vietnam War "a tragic national mistake" and noting that, "if anyone is to blame, it is people like me for not speaking up and speaking out sooner—for not asking 'what goes on here?' "[103] Lundborg and some of his fellow executives then carried their antiwar views to peace groups, colleges, and meetings of businessmen, giving their institution the reputation of "the antiwar bank"· and quickly making it the leading corporate opponent of the Vietnam War. At the corporation's annual meeting a year later, Lundborg was asked if the bank's management felt the war was "morally and economically bad." He replied, "Yes it is,"[104] and indicated that he was speaking "for the whole corporation." The bank, however, did not close its Saigon branch. It contended that to do so would be to usurp responsibilities that belong to elected public officials. According to the *New Republic*, bank officials privately added that "it would be dangerous for a company involved in such a closely regulated industry as banking to challenge the federal government too actively."[105]

One of the most important impacts of the antiwar protests was to help make some elements of the business community more skeptical of the value of the war. By raising its cost to business in a way that pressures directed exclusively toward the state would have been less likely to do, it exacerbated divisions among the elites of the nation's dominant institutions. The range of concerns that the protests raised within the business community following the spring of 1970 is revealed in a report that the Conference Board, an independent, business-sponsored research organization, published in 1971. Entitled "Handling Protest at Annual Meetings," the seventy-six-page booklet was an attempt to pool the experiences of the seventeen major corporations that had been the objects of protests in 1970. In his forward, the board's president, Alexander Trowbridge, a former secretary of commerce, wrote:

These incidents seemed to merit investigation because of the extent to which they represented direct confrontation between the corporation and those who are critical of its role in society. They were another facet of a growing pressure on corporate leadership—and ownership—to accept a greater degree of social responsibility for their business enterprises.[106]

Under the heading "Security Arrangements," the report covered such topics as "Obtaining Intelligence on Protesters' Intentions," "Protection Against Bombing," "Protection for Directors Attending Meetings," and "Removing Disorderly Persons." A virtual corporate counterpart to the NARMIC Movement Guide, the Conference Board study, appropriately enough, included two pages of comments by Carl Gerstacker. Giving his fellow executives "some free advice," Dow's chairman cautioned:

You may be outraged and much of the time you should be, by such behavior, but the first and most important thing of all is to keep your cool, in spite of their efforts.

The key to dealing with demonstrators, he suggested, is to

know your position so thoroughly that you deal from a position of overwhelming strength and being so confident in this strength that you can deal with the protestors with a maximum of patience, diplomacy and grace.[107]

### HONEYWELL AND ANTIPERSONNEL WEAPONS

The most disruptive and bitter confrontation between antiwar activists and business in 1970 occurred at Honeywell's annual meeting, held on April 28 in Minneapolis.[108] The previous evening, 3,000 people had attended a rally at Macalester College. The next day 2,000 demonstrators met at a Minneapolis city park and conducted an orderly march to the site of the stockholders' meeting. Approximately 1,000 were legally entitled to attend the meeting by virtue of their ownership of shares or control of proxies. By the time the meeting was due to begin, due to stringent security measures, only 300 proxy holders, largely protestors, had been admitted. Honeywell's chairman had previously assured the corporation's critics that "they have the right to attend the meeting and express their opinions and we will respect that right."[109] However, once the meeting began, the tension both inside and outside the hall made its continuation impossible. Binger declared that he possessed enough proxies (87.7 percent of the outstanding shares) to be reelected by the corporation's directors, and amid shouts of *"seig heil"* he immediately adjourned the meeting—only fourteen minutes after it began. The meeting represented the most dramatic moment of six years of continuous challenge to the corporation's production of antipersonnel weapons. The campaign against Honeywell was the longest lasting of any countercorporate effort; it employed at one time or another virtually every mechanism of citizen pressure described in this study.

The public challenge to Honeywell resembled those directed at both Eastman Kodak and Dow Chemical. As in the case of Dow Chemical, Honeywell was a focus of considerable criticism from those opposed to the war in Vietnam because of its manufacture of a military weapon perceived as particularly abusive to noncombatants: in this case antipersonnel weapons. On the other hand, unlike Dow but like Kodak, Honeywell had a strong geographical identity. It was the largest private employer in Minneapolis and occupied a position in the political and social structure of Minneapolis like that of Kodak in Rochester. Also, like Kodak, Honeywell enjoyed the reputation of being a relatively liberal and enlightened corporation. It was apparently highly conscious of its responsibilities to the city and state in which the greater part of its facilities were located and had played a particularly progressive role in the area of equal employment.

In 1968, the Reverend Al Currier of Macalaster College in St. Paul, Minnesota, attending a conference in Berlin, was given an unexploded fragmentation bomb by an official of North Vietnam. The official had informed him that the bomb had been made by a Honeywell plant in Minneapolis and inquired if the people of Minneapolis would continue to "permit the production of such weapons."[110] Shortly afterward, a coalition of antiwar groups in Minneapolis established the Honeywell Project. Staffed by Marv Davidov, a former civil rights worker then involved in community organizing, it announced as its goal:

to bring world-wide pressure to bear upon Honeywell to stop not only the immoral production of antipersonnel fragmentation bombs, being used in a campaign of genocide in Vietnam, but also to persuade Honeywell to cease all aspects of defense production.[111]

Radical in its orientation and constituency, the project established an off-shoot, Minnesota Proxies for People (MPP). The purpose of this group was to use the proxy mechanism to involve as broad a political base as possible in the struggle against Honeywell. Students, educators, local businessmen, housewives, and local educational and clerical institutions were encouraged to use their Honeywell stock either to attend personally the corporation's annual meeting or to turn over their voting rights to MPP.

The project's goal was not simply to force Honeywell to stop producing antipersonnel weapons; they wanted it "to reconvert its means of production to help in the solution of ecological, urban and community problems ... [as well as to] change its corporate structure to allow for representation from the workers of Honeywell and members of the larger community to have a real voice in determining company policy."[112] Clearly, these demands went far beyond any previously addressed to corporations by a citizens' group; it was impossible that Honeywell would consent to them. The MPP saw its campaign as part of a long-term effort which it hoped would be duplicated by similar middle-class community organizations in different parts of the country. Their goal was to accumulate a large enough number of individual and institutional proxies in order to force corporations to pursue less profit-oriented objectives. The Honeywell Project represented the most active involvement of the New Left in organizing against a corporation; its goal was essentially that of socialism in one company.

Following the abbreviated 1970 meeting, a number of leaders of both MPP and the project formed a new organization, the Council for Corporate Review. It attempted to disassociate itself from the more radical and ideologically oriented project in order to build a "mass citizen support" capable of making corporations in the twin city area "more accountable to the differing publics they affect."[113] Honeywell was picked as its first target. Working with an annual budget of $15,000 and four full-time staff members (two of whom were paid), the council began an intensive two-year pilot study of "every facet of Honeywell's operations."[114] Throughout the winter of 1970 and the spring of 1971, the council sponsored a series of demonstrations, including a "balloon day" and a "peace fest" designed to call public attention to Honeywell's involvement in the production of antipersonnel weapons. Due in part to the public leadership of Charles Pillsbury, grandson of the flour company's founder and a local resident, the council received considerable press attention. It was relatively successful in projecting itself as a "liberal reform group" and was able to form an alliance with the Greater Metropolitan Federation, a middle-class organization with 10,000 members. For a period of nearly one year, the council's challenge to Honeywell was the focus of considerable public interest and attention in Minneapolis.

The council decided to use legal channels to present its position at Honeywell's 1971 meeting. Five proposals were formally submitted for inclusion in the corporation's proxy statement. This would insure that the group's concerns would be part of the meeting's official agenda and would also be brought to the attention of all the firm's shareholders. All five were rejected by Honeywell's management, but the SEC ordered the three that dealt with the corporation's decision-making processes be included. These required Honeywell's management to establish a Shareholder Committee on Corporate Responsibility; to expand the board of directors to include two members with expertise in the areas of consumer protection, ecology, and economic conversion; and to forbid board members from holding positions in more than one corporation.

The annual meeting began rather dramatically: several shareholders carried boxes of rolled petitions containing 20,000 signatures demanding that Binger and Honeywell cease producing antipersonnel weapons and convert its facilities from war to peacetime production. Reverend Hudnut, president of the Greater Metropolitan Foundation, asked Mr. Binger to respond personally to the signatures rolled at his feet. Mr. Binger remained silent. The climax of the meeting came when Charles Pillsbury concluded his presentation of the council's three proposals by saying to Honeywell's chairman: "Mr. Binger, I have been waiting twelve months to ask you a personal question. How does it feel to be the Mr. Krupp of Minneapolis?" After a long silence, Binger informed Pillsbury that he found the question "personally disagreeable."[115]

THE NATIONAL CAMPAIGN

In 1972, the issue of Honeywell's military production assumed a national dimension. Seven years earlier, in 1965, a group of Protestant and Catholic church and church-related groups had formed an organization to oppose U.S. involvement in the war in Vietnam. Its founders included most of the religious leaders prominent in the antiwar movement, including the Berrigan brothers and William Sloan Coffin. Beginning as a coalition of existing organizations, Clergy and Laity Concerned About the War in Vietnam developed into a nationwide organization with fifty chapters and more than 40,000 dues-paying members. In 1972, its name was changed to

Clergy and Laity Concerned, reflecting its change from a predominantly religious organization interested in one particular public issue to a more politically oriented group questioning the structure of power in American society. Both these sets of interests led them to confront the American business corporation. At its national organizing conference held in the summer of 1971, CALC (its initials remained the same) discussed the "development of a corporate strategy relating to major war industries."[116] Subsequently, four corporations were targeted for a nationwide campaign: General Electric, Honeywell, Standard Oil of New Jersey (now Exxon), and International Telegraph and Telephone (ITT).

Trudi Schutz, CALC's codirector, cited three reasons for choosing these particular corporations:

(1) they are among the top 30 defense contractors, and are engaged in production of air war and anti-personnel material, (2) more than six of the major denominations hold stock in each of them, (3) they each have local plants and operations throughout the country where church and CALC people can focus their attention and actions.[117]

CALC was interested in achieving a number of objectives. The most obvious was moral: it wanted to make corporate executives feel responsible for the uses of the products their firms produced. CALC's other director, Richard Fernandez, noted, "We want to make businessmen self-conscious, to redefine the boundaries of appropriate corporate conduct in order to create a climate in which certain things are less easy to do."[118] The second objective was educational. Schutz reflected:

We saw the challenge as a teaching vehicle. It would enable middle-class people of conscience to begin to understand the lines of power in the society. It would be giving people a sense of how things got done. There were many avenues leading to the war in Indo-China and Honeywell was one of them. By choosing firms that also had consumer products, we could bring the war into an arena which people could understand. They would learn that everything you consume connects you with the war.[119]

CALC also had a more specific purpose. By 1971, the withdrawal of American combat troops from Vietnam was virtually completed. As a result, the salience of the military conflict in Indochina had declined considerably in the United States. The American military participation was largely confined to bombing and support missions. By challenging corporations that were producing military material specifically used by the Air Force, CALC hoped to call public attention to the continuation of American involvement in Vietnam. Citizen protests against business represented a strategy for keeping alive a political issue whose public visibility had become reduced.

In addition, CALC regarded its corporate campaign as an effort to mobilize its own constituency. It would provide a mechanism through which members of churches and church-related groups all around the nation could oppose the war. Just as the effort to keep recruiters from Dow Chemical off campus provided students with an opportunity to challenge and change the authority structure of the university, so the CALC air war campaign provided socially committed clergy and laymen the opportunity to question the investment policies and proxy votes of the church hierarchy. The issue was not simply symbolic: a research unit of the National Council of Churches revealed that three of its member churches owned almost 40,000 shares of Honeywell stock worth about $5 million.[120]

Shareholder resolutions were proposed and boycotts organized against each of the four firms. For example, the Women's Strike for Peace picketed ITT's international headquarters in New York City and attempted to encourage supporters of the peace movement to refuse to buy two consumer products made by ITT, Hostess Twinkies and Wonder Bread. Ethel Taylor of the Philadelphia Women's Strike for Peace said that the group decided to

dramatize the electronic battlefield by attacking ITT just as peace groups earlier dramatized the horror of napalm bombing by attacking Dow Chemical Company.

She said that

ITT was picked as the target not because of its problems in Washington—which came to light much later—but because it makes bread which everybody sees as well as sophisticated weaponry which hardly any of us see.[121]

The War Resistance League, as well as several other peace groups, also engaged in civil disobedience activities outside ITT's New York offices; they passed out leaflets in the form of antipersonnel weapons. However, CALC's campaign against Honeywell was the most important of the four. Their national steering committee reasoned: "We believe that Honeywell, Inc., symbolizes the heinousness of the entire South East Asia war because it produces 70 percent of all anti-personnel weapons used in the war."[122]

THE HONEYWELL CAMPAIGN

Much of the campaign employed strategies similar to those used to pressure Dow Chemical. These included efforts to prevent Honeywell from recruiting on campuses and attempts to boycott Honeywell's products. Thirteen British nuclear scientists told the electronics company that they would not recommend purchase of its products as long as it continued to make antipersonnel weapons, and in the United States members of the Society of Professional Architects boycotted Honeywell heating systems while the editors of the magazine of the Association for Computing Machinery denounced the company. Honeywell officials were visited by church delegations in about twenty-five cities.

What distinguished the Honeywell campaign from that directed against Dow was the use of the corporate proxy both as strategy for involving large numbers of people and for focusing attention and pressure upon management. In 1972, CALC had succeeded in forcing Honeywell to include two resolutions on its proxy statement. These called for the corporation to reveal all its military contracting and to establish a committee to make plans to manufacture the conversion of its facilities from war to peacetime production. The second was cosponsored by the local Council for Corporate Review. A year later, the SEC required Honeywell to include a resolution calling for an amendment to the corporation's charter that would ban the production of antipersonnel weapons. Since none of these resolutions received the minimum 3 percent of the shares voted that would enable them to be resubmitted, in 1974 CALC produced two new resolutions that dealt with a similar theme. An official of the National Council of Churches who had been working with CALC stated in April of 1972:

It is important . . . that socially and morally concerned investors make their voices heard, not only through letters to management or conversations, but also on the proxy. Otherwise it would seem likely that this most legitimate and legal means for expressing shareholder concerns, which have very real long-term human and financial implications, may fall into discredit.[123]

Fernandez, however, also shared the ambivalence of many within the antiwar movement about the usefulness of the electoral process—whether corporate or governmental:

But voting one's shares, like voting for a new U.S. President, is not enough. We need people, ideas, time, energies and commitment. It's going to be a long and difficult struggle that will require more than a ballot.[124]

By encouraging its members and supporters to "buy a share" in the four corporations (CALC itself bought four shares in each of the companies at the outset of its campaign in order to make it eligible to submit proxy resolutions), CALC hoped both to educate the public about the nature of corporate responsibility for the savagery of the weaponry used by the United States in Indochina and to make the annual shareholders' meeting a focus of antiwar pressure.

In spite of its attempt to advance a radical analysis of the distribution of power in American society, the campaign against Honeywell was dominated by moral themes and issues. It invoked the historic clash between religious and economic imperatives more dramatically and starkly than any other citizen challenge of the decade. Thus, the night before Honeywell's 1972 meeting, 1,000 people attended an ecumenical worship service for the conversion of Honeywell's corporate soul. Rabbi Balfour Brickner, Director of Interfaith Activities for the Union of American Hebrew Congregations, told the gathering:

We weep for the pervision of conscience that permits good men to act evilly and not feel pain. We weep for America's "successful" men, who, in the name of profit, have no ear for the words of the prophet. And we pray, O Lord, for life.[125]

Dr. Robert McAfee Brown, a Protestant theologian and professor at Stanford University, based his sermon on the text Micah 4:1–5: "Beat your swords into plowshares and your spears into pruning hooks." He concluded by expressing the hope that

there are enough decent people among them [Honeywell stockholders] so that they will recoil from making profits for themselves at the price of lacerating and destroying the flesh of innocent people they have never met.[126]

A year later in 1973, the meeting itself became the setting for a moral dialogue between representatives of CALC and Honeywell. Largely as a result of extensive grassroots organizing, "Honeywell Campaigners" from seventeen states attended. The participation of between 150 and 200 CALC representatives—seventy-three of whom individually took to the floor to ask questions of the six directors present in the course of the four-hour meeting—made it one of the best attended in Honeywell's history. In a typical exchange, a shareholder from California asked Stephen Keating, Honeywell's president, "What kind of considerations are important as you decide whether to produce and develop weapons systems?" Keating replied: "Whether the proposal is technologically feasible, whether it's economically viable, whether it has a future." Binger was then asked: "Would the company accept a contract to build gas ovens for extermination?" Binger replied that he could not accept the question. The shareholder's response touched the core of the political ambiguity about the concept of corporate social responsibility:

I can't believe that you operate in a moral vacuum. You exercise moral judgment. Your minority recruitment and minority business programs indicate that you do. Can you give us any other clue at all what your moral standards are?

Binger concluded the exchange by acknowledging the legitimacy of moral considerations in corporate policy, but insisted that management's own judgment, "with the help of those whose views we value and respect," is the basic measure of the morality of corporate decisions.[127]

The Reverend Howard Schoner of the United Church of Christ told Binger and the assembled shareholders that the International Committee of the Red Cross had recently convened a conference to help prepare additions to the 1925 Geneva Protocol that might include weaponry currently being produced by Honeywell. Reverend Schoner stated:

I submit that a good corporate citizen, such as this company prides itself on being, does not persist in dubious business right down to the hour that it becomes a punishable offense. I argue that enlightened management—and all the more so when it is made up of men whose consciences have been shaped and alerted by their personal religious traditions—does not hide behind government policies which it knows to be dubious.

He dramatically concluded:

Let Honeywell freely withdraw from the anti-human weapons trade, as others once did the slave trade, before it is abolished by international agreement. In such moral matters, it does not hurt to be at least a little precocious.[128]

Paralleling the moral issue raised by CALC was a purported legal one: were Honeywell's executives liable for prosecution under the provisions of the Hague Convention of 1907 and the Nuremberg Military Tribunals? Richard Fernandez, a minister of the United Church of Christ, argued that

antipersonnel weapons are illegal according to the definition of law under the Hague Convention, Article 23, where it states, "It is especially forbidden . . . to employ arms, projectiles or material calculated to cause unnecessary suffering.[129]

After an extended analysis of the contemporary relevance of the Nuremberg decisions in which the managers of Krupp, Flick, and I. G. Farben were held individually responsible for their participation in violations of international law in spite of the fact that they were acting in cooperation with government orders, Richard Falk, a professor of international law at Princeton University, concluded:

There exists the potential basis for imposing criminal responsibility upon corporate officers who knowingly aid a government to commit war crimes. Given the properties and battlefield uses of anti-personnel weapons there seems to be an ample basis for regarding the profitable sale of weapons as a sufficient link to their subsequent use.

Falk urged Honeywell to discharge its social responsibility by refusing to satisfy the government's procurement needs in the area of antipersonnel weapons and offered to help its officers "to explain and justify this decision to the government."[130]

To dramatize the Nuremberg analogy, the Honeywell Project sponsored eight days of "Corporate Crimes Hearings" in 1972. By invoking the principle under which business leaders were convicted at Nuremberg, Honeywell's religious and political critics were attempting to establish a single and precise standard of conduct for governmental and corporate officials. Since it was obviously unrealistic to expect the U.S. government to bring charges against officials in its private sector for "war crimes," the only way this issue could be raised was through a citizen challenge. Assessing the campaign's first year, CALC wrote to its members in 1973:

The Honeywell Campaign is the first long-term campaign that CALC people around the country have worked on together; we are beginning to learn about the amount of patience, persistence and hard work that is needed to carry on such a long-term project. . . . [It] is probably the first corporate responsibility campaign to have an organized nationwide network. We are beginning to recognize the large amount of time, energy and serious commitment that is needed to change corporate policy and practice.[131]

Trudi Schutz subsequently remarked:

We had to watch the corporations to see where we were hurting them. We started out very ignorant. We didn't know what our definition of success was. We began with simple moral outrage and came to understand power.[132]

Honeywell's positions as well as its policies remained consistent and firm throughout the seven-year dispute. The firm's basic defense was that it was up to the government, not a corporation like itself, to decide what U.S. military requirements should be; the alternative would result in each corporation having its own domestic and foreign policies. Honeywell further contended that antipersonnel weapons

have the same purpose as hand grenades, conventional bombs or bullets. They were not developed for use against civilian population as has been charged . . . but for use against military targets.[133]

Honeywell acknowledged the possibility that international rules of warfare might be changed to prohibit weapons that it was currently manufacturing, but concluded that that "contingency . . . was remote."[134] In fact, in April of 1972, as the national campaign was first getting underway, Honeywell publicly announced that it was continuing to produce only one of the five weapons for which CALC had criticized it, a munition called Rockeye II, officially designated as an antitank weapon. This decision, however, simply reflected a shift in the government's procurement policies, and Honeywell officially stated that "we are prepared to resume production should the government request us to do so."[135] The company's normal business operations appear to be less affected than Dow's or Kodak's had been: none of Honeywell's consumer products ever acquired the visibility of Saran Wrap and the company experienced minimal interference with its recruiting activities. While it is highly unlikely that the price of Honeywell's stock moved upward as a result of CALC's "Buy a Share" campaign, this strategy at least did not place any financial burden on the company.

Shortly after CALC's campaign began, Honeywell issued a press release in which it expressed puzzlement as to why it had been singled out as part of a nationwide campaign and denied producing five of the twelve weapons attributed to them by a local CALC leaflet. Prior to the 1972 shareholder meeting, the corporation took out several full-page ads in local newspapers explaining what antipersonnel weapons they had actually produced. (Ironically, these ads probably did more to acquaint the residents of Minneapolis with Honeywell's involvement in defense contracting and antipersonnel weapons production than all the efforts of the antiwar movement.) The firm also made arrangements with the Federal Bureau of Investigation to exchange information about the plans of demonstrators; this cooperation subsequently became the basis for a lawsuit filed by the American Civil Liberties Union against officials in both organizations.[136]

Throughout the challenge, Honeywell's chairman Binger played an important personal role. He met both formally and informally with his firm's critics on innumerable occasions, several times inviting them to his home. Binger described Falk's references to the Nuremberg war crimes trials as "eloquent"[137] and told Dr. Howard Schomer of the United Church of Christ that his comments were "thought provoking" and that he "found himself in agreement with much of what you said."[138] Privately, Binger frankly acknowledged that management found it very hard to draw lines on what military products would be morally acceptable to produce and did not try to do so.[139] There is also evidence that the corporation's attorneys did, in fact, look into the applicability of war crimes prohibitions to their position. When he was presented with a plowshare at the corporation's 1972 meeting in recognition of the company's discontinuance of all but one antipersonnel weapon, a reporter noted that "Binger gave the distinct impression of being a little pleased and a little puzzled, by the award."[140]

After a meeting with three of Honeywell's executives, CALC's representative noted, "The whole question of image was one of great concern to the corporation. . . . They do not want Honeywell to become the Dow Chemical of the seventies."[141]

### THE MANAGERIAL REVOLUTION

The tone of the criticisms leveled at corporations during the late sixties and early seventies reveals much about the nature of modern American capitalism. A headline in the student newspaper of the University of Minnesota on February 14, 1972, read, "Honeywell: Switches Pulled in Minneapolis make Death in Southeast Asia." Similarly, one of the most popular antiwar slogans was "Dow Shall Not Kill" and its corollary, "Dow Kills." Student supporters of an electrical workers' strike in 1969 chanted: "Warmaker, strikebreaker, Fight GE." These slogans concretized an abstraction by personifying an institution. It is rather dramatic testimony to the public impact of the managerial revolution that throughout the late sixties and early seventies, a period of the most bitter and violent attacks on business since the struggles for union recognition of the thirties, it was the institutions of business that were criticized, not individual businessmen. Gerstacher of Dow Chemical and Binger of Honeywell were certainly not ignored by their critics; Binger's church, for example, was picketed. But when compared to their counterparts in the public sector, the chief executives of profit-making institutions never really lost their anonymity during the Vietnam War. This is in sharp contrast to the pattern of political conflict earlier in this century. The famed "merchants of death," investigated by Congress after World War I, were individuals such as the DuPonts and J. P. Morgan, rather than the firms with which they were associated. Similarly, it was John D. Rockefeller himself, rather than the Colorado

Mining Company which he controlled, who was vilified for the Ludlow massacre.

### THE B-1 BOMBER

Just as the strategies and goals of PUSH outlasted the civil rights movement in which they were formed, so the campaign against the B-1 bomber, organized by the American Friends Service Committee and CALC in 1974, represented a continuation of the antiwar movement after the termination of American involvement in Vietnam. In both cases, direct challenges to business continued as an important form of political expression for individuals and organizations that had become involved during the "popular" phase of these movements. Organizationally, the continuity is direct; CALC's interest in the B-1 bomber began in 1974, the year it officially abandoned its campaign against Honeywell.

The goals of the "Stop the B-1 Bomber/National Peace Conversion Campaign" were threefold. The most obvious and immediate was to stop production of the B-1 bomber. The second two were addressed not to business or government, but to the public. They were to make people aware and critical of the interrelationship of business, the government, and the military, and to build public support for the long-term goal of converting American industrial production away from military contracting and toward "the production of goods and services which meet pressing human needs for health, transportation, education, environment and more."[142] As a newsletter assessing the campaign's first three years put it:

We hoped to use the B-1 Bomber as a classic "tip-of-the-iceberg" example in order to build a broadly-based coalition to challenge the B-1 and its corporate backers and to demonstrate how corporate power, operating in concert with the military and government, becomes one of the prime obstacles to meeting human needs.[143]

It would probably be unrealistic for the board of directors of a corporation, or any significant proportion of its employees or stockholders, to entertain any serious qualms about the acceptance of a contract with potential values in the billions of dollars. Not only is the production of a new generation of aircraft of far greater financial consequence to the firms involved than to the predominantly civilian-oriented companies such as Dow Chemical and Honeywell (or even Standard Oil and ITT), but producing a new jet plane carries with it few of the moral questions that became associated with weapons alleged to be inappropriately employed against civilians. Yet, while direct pressure on corporations represented a relatively smaller component of the effort to prevent manufacture of the B–1 bomber than it did in the issues explored above, it nonetheless was important. Shareholder resolutions aimed at B–1 production were filed with General Electric in 1974, and with Rockwell International and Boeing as well as GE in 1975 and 1976. Over 1,200 individuals attended Rockwell's 1976 annual meeting, most of them quite angry and vocal; outside demonstrators pushed around a five-foot-high white elephant labeled "B–1."[144] The headquarters of Rockwell International in Pittsburgh were picketed every Thursday for a year—an effort that climaxed with a twenty-five-hour sit-in. The campaign was, in fact, able to put together a relatively broad coalition, including church groups, five trade unions, and a number of environmental and public interest organizations. Studies were also produced detailing the role of Rockwell in promoting the plan and describing its adverse environmental and economic impact.[145]

According to Gordon Adams, a research associate specializing in the military with the Council on Economic Priorities, the campaign's energies were about evenly divided between the private and public sectors. This strategy flowed "from the logic of the military-industrial complex."[146] Underlying the direct focus on corporations was the notion that the government's defense policy was decided not only by governmental institutions. While "it is the U.S. Congress which will make the necessary decisions affecting the future of the B–1 program," as General Electric argued, the sponsors of the "Peace Conversion Campaign" contended that the corporation's role was not a simply passive one.[147] On the contrary, the corporate interest constituted a major source of political pressure upon the government and thus was a major obstacle to any effort to reshape public priorities.

The focus on business, Adams suggested, was "critical for educating people about what the conflict looked like. It represented a way of telling people that there is more to the military than government and Congress, even though we obviously have little ability to directly influence business."[148] Schutz echoed this assessment: "What we learned from the campaign against Honeywell was that challenges to business in this area must take place on various fronts. You can't just lobby or challenge a corporation or the government. You have to do both."[149]

The success of the campaign against the B–1 bomber, while not attributable to direct citizen challenges, is likely to encourage organizations and coalitions opposed to other defense procurement policies to focus their pressures on institutions in both the private and public sectors.

## Conclusion

In evaluating the impact of the antiwar and civil rights movements on the subsequent development of citizen pressures on business, 1967 is a convenient bench mark. That year marked the first time that large numbers of political protestors appeared at the annual meetings of American corporations. Political criticism of management policies took place at the meetings of Chase Manhattan Bank, General Motors, First National City Bank, Eastman Kodak, and Xerox.[150] All were challenged on various racial issues; the first three about their presence in South Africa and the last two on their domestic employment policies. Nineteen sixty-seven is also the year that campus protests against Dow Chemical began in earnest, and it marked the first attempt to use proxies to pressure management policies on social issues. Since 1967, the annual round of stockholders' meetings each spring has been the occasion for widespread criticisms of the political and social impact of corporate decisions. Indeed, for several corporations the absence of highly visible, politically oriented shareholders has become as newsworthy as their presence once was.

What also makes this year significant is that before 1967 public pressures on business were not linked to general antibusiness sentiment. However, 1967 marks the beginning of the current period of public mistrust of the large corporation—a change documented by public opinion polls and symbolized by the publication of Galbraith's widely read and discussed *New Industrial State*. Galbraith's best seller both reflected and reinforced the central assumption of the corporate accountability movement, namely that neither the market nor the state exercised adequate control over the corporation. Thus it is appropriate to date the contemporary movement for corporate accountability from this period. The next two chapters trace the development of two particular tactics for making corporations more publicly accountable—the proxy resolution and pressures for increased disclosure.

# CHAPTER III

## The Resurgence of Shareholder Participation

IN 1970, for the first time, the governance of the corporation became the primary focus of a citizen challenge. This effort, popularly labeled "Campaign GM," was one of the most politically sophisticated challenges to the authority of management. Its participants, predominantly lawyers, devoted an extraordinary amount of effort to articulating and publicizing their philosophy of corporate accountability. The Project on Corporate Responsibility (PCR), the sponsor of Campaign GM, was also the first citizen group to make the public interest proxy resolution central to its strategy. By forcing General Motors to include two of its resolutions on the 1970 proxy statement, it inaugurated a tactic that has developed into the mainstay of the corporate challenge movement.

This chapter traces the politicization of the shareholder role as it developed between 1970 and 1977. Following a lengthy analysis of Campaign GM, it discusses another campaign for corporate accountability that was directly inspired by and closely paralleled the PCR's efforts: the attempt of a citizens group in Minneapolis to place a public interest representative on the board of directors of their local utility. It also examines three related developments: the increasing use of the public interest proxy resolution, the role of institutional investors in the politics of corporate accountability, and the changing policy of the SEC toward the expression of political views by investors. Finally, the chapter discusses the implications of illegal domestic campaign contributions by corporations—often referred to as the "Corporate Watergate"—on the politics of corporate governance.

## Campaign GM

In February of 1970, a small group of young lawyers who had formed an organization called Project for Corporate Responsibility called a press conference to announce that by virtue of their collective ownership of twelve shares of General Motors, they were submitting nine resolutions to the auto company's 1.3 million shareholders.[1] Their action signaled an important event in the recent history of citizen pressures on business. Previous challenges had not centered on the corporation *per se*, largely viewing it as an instrument for changing public policy. Campaign GM departed from this pattern; both its goals and tactics focused predominantly on the corporate sector.

General Motors was chosen by the PCR not so much because of anything it had done or neglected to do, but because of its status as a symbol of the prototypical American corporation. Largely because of its size and the unusual visibility of its basic product, General Motors had come to personify American business. It is the subject of Drucker's classic study of modern business organization, *The Concept of the Corporation*,[2] and for nearly a decade the firm invariably has been cited by scholars seeking to demonstrate the public or governmental nature of the large corporation. Thus, Phillip Blumberg wrote:

General Motors from many points of view can be regarded as a political or quasi-governmental institution. With 1969 . . . total revenues of $48.6 billion, with 793,924 employees, economically dependent on it with annual wages of almost $7 billion and with an international production of 7.2 million cars and trucks in 1969, the decision(s) of General Motors . . . represent decisions of vast implications for the countries, communities and individuals involved.[3]

After a complementary recitation of facts, Robert Dahl had concluded his essay on business authority in *After the Revolution*, "In the circumstances, to think of General Motors as *private* instead of *public* is an absurdity."[4] As one of PCR's founders put it, "We couldn't do anybody but General Motors. It just had to be GM. It had the greatest impact on our lives."[5] Moreover, by virtue of Nader's "David and Goliath" type struggle with the automobile manufacturer which marked the consumer advocate's public debut in 1966, it seemed to present an ideal target for a campaign concerned with the abuse of corporate power.[6]

Campaign GM directly flowed from the civil rights movement. Three of its four founders, Jeff Cowan, Joe Onek, and Phil Moore, had been active in the movement, one of them working with Alinsky in Rochester. It was from the civil rights conflict in general and Alinsky's challenge to Kodak in particular that the project's members learned the tactic of focusing national publicity on a particular corporation in order to highlight an issue. The civil rights movement also inspired its underlying political perspective. This stressed the importance of increased democracy and the fostering of opportunities for political participation in all institutions. Onek noted:

This had worked both in voter registration in the south and in the reforms of the Democratic Party. The basic idea was captured by the slogan "power to the people!" If blacks could get the vote in the south, why shouldn't the constituencies of General Motors also be enfranchised?[7]

If the tone of the campaign and its general objective derived from the civil rights movement, its specific interest in the corporation owed much to both the frustrations and influence of the antiwar movement and the New Left. The theme that pervades the large numbers of articles, position papers, and bulletins produced by the project's extremely prolific staff is the notion of the corporation as a political institution with impact over the direction of the entire society—including the state. Phil Moore, PCR director, wrote:

Corporate reform today is a natural and appropriate extention of the social and political movements of the sixties. We directed our efforts then toward institutions of government and the courts—to begin facing an entire spectrum of social wrongs. But it never really worked . . . we sapped our energies with illusory victories. We discovered what we practically probably knew—that regardless of new laws or consciousness, their objectives would not be accomplished without a commitment of our corporate institutions which have enough power to implement or defy national goals. *So now the movement of the sixties is redirecting its energies from institutions of government to institutions of private power.*[8] (emphasis added)

PCR counsel, Donald Schwartz, added:

. . . in the spring of 1970, a new tactic was adopted by some dissenters who saw corporations to be the core of the problem. They analogized corporations to the State, and saw them as the maker of economic policy. To affect national policy, the dissenters concluded, required them to influence economic policy and this in turn meant that they had to work *within* the organizations that make such policies.[9]

In its conception of all power in American society as "in the last analysis" derivative of corporate power, the PCR was not simply echoing the populist charge of the domination of government by big business.[10] Nor was its unit of analysis primarily the imperatives of the market or capitalist system. What concerned the project and its supporters was their perception of the relatively large degree of autonomy employed by corporate management; the project owed more to Weber than to Marx. Thus, in one of its official statements, the PCR asserted that "there are corporate leaders who could do more to eliminate job discrimination or air pollution than any U.S. Senator."[11] At a press conference that announced Campaign GM,

Nader ascribed General Motors' "half-century of delay in installing a collapsible steering wheel" to "the vested interest of an authoritarian psychology" and to "rigidities of a bureaucratic . . . nature," rather than to economic factors. He concluded:

This microcosmic episode illustrates the enormous power in the hands of those who decide manufacturing priorities and product designs. (The ramrodding steering column is estimated to have fatally injured over 200,000 Americans since 1900).[12]

In his appearance at GM's 1971 annual meeting, Dahl made a similar point. Corporations, he noted, are "political systems led by a group of leaders . . . who are in many of their decisions . . . substantially unchecked by any outside forces, including those of the market, those of the stockholder, those of consumers and those of the government."[13]

For Campaign GM the issue was not whether the corporation could be appropriately defined as a political institution by virtue of its public impact. Nor was it whether its directors had authority which they were exercising in socially irresponsible ways. Rather, it was that given both these assumptions, did the current processes of managerial decision making insure that the wide diversity of interests affected by a firm's decisions were adequately considered? The project argued that they did not. They diagnosed the source of the problem as structural: the priorities and needs of General Motors' various constituencies were not reflected in the corporation's policies because they did not participate in its formulation. Donald Schwartz contended:

. . . the political structure of the corporation was too narrow. . . . Unbridled power . . . in the hands of managers raises the likelihood that arbitrary policies will emerge. Political experience teaches us that the restraint of power through principles of law and republican government best serves the collective interest.[14]

The PCR wanted to do for business what the Progressives had accomplished for urban government and the McGovern Commission had achieved for the Democratic Party.

As political reform should end decisions made behind closed doors by bosses, so should corporate reform end the insulated decision-making of corporate executives. . . . We want corporate leaders to be accountable to all people affected by corporate decisions. . . . We think that American corporations can draw from the lessons of American democracy and become truly responsive.[15]

Their long-range goal was thus rather simple and unambiguous. It was

to work toward a reform of the corporate system that will give the public interest a permanent and persuasive voice in the corporate decision-making process.[16]

### TACTICS

Campaign GM was distinguished by its emphasis on one basic tactic: the public interest proxy proposal. The decision to focus on this tactic—which set the entire framework for both Campaign GM "Round I" (1970) and "Round II" (1971)—was dictated by several factors. Most obviously, it was a mechanism ideally suited to a group of lawyers who were interested in using their occupational skills to bring about changes in the society. It provided an ideal opportunity for the practice of what was gradually becoming known as "public interest law": the use of the legal machinery to achieve social and political objectives. Campaign GM's lawyers were interested in taking the notion of "working within the system" one step further: they wanted to work within the corporation itself. Corporate law was certainly not one of the more likely places one would look to bring about social reform; the very novelty of their strategy, however, constituted an important source of public and corporate interest in their effort.

Secondly, if one wanted to reform the government of the corporation, then the most logical place to begin was the corporation's existing legal or constitutional structure. The nineteenth-century corporation has been described as a "republic in miniature."[17] The legal scholar Abram Chayes noted:

The analogy between state and corporation has been congenial to American lawmakers, legislative and judicial. The shareholders were the electorate, the directors the legislature, enacting general policies and committing them to the officers for execution. A judiciary was unnecessary, since the state had kindly permitted the use of its own.[18]

By the 1930s, however, the corporation could be more accurately characterized as an "oligarchy writ large." As economic power became more concentrated among corporations, authority also became more centralized within each firm.[19] Campaign GM sought to appropriate the symbols of corporate constitutionalism both in order to emphasize the political nature of the corporation and to expose the hollowness of shareholder democracy. Since the structure of the corporation is historically derived from democratic theory—reinforced by the Securities and Exchange Act of 1934's emphasis on the concept of "fair corporate suffrage"—Campaign GM wanted to use the principles of democracy to criticize the narrowness of the constituencies to which GM's managers were actually accountable. One supporter of the project noted:

What we need is not shareholder accountability, but public accountability. To the extent that the shareholder democracy approach confuses the real issue it is harmful. To the extent that it understands that distinction and comes out on the public side of it, it is helpful.[20]

The paucity of proxy challenges proposed by shareholders during the act's first thirty-five years suggests that the floor of the stock exchange rather than that of the annual meeting is the arena most frequently employed to define the relationship between management and shareholders. The proxy mechanism has proved peripheral in protecting the financial interests of shareholders: when displeased with the performance of management (for whatever reason), they sell their shares. But the project wanted investors to express their displeasure with General Motors' social performance by voting their shares on various proposals against management, not by selling them. This strategy was central to the project's political perspective. Its organizers were not interested in making an analogy between consumer or investor sovereignty—as expressed through purchase decisions—and popular sovereignty as expressed through elections. The project's choice of tactics implicitly argued that one had no more choice about whether or not one was affected by General Motors than one had about being an American. As Nader noted: "For most Americans there can be no rejection or escape from the corporate embrace."[21] (Indeed, there is a revealing parallel between the "love it or leave it" argument and that for consumer and investor sovereignty. Both are used by conservatives to limit political dissent. One discourages the challenging of governmental policies and the other avoids public disagreement with corporate policies.)

Campaign GM appealed to the company's shareholders in their roles as citizens. It wanted to use them as a surrogate to represent the public interest. Why shareholders rather than workers or citizens acting in their traditional role vis-à-vis the state? On one hand, workers were simply too narrow a constituency. They were certainly regarded as a necessary and legitimate part of corporate governance, but not a sufficient one. The project also rejected the alternative of nationalization. Schwartz wrote:

I am not talking about [public ownership]. I do not prefer magnifying bureaucratic power with its monopolistic and unimaginative approaches to our problems. I still find hope in a pluralistic and diverse society.[22]

Nader, whose opinion of governmental bureaucracy is also highly critical, echoed this point:

As a bureaucratic structure, the corporation is here to stay and whether it comes in private, public utility or Comsat-type dress is less important than its dynamic relationship with its total constituencies.[23]

On the other hand, more individuals are eligible to participate in the election of the board of directors of General Motors than that of most elected officials in the United States. The ownership of stock thus appeared to provide a vehicle through which the "public" could participate in corporate decision making without directly increasing the authority of the government over business.

For all their vast numbers, General Motors' shareholders of record were not by any means a representative sample of the American citizenry. As of 1970, 42 percent of the shareholders owned fewer than twenty-six shares, and 79 percent fewer than 101. At the other end, 10.6 percent of the shareholders, consisting of 143,948 individuals or families, owned 89.5 percent of the equity in GM.[24] (In its degree of concentration of share ownership, General Motors is not atypical.) If a majority of the affluent could not be counted upon to support economic reforms proposed through the governmental process, where at least the principle of "public spiritedness" was operative, they were obviously not about to support similar reforms when they were presented in an arena much more identified with their economic self-interest. Campaign GM was well aware of this reality: they made it quite clear that they expected their proposals to lose and that their success would not be defined by the number of votes their proposals received.

Instead, the PCR's goal was to encourage as much debate as possible about the relationship between corporate responsibility and managerial authority. Thus, campaign GM addressed all its communications to the public rather than to GM's shareholders and unlike in traditional proxy conflicts, the campaign made extensive use of press conferences and press releases. By engaging in as public a debate as possible with management about GM's social performance, the project hoped to encourage individuals, institutions, and organs of opinion throughout the society—regardless of their status as shareholders—both to examine and to evaluate General Motors. The project wanted to do for the issue of corporate governance what the antiwar and civil rights movements had done for the issues with which they were preoccupied: to make them a focus of debate in every institution in the land. In short, the project's means was one of its most important objectives: "the mere engaging in open debate is at least a partial victory . . . to engage in public debate with management so that the issues would be discussed in broad terms . . . was not just a tactic; it was one of the main objects of the campaign."[25]

The two proposals that General Motors was forced to include on its proxy statement managed to encompass virtually all of Campaign GM's substantive concerns. The first dramatized the limited decision-making base of the corporation. It requested that management expand the board of directors to twenty-six in order to make room for three additional directors. Campaign GM intended that these directors be drawn from those constituencies currently not represented on the corporation's formal governmental body. To personalize their demand and make the contest more closely resemble that of an ordinary election, the campaign announced its nominations in advance. They were Betty Furness, the consumer advisor; the Reverend Channing Phillips, a black Democratic National Committeeman for the District of Columbia; and René Dubos, a biologist and environmentalist.

The second proposal asked GM to create a "Committee for Corporate Responsibility," consisting of between fifteen and twenty-five individuals. They would be chosen by three representatives: one from the board, one from the PCR, and one from the United Auto Workers. The doctrine of corporate social responsibility—publicly endorsed by nearly all corporations by 1970—contended that management was indeed responsible for the welfare of all its constituencies, not simply its shareholders. Campaign GM demanded that this commitment be institutionalized. The principle of corporate responsibility still left too much authority in the hands of a self-appointed elite. Campaign GM argued that the only way GM's managers could be made more responsible was to make them accountable.

If the New Left had sought to use the corporation as a vehicle for raising issues that were of more direct concern to the governance of the university, then Campaign GM tried to use universities as a vehicle for raising issues that directly affected the governance of the corporation. Universities owned very little GM stock—the largest single holding was MIT's with only 291,000 shares. Universities did, however, include among their own constituencies a group Campaign GM targeted as one of its most important potential allies: college students. Since virtually each university would have to make some decision as to how it would vote its shares on the project's proxy proposals, Campaign GM hoped that the nation's campuses, which only a few years before had been the center of two hundred demonstrations against Dow Chemical recruiters, would now become the setting for a discussion of corporate governance. One reporter commented in *Science*:

The corporate responsibility issue arises at a time when university students, who remain in a continuing state of ferment, seem especially susceptible to arguments for corporate reform. Fairly or not, large corporations are identified by many students with the Pentagon and the Vietnam War. . . .
In Campaign GM, students . . . have . . . an ingenious alternative to staging sit-ins and picketing corporate recruiters . . .[26]

### THE ROLE OF THE SEC

Campaign GM achieved one of its most important objectives when the SEC ordered General Motors, over the corporation's strenuous objections, to include two of the project's nine proposals on its proxy statement. When reinforced by the *Medical Committee* decision, this had the effect of opening up the proxy machinery to "public interest proposals." Because of the large number and geographic dispersion of shareholders in the modern corporation, the proxy provides the only legal mechanism by which the corporation's nominal owners can communicate with management and each other. The legislative history of the Securities Exchange Act reflects this concern:

The proxy solicitation is now in fact the only means by which a stockholder can act and can perform the functions which are his as owner of a corporation. It, therefore, seems clear to us that only by making the proxy a real instrument for the exercise of those functions can we obtain what the Congress and this committee called for in the form of "fair corporate suffrage."[27]

While any shareholder does have the right to mail a proposal at his own expense, the cost is prohibitive. (This is the method employed by those seeking to gain financial control of the corporation; if successful they are then in a position to receive reimbursement for their expense.) The issue of shareholder access to management's proxy mechanism thus raises issues similar to those posed by public financing of elections. The principle at stake is identical: the fairness of the electoral process is intimately connected with the control of financial resources.

However, the democratic accountability of management to shareholders was not meant to be taken literally by the writers of the Securities Exchange Act; corporations, after all, are also businesses and those legally responsible for supervising their day-to-day affairs were presumed entitled to be free from too much interference with their work. Moreover, the preparation, distribution, and tabulation of proxy proposals involves some expense, all paid for by the corporation, and thus all its stockholders.

79

Rule 14a–8 of the SEC proposed three principal grounds for excluding proxy proposals. Management need not include proposals from shareholders that under the law of the state in which the corporation is chartered are "not a proper subject for action by security holders." Secondly, a proposal may legally be excluded if it "consists of a recommendation or request that management take action with respect to a matter relating to the conduct of the ordinary business operations of the user." The final limitation is that the proposal cannot "clearly appear [to be] submitted by the security holder . . . primarily for the purpose of promoting general economic, political, racial, religious, social or similar causes."[28]

These regulations, like most legal principles governing complex political and economic issues, are susceptible to a wide range of interpretations. The paucity of case law on this issue suggests that the enforcement of the "gate keeping" function has generally been left to the discretion of the commission. Significantly, one of the few exceptions involved a civil rights issue. In 1951, a shareholder of the Greyhound Corporation asked the firm to include a proposal that management "consider the advisability of abolishing the Segregated Seating System in the South."[29] The corporation's refusal was upheld by the commission on the grounds that it covered "matters of a general political . . . nature," that were more appropriate for the governmental process.[30] The SEC ruling was appealed and a New York district court refused to issue a mandatory injunction compelling the corporation to include the proposal. The court based its decision on procedural grounds, that the "stockholder had failed to exhaust his administrative remedies," thus never addressing the substantive issue.[31]

Throughout the fifties, the SEC regularly refused to require management to include a number of socially oriented proposals on the grounds that they were motivated by political purposes. Thus, RCA was able to exclude a resolution prohibiting the hiring of communists, and Standard Oil of New Jersey legally excluded a resolution prohibiting discrimination on the basis of race or religion.

In 1970, General Motors, with all the legal precedents on its side, notified the SEC and the PCR that it would exclude all the project's proposals. It rested its decision largely on three grounds. First, it cited the PCR's own literature and statement of propose to argue that the project was only interested in GM as a symbol. Its real objective was to influence public opinion as evidenced by the fact that the PCR sought to address shareholders about issues that concerned them as citizens rather than as shareholders. Secondly, GM's counsel contended that the resolutions required action, either not permitted by state law, already required by state law, or reserved by state law to the board of directors. Finally, the firm suggested that all but one of the nine represented interference with "the conduct of ordinary operations." GM added that there was nothing, of course, to prevent the PCR from engaging in its own proxy solicitation at its own expense.

The project responded:

It is too glib to say that the proponents of the resolutions can undertake their own proxy solicitations. As Management well knows, the cost is virtually prohibitive except to extremely well-heeled shareholders. . . . This is not an ordinary dispute with management. . . . The issues here lack . . . personal pecuniary basis. Denial of access to the shareholders through Management's proxy solicitation is total denial.[32]

The PCR did not dispute the social orientation of its resolutions. Rather, they argued that "modern notions of the corporation rendered social concerns legitimate areas for corporate activity and for shareholder consideration," and that, furthermore, "it was good business for the corporation to weight social factors in business decisions."[33]

The SEC found seven of the proposals to be clearly excludable while the proposal that the corporation's bylaws be amended to expand the number of directors was judged to be within the prerogatives of shareholders. The SEC turned its attention to the proposal to create a shareholder committee. The commission's staff was divided: the Division of General Counsel favored inclusion, while the Division of Corporate Finance opposed it. Two of the commissioners who would have sided with the recommendations of the Corporate Finance Division were absent on the day the commissioners resolved the dispute two to one in favor of the PCR.[34] The implications of the decision were far-reaching: it represented the first time that the commission had required management to include a resolution whose implications were clearly social rather than financial. Campaign GM's counsel wrote:

In finding that the proxy rules required *any* of the proposals to be included, the Commission was finding that a proponent's concern more for the impact of the corporation on society rather than with the corporation itself does not render his proposal one which is *ipso facto* "primarily for the purpose of promoting general . . . causes." Rather, the proposals are raised in a proper forum when shareholders consider them because they are within the corporation's scope of action.[35]

A two-to-one ruling with two abstentions was obviously a somewhat precarious "victory." It received a much firmer foundation by the ruling of the court of appeals in the *Medical Committee* case that was issued shortly afterward. Two additional factors also reinforced the commission's decision: it received a considerable amount of favorable press coverage for what was obviously a breakthrough ruling, and shortly afterward a new commission chairman, more sympathetic to the principle behind the public interest proxy, was appointed. The consequence was that the mesh in the 14a–8 screen became more transparent.[36]

THE PUBLIC DEBATE

The responsibilities of General Motors' management to its nonshareholder constituents did manage to become the subject of considerable public discussion. Contrary to most press accounts, Ralph Nader neither organized nor directed Campaign GM. His appearance, however, at its first press conference did attract considerable initial attention. Between February and May of 1970, the project received a great deal of national press coverage and was publicly endorsed by sixteen congressmen. General Motors' annual meeting in 1970 was attended by 130 reporters—a far cry from the usual press coverage given such events and clearly attributable to the public interest generated by the project's campaign. General Motors' response confirmed Schwartz's prediction that "when corporate policy gets debated in a national forum, management's concern must turn outward."[37] The company accepted the terms of debate that Campaign GM had defined and sought to convince its shareholders—and through them the general public—that it was adequately fulfilling its social responsibilites. GM reportedly spent over half a million dollars to counter the PCR's $35,000, financed by a grant from the Stern Family Fund. The company mailed to each of its 1.3 million shareholders a twenty-one-page booklet detailing "GM's record of progress in automobile safety, air pollution control, mass transit, plant safety and social welfare."[38] It also ran full-page advertisements in about 150 daily and college newspapers documenting its interest in cleaner air. In addition, GM scheduled an all-day program in order to provide reporters with the details of the firm's efforts to curb industrial air and water pollution. At the annual meeting GM showed a specially prepared twenty-five-minute film describing the corporation's commitment to environmental protection and racial justice. Geoffrey Cowan wryly noted, "At least we succeeded in changing their rhetoric, now if we can only get them to live up to their rhetoric."[39]

The PCR sent out a fifteen-page statement to 200 institutional investors defending the merit of its proposals. GM relied more upon personal contacts with those responsible for the voting of their institution's portfolio. A banker in Detroit told the *Wall Street Journal* that GM officials had been making calls almost daily to banks' trust departments, "to make sure that the proxies are being returned and that they are being voted the right way."[40] The vice-president for finance at Antioch College commented, "Aside from feeling occasionally like our 1,000 shares is a majority holding in GM, there hasn't been any pressure at all." But one foundation officer noted: "GM doesn't have to tell the banks, foundations, and institutional investors what to do, because their leaders' own corporate philosophies make them prone to vote for management anyway." A bank trust officer close to GM's management described their efforts as a "classic example of corporate overkill."

The principal locus for the conflict between the project and General Motors' management was the corporation's nonprofit institutional shareholders, particularly universities. Support groups of students and faculty were established on a number of campuses. The project was particularly visible at Harvard and MIT: Harvard polled its students, faculty, and alumni on the issue of how its shares should be voted, while at MIT a formal public debate was held between representatives of the campaign and the corporation. Only a few universities, including Tufts, Brown, Antioch, Boston University, Iowa State, and Amherst actually voted for any of the project's resolutions. A few gave the campaign a partial victory by abstaining.* These included Yale, Williams, Stanford, Swarthmore, and Rockefeller University. At Harvard, the trustees ignored the vote of each of the university's constituents and voted in favor of management, while the governing committee of MIT indicated that it would formally request the corporation to concern itself with socially desirable goals.

The project had less success with other institutional investors. Aside from a few churches, the only noneducational institution to support the project was the New York City Pension Fund. Two foundations, Carnegie and Rockefeller, while voting their shares in favor of management, did indicate their uneasiness with GM's social performance and their willingness, in principle, to sacrifice short-term earnings "for assurance of the longer-term viability and profitability of the company."[41] The Rockefeller Foundation publicly castigated GM for its "defensive and negative attitude toward its critics."[42] A total of thirty-five institutional investors, primarily foundations and colleges, wrote to General Motors' management to express their concern about the issues raised by the PCR.

---

* The percentage of votes in favor of a proxy proposal is based on the number of votes *cast*. An abstention is generally regarded as a vote against management, since it makes it easier for the proponents of a proxy resolution to achieve a higher percentage of the total votes.

## THE 1970 ANNUAL MEETING

Following the precedent set by Alinksy in his dispute with Kodak, GM's shareholders' meeting became the climax of the corporate challenge. It amply confirmed Nader's expectations made at the outset of the campaign that "on May 22, 1970, GM may be the host for a great public debate on the giant corporation rather than a wooden recital of aggregate financial data."[43] The meeting was virtually dominated by Campaign GM's agenda. Its tone fully reflected the professional and legal orientation that had been one of the campaign's most distinctive characteristics. In sharp contrast to the disruption that marked many other annual meetings in 1970, both the campaign's spokesman and GM's chairman, James Roche, behaved toward each other with considerable civility throughout the six and one-half hour meeting. The 3,000 individuals who attended were an all-time record for a GM shareholders' meeting. Among those who took the floor to support the PCR were Leonard Woodcock, recently elected president of the United Auto Workers Union; Stewart Mott, heir to the largest individually owned block of GM stock; George Wald, the Nobel laureate biologist from Harvard; and Robert Townsend, former president of Avis turned corporate gadfly. The meeting's most celebrated exchange occurred between Barbara Williams, a black law student at UCLA, and Roche over one of the project's most central concerns: the narrowness of the composition of GM's governing board. It went as follows:

WILLIAMS: Why are there no blacks on the board?
ROCHE: Because none of them have been elected.
WILLIAMS: I expected better of you. Why are there no blacks on the board?
ROCHE: No black has been nominated and no black has been elected.
WILLIAMS: Why are there no blacks on the board?
ROCHE: I have answered the question.
WILLIAMS: You have failed not only the shareholders, but the country. Why are there no women on the board?
ROCHE: Our directors are selected on the basis of their ability to make a contribution to the success of General Motors.
WILLIAMS: You have not adequately answered those questions. We will be back with that same question next year and we expect you to have done something about it.[44]

The tone of this exchange was repeated with respect to a number of other issues: the meeting probably provided the most pointed and intensive public questioning of a corporate executive outside of a congressional hearing or courtroom in modern business history.

As expected, the vote on the PCR's proposals was anticlimactic. The project's two proposals received 2.73 and 2.44 percent of the shares voted. This represented the support of 61,000 and 53,000 shareholders, respectively. Schwartz complimented Roche on his courtesy and stamina and told him that "we look forward to seeing you next year."[45] Roche, in turn, thanked the shareholders for "a most gratifying expression of confidence" and added, "we leave this meeting more determined than ever to fulfill our responsibilities."[46] At a press conference afterward, Roche remarked that he was impressed with the project: "They were very precise. It was obvious they did a lot of homework. I'm sure there is going to be continued interest."[47] On the other hand, John Conner, a member of GM's board and a former secretary of commerce, noted that he ". . . was quite upset by the nature of the questions and the tone of the questions—as if the board was a public body whose deliberations were a matter of public record."[48]

However decisive its numerical victory, GM's management was somewhat disconcerted by the dissatisfaction that some of its institutional owners had expressed with the firm's social contribution—even though they had supported the management with their franchise. It was also concerned with the degree of public dissatisfaction which the social performance of the project both reflected and reinforced. General Motors subsequently took two concrete steps to diffuse some of the issues raised by Campaign GM. Only three months after their shareholders had been persuaded of the lack of a need for a "Committee for Corporate Responsibility," the corporation reconstituted five members of its board into a Public Policy Committee. Conner, one of the five chosen, acknowledged that the committee was formed as a "response to the questioning of Ralph Nader, his associates and GM stockholders."[49] (Phillip Moore, Campaign GM's director, was unimpressed; he stated that the GM committee "suffers from the same parochialism as the board itself. . . . It has no blacks, no women, no consumer representatives, no environmentalists.")[50] Far more significantly, three months after its annual meeting, GM announced the appointment of the Reverend Leon Sullivan to its board. Sullivan, who had founded a job training organization in Philadelphia, thus became the first black to be "elected" to the official governing body of the largest American industrial corporation. While his identification with a sort of "black capitalism" approach to racial problems presumably made him acceptable to GM's management, Sullivan made clear that he defined his position as a director in quite unorthodox terms: he viewed himself as representing the special interest of black people. Sullivan informed Roche:

I will not be tied to the board's traditions. . . . I'm more interested in human returns than capital terms. My main concern is helping to improve the position of black people in America. I want to be a voice from the outside on the inside.[51]

Black membership on the boards of nonblack-owned corporations, though infrequent, was not unknown before 1971. What made Sullivan's appointment both unique and significant was that he was chosen, in part, because of his close political ties with the black community, rather than because of his business or legal skills. By choosing an individual whose major "constituency" was a group of citizens rather than the state or a legal or economic institution, GM was implicitly acknowledging the growing importance of the nongovernmental political environment of the firm. Campaign GM did not choose Sullivan, nor did he consider himself accountable to them; he did, however, represent their most important immediate impact on the government of General Motors.

The first round of Campaign GM clearly had promoted widespread public discussion of the problem of corporate accountability, but that accomplishment, though impressive, begged the far more difficult question: in the absence of additional government regulation or voluntary concessions by management—both of which Campaign GM deliberately deemphasized—how was this new accountability to come about? How was the PCR, which lacked the thousands of "bodies" that had made the demands of the anti-war movement and the civil rights movement credible, going to succeed in reforming business in a way in which these movements had obviously failed?

### ROUND II

This was the problem with which Round II sought to come to grips. Far less glamorous and dramatic than the effort in 1970, it nevertheless did suggest a serious, politically viable solution to the problem that it had posed. Its goals could not only be measured, but also appeared to be obtainable. By its own criteria, Round II represented a major defeat for the PCR. Yet by suggesting a way in which the issue of corporate accountability could be brought down from the clouds of consciousness to the reality of actual political practice it had a far more significant, long-term effect than the more symbolic Round I.

The strategy for Campaign GM, Round II, was novel in two important respects. First, while the stockholder proposals offered in 1970 were chosen because of their political attractiveness, the three resolutions proposed for 1971 had a more legally oriented focus. They sought to change not so much what GM did, but how it did it. Moore told an interviewer:

We couldn't just go back with the same proposals and get bashed all over again. It would just be the same old debate, our saying GM isn't doing enough about pollution and GM's saying they're doing fine. . . . It doesn't do that much good to deal with a corporation's decisions, even to force Roche to produce a more pollution-free car. You have to deal with the way a corporation's decisions are made. You have to deal with the power base itself.[52]

The project's three proposals were designed to institutionalize social concerns within the corporation. The first, a "Proposal for Shareholder Democracy," required GM to list on its proxy statement directors nominated by shareholders as well as those nominated by management. A "Proposal for Constituent Democracy" provided that three of GM's constituencies—employees, dealers, and vehicle owners—could nominate a candidate for director. The final proposal required GM annually to disclose its progress in the areas of minority hiring, air pollution, and auto safety to its shareholders. Each of these proposals was closely modeled after both the letter and spirit of the Securities and Exchange Act: they essentially expanded the prerogatives of shareholders vis-à-vis management in order to expand the range of concerns to which managers could be made accountable.

Secondly, the PCR decided to concentrate the bulk of its energies on securing the support of institutional investors. Twenty institutions—five banks, two insurance companies, two foundations, ten universities, and one pension fund collectively either owning or controlling approximately 13 million shares—were chosen as the project's targets. All told, these institutions controlled about 6 percent of GM's common stock. The PCR publicly stated that its goal would be to have its proposals supported by 3 percent of the company's shares voted. The 3 percent figure was chosen for two reasons: it would represent a slight improvement over the 1970 results and it would make the proposal automatically eligible for resubmission the following year under SEC regulations. The 3 percent figure was still in a sense a symbolic one. What gave Round II its political content was the project's judgment that the way to get at the power of the corporation was through its institutional shareholders. By including seven financial institutions on their widely publicized target list, Round II, unlike Round I, was not targeting institutions on the basis of their vulnerability to popular pressure, but because of their actual economic importance.

To concentrate on financial institutions was to address the "jugular vein"[53] of the business system. While the decision-making structures of the universities had been previously raised as a political issue, that of banks, insurance companies, and foundations had been relatively ignored. If traditional liberal theory had designated the state as the crucial mediating institution between public demands and private purposes, then Campaign GM sought to target a new set of intermediaries for this purpose. In effect, Campaign GM sought to use the nation's most important institutional investors in the same way that the antiwar movement had used pressures on corporations: in both instances the goal was to change the policies of an institution by separating it from its support structure. Near the outset of the unveiling of the new strategy, Moore noted:

One really major institution, one really big stockholder, just one that will break away from management. That's all we need. It would so worry General Motors, so *scare* them. Because they just wouldn't know whether it wasn't the beginning of a trend. They couldn't be sure. The effect on GM's management would be profound.[54]

This "end run" around the corporation produced meager results. None of Campaign GM's targeted financial institutions agreed to vote against management, though most were willing to agree to meet with PCR representatives. The project received its most important victory from an unexpected source: thanks to the support of John Bunting, the First Pennsylvania Bank's controversial chairman, the bank voted its approximately one-half million shares in favor of the disclosure proposal. This decision had an enormous impact on the financial community; it was the first time one profit-making institution had publicly dissented from the position of another on a public interest proxy issue. With this notable exception, the project was unable to have much impact on institutional investors. Only those pension funds whose managers were at least partially democratically chosen by their beneficiaries were even in a position to vote their preferences. For example, while the United Machinists decided to support Campaign GM, the banks that managed their pension funds did not honor their requests.

On the other hand, several pension funds that were controlled directly rather than through financial intermediaries voted in favor of at least one of the PCR's reform proposals. They included those of the State of Iowa, New York City, San Francisco, and most important in view of its 715,000 shares, the College Retirement Equities Fund. In addition, two important nonprofit institutions, the Rockefeller Foundation and Harvard University, abstained on the disclosure proposal, thus giving the project a partial victory. Overall, the strategy of challenging institutional investors proved disappointing to the project. None of the three proposals did as well as in 1970: the most popular, the disclosure resolution, received the support of 2.36 percent of the shares voted. Campaign GM's organizers were stunned by the defeat and announced that they would "have to reassess the kind of strategies we pursue in the future."[55]

Round II also had considerably less public impact. The annual meeting was attended by 30 percent fewer people and received far less public attention than during Round I, although it was attended by Irving Bluestone and Olga Madar, two top officials of the United Auto Workers; Robert Dahl, a professor of political science from Yale University; and Richard Ottinger, a former congressman from New York active in consumer affairs—all of whom took the floor to support the project. Not only did the 1971 campaign lack the element of novelty that gave Round I much of its impact, but importantly, the structural proposals appeared less attractive to potential protest constituencies. By raising its contest with GM from one of principle to one of power, the PCR took a gamble, and it lost. Press accounts of the 1970 meeting are dominated by Campaign GM's impact; those of Round II by management's "smashing victory."[56] By accepting, without objection, all the campaign's resolutions and refusing to engage in a publicity battle with the PCR, GM received far less adverse publicity than it had the previous year.

The change in the relationship between the project and GM was reflected by Roche's handling of the 1971 meeting. While he was outwardly courteous to the project's representatives, his conduct appeared to be less impartial than during the previous year. In what became probably the worst gaffe uttered by a chief executive at a modern stockholder meeting, Roche replied to a question about GM's accountability by affirming that "yes, we are a public corporation owned by free, white . . ." Following the crowd's gasp, Roche hastily added, "black and yellow people all over the world."[57]

## CAPUR

There was, in fact, one notable effort to sustain the momentum generated by Campaign GM: the effort of the Council to Advocate Public Utility Responsibility (CAPUR) to elect a public interest director to the Board of Northern States Power Company, a utility serving 3 million people in Wisconsin, Minnesota, North Dakota, and South Dakota.[58] In 1972, the Council for Corporate Review, a Minneapolis-based public interest organization that grew out of local efforts to challenge Honeywell's production of antipersonnel weapons, broadened its focus. It became concerned with the more general issue of the conversion of military production to peacetime uses. Proxy resolutions were submitted to five corporations with extensive military production facilities in the Minneapolis area. In addition to Honeywell, they were FMC Corporation, Control Data Corporation, Sperry Rand Corporation, and the Donovan Corporation. These resolutions requested that the companies establish Committees on Economic Conversion.

A resolution was also submitted to Northern States Power Company (NSP) calling for an increase in the board of directors in order to allow for a public interest representative. The latter resolution received the support of 9.1 percent of the shares voted—a record high at the time for a public interest proxy resolution. Because under NSP's system of cumulative voting for directors only 7.2 percent of the shares voted were necessary to elect one of the corporation's fourteen directors, the corporate challenge movement thus appeared to be presented with its first opportunity to actually use the corporate electoral process to affect the governing of a corporation. Believing that stockholder activism could make corporations literally accountable to a broader public constituency, a coalition of eleven environmental, consumer, and community organizations representing about 150,000 of NSP's consumers and small shareholders formed CAPUR.

CAPUR represented the culmination of an unsuccessful thirteen-year effort on the part of a wide variety of local groups, as well as local governmental agencies, to change Northern States Power's consumer and environmental practices. In its founding document, CAPUR specifically listed eighteen occasions since 1960 when various local interests had tried to challenge a wide variety of NSP's activities, including overcharging, water pollution, and the use of nuclear power. Most strikingly, Minnesota was one of only three states without a utility regulatory commission, thus giving citizens opposed to the utility's decisions no effective mechanism for having their views reflected in its policies.

If the ineffectiveness of government regulation created the necessary conditions for the mobilization of a wide variety of local groups and interests—ranging from the Minnesota Tenants Union to Consumer Action Now to the Minnesota Environmental Citizens Control Association—then the strategy of the Project on Corporate Responsibility furnished these groups with a solution to their impotence. This solution involved internal corporate reform. Campaign GM's argument was echoed by CAPUR:

Corporate policy is the responsibility of the Board of Directors and clearly reflects the present Board's composition. For .4 percent of NSP's customers, the larger commercial and industrial users, to be represented by the present directors to the exclusion of all other interests, including the majority's, is a mockery of the democratic process. On the Board of Directors of a public utility from whom we all have no practical choice but to buy our electricity, common sense, decency, and the most minimal standards of justice, all demand a Public Representative.[59]

In a letter to the author, one of CAPUR's members spoke of the evolution behind the organization's political perspective:

When the Council for Corporate Review—really the driving force behind CAPUR—first began we were talking of "corporate responsibility." We soon changed and spoke of "corporate accountability." The first, to us, means pressuring business to clean up their acts a bit. The second means developing new constituencies into organizations that will be able to join management at the decision-making table. Is good government, in other words, an adequate substitute for self-government? If yes, then corporate responsibility is adequate. If no, then corporate accountability is a necessity.[60]

NSP's management stated that it was not opposed in principle to the selection of an additional board member with a particular sensitivity to the firm's nonfinancial constituencies. After all, GM had previously selected Sullivan for a similar role, though after enormous pressure. In December of 1972, NSP invited CAPUR to submit a list of nominees, but none of its five nominees was satisfactory to the utility. A month later, CAPUR announced its own nominee: Alma Smaby, a sixty-three-year-old Minneapolis resident with a long and well-known record of involvement in civic and political issues. Like Kodak-FIGHT, the fundamental issue that divided CAPUR and NSP was not whether the firm should "be responsive and fair to the public [and seek] community input on important decisions";[61] the board's official statements said as much. It was rather over the concept of representation: who should select the "guardians" of the public interest—management or a faction of the firm's shareholders?

### THE ELECTORAL CONTEST

The significance of the contest was fully appreciated by all participants: it was the first public interest–oriented shareholder election in which the outcome was not preordained. By emphasizing the personal views and qualifications of their candidate, CAPUR was able to make this corporate election more closely resemble one for government office. Those who organized CAPUR saw themselves as "planning for a history-making breakthrough in the field of corporate accountability."[62] At the same time, the strategies employed by the company's officials to counter CAPUR indicates that the principle of management selection of the board was not one they were prepared to see undermined.

In March, Smaby filed her credentials with the SEC. CAPUR then filed its proxy materials with the commission and mailed them to NSP's shareholders at a cost of $10,000. At the same time, NSP quietly hired Georgeson and Co., an investor relations consulting firm based in New York. The firm made two suggestions. The first was for NSP to deny access to the shareholders list to CAPUR shareholders who might request it—in order to "force [CAPUR] to bring suit."[63] The firm advised NSP that they "could get the case transferred to a Federal court shortly with the possibility that the SEC might join in," adding that NSP "would be a hero to the managements of other companies who are harassed by similar groups and I suspect the SEC would welcome such a suit."[64]

The firm's second suggestion proved considerably more controversial. Exactly a month before the election, NSP announced a change in the system of electing directors. Their number was reduced from fourteen to twelve, and the corporation's bylaws and articles of incorporation were to be amended so that only four directors would be elected each year by the company's shareholders. The changes would be submitted to the forthcoming annual meeting and, if approved, would apply to the coming election. In its press release on April 6 announcing the change, NSP frankly admitted that the new election procedures would make it "more difficult for small groups of shareholders who oppose management to gain representation on the board."[65] In fact, it would require a candidate to receive more than 20 percent of the shares voted to be elected, rather than the 7.2 percent required under the existing rules—far beyond the capacity of any candidate opposed by management. The resulting public furor resembled that following Kodak's repudiation of the agreement one of its officials had negotiated with FIGHT. Suddenly the proxy contest, which up to then had aroused relatively little public interest, received major press attention, much of it critical of NSP. The issue of NSP's governance had, in fact, become a public one.

After considerable deliberation, CAPUR decided to take NSP to court. Since legal precedent overwhelmingly suggested that management could do virtually anything it wanted with its bylaws, providing a majority of the shareholders approved, CAPUR was not optimistic about the outcome. However, on April 12, a temporary restraining order was issued, preventing NSP from holding its meeting, and on April 24, a preliminary injunction was issued against NSP and its solicitation of proxies. In the decision, the court noted that the plaintiff (CAPUR) was not bringing injury to the company, as the firm alleged, but was simply trying to preserve the same election procedures that had existed since 1902. The court ruled:

> The public interest aspects of this case may prove to be quite important. NSP, as the provider of vital public services for a four-state area, is a unique corporation in that its position imposes upon it certain public responsibility and public duty. As a consequence, it may be that the motives and actions of the Directors and Officers must be scrutinized all the more carefully to insure that NSP's obligations to the public are carried out.[66]

The ruling forced a postponement of the annual meeting, and a trial date was set for June. To CAPUR's surprise, only hours before the trial was to begin NSP offered to settle out of court. The company agreed to pay CAPUR's court costs and attorney fees, totaling about $24,000, and to postpone the effective date of their proposal to stagger the elections of their directors until 1974. On the other hand, it insisted on reducing the size of the board from fourteen to twelve members. Although the latter change would make it marginally more difficult for CAPUR to elect Smaby, CAPUR felt that it would be still likely to win. The utility also agreed to send CAPUR's proxy to its shareholders—at the corporate challenge group's expense. CAPUR and much of the press considered NSP's overall offer "a major victory."[67]

The NSP proxy election differed from that of all other public interest shareholder challenges in that it was legally defined as an adversary relationship between the board and CAPUR. Management can be required to include various changes in the corporation's policies proposed by shareholders on its proxy statement when they are matters deemed relevant to the interests of shareholders. That is the case in a public interest proxy proposal. On the other hand, when a nominee to the board itself is formally proposed by shareholders, the election then legally resembles an actual fight for the control of the corporation, and each side sends its own proxies. Each shareholder's proxy was thus solicited by both NSP and CAPUR. CAPUR initially received about 14 percent of the votes, sufficient for Smaby's election. The company then took the unprecedented, though legal, step of sending out a second proxy to all shareholders. According to corporate law, only the most recently dated proxy counts. Smaby recalled:

> It was that mailing that did us in . . . that 14 per cent fell to 4 per cent as the results of the second mailing were tallied. What caused the drastic change is a subject for speculation. . . . We did determine that there was genuine confusion when the second proxy came from the company; after all, it had never hap-

pened before. We learned, too, that many shareholders did not understand that merely by returning management's proxy signed, they were voting for the company.[68]

On September 27, CAPUR called a press conference and admitted defeat, but claimed a "moral victory."[69] Shortly afterward, in a move reminiscent of GM's, the company itself selected two more directors, a woman and the vice-president of a large farm cooperative, adding that "the Smaby campaign encouraged the company to seek new viewpoints on its board."[70]

Smaby's defeat was a major blow to CAPUR and the Council for Corporate Review, both of which were dissolved shortly afterward. Not only did it bring to a halt the momentum of corporate challenge efforts in the Minneapolis area, but it had important national implications. CAPUR's challenge was made possible by a variety of unique circumstances: the election procedures of NSP, the lack of a public utilities commission, and the history of grass roots organizing against corporate authority in the region. Moreover, as the district court's decision argued, as a utility NSP enjoyed a "public" status that made it atypical of investor-owned corporations. Nevertheless, it had created considerable interest and excitement among corporate activists around the nation. What made NSP's victory particularly important to those interested in using proxies as a vehicle for popular organizing and corporate reform was that it revealed the extent to which the entire proxy mechanism was rigged in favor of management. Smaby noted, "[We] had worked in campaigns and public-cause groups. But none of us had experienced a proxy contest, no one had anticipated the lengths to which NSP would go to defeat us."[71] CAPUR also had seriously underestimated the considerable expenses that a proxy contest involved; their proxy mailing alone cost $15,000, a considerable sum for a coalition of local citizens groups. CAPUR's demise dissipated much of the momentum generated by Campaign GM: it was the first and last effort to base a grass roots corporate challenge primarily on a proxy election.

## Institutional Investors: Nonprofit

The most important long-term impact of the Campaign to Make General Motors Responsible was that it began to erode the practice of institutional neutrality in stockholder elections. While Blumberg's conclusion that "as a result of Campaign GM, American corporate electoral processes have become fundamentally changed" is an exaggeration, after 1970 one can discern the beginnings of a shift in the relationship between shareholders and management.[72] When seen in the context of the history of the structure of authority of the corporation, the year 1970 marks an important watershed: after roughly thirty-five years of relatively steady increases in the authority of management over shareholders, a number of important institutional shareholders began to reassert the prerogatives of ownership. The vehicle for this gradual transformation was the public interest proxy introduced by Campaign GM.

The displacement of entrepreneurs by professional managers at the apex of the corporate hierarchy is one of the characteristic features of twentieth-century American capitalism. The formal separation of ownership and control had continued to increase since Berle and Means published the first study of the phenomenon in 1932. In 1963 an update of the Berle and Means data revealed that the percentage of the 200 largest nonfinancial corporations controlled by management had nearly doubled—to 84 percent.[73] The number of shareholders also steadily increased throughout the postwar period: 6.49 million Americans owned stock in 1952, while nearly five times that number held at least one share in a corporation twenty years later. At the same time, an increasing percentage of stock became owned or controlled by financial institutions. Between 1949 and 1972, institutional investors increased their holdings of securities listed on the New York Stock Exchange from $9.7 billion to $258.3 billion. This latter figure represented 29.6 percent of all the outstanding shares traded on the exchange. Slightly more than two-fifths of this total consisted of stock purchased by private and government pension plans. The remainder largely consisted of securities owned by investment and insurance companies.

The result is that while stock ownership may have become somewhat more widely distributed, thanks to the dramatic growth of institutional investment, control of stock remained centralized. In 1972, the total institutional holdings of New York Security Exchange stock were estimated at more than 45 percent—a 25 percent increase in just a four-year period. As a result, the formal control of corporate stock was not substantially different in the 1970s from what it was during the previous century. Rather than being concentrated in the hands of those who owned their own corporations, it was now almost equally concentrated in the hands of those who administrated stock portfolios: the formal locus of control had shifted out of the firm to the financial community.

While Berle and Means's *The Modern Corporation* had predicted that the stockholder franchise would "diminish . . . in fact to negligible importance as the corporations become giants,"[74] throughout the fifties and sixties, a number of attentive students of the corporations, including Berle himself, noted the growing importance of institutional ownership. They spoke of the growth of institutional investment in somewhat the same sense that Marx, in the 1840s and 1850s, had remarked on the creation of the industrial proletariat. Both had sprung up behind the backs of the industrial bourgeoisie as a response to the imperatives on capitalist development: one reflected the need for increasing numbers of laborers, whereas the other reflected the need for increasing sources of capital. Investors became for students of advanced capitalism what the proletariat represented to observers of industrial capitalism: a sort of "sleeping giant" whose potential could, at any moment, suddenly become realized and, in so doing, fundamentally transformed the power structure of the industrial economy. What most impressed Marx in the 1840s was similar to what intrigued Drucker and Berle in the 1950s: a growing objective potential for power over business was going unused. Thus, Berle wrote in the late fifties:

Pension trusts grow as a matter of necessity. . . . If part of their investments must go into common stocks . . . the time will certainly arrive when their power position cannot be avoided. . . . honest managers of funds cannot honorably refuse interest in or decline concern with management of those enterprises in which they have large investments. . . . Thus we must forecast a time when these funds now valuting to comparable size with the other great pool of private investment—insurance companies—will emerge as a major and perhaps decisive element in choosing the managers and influencing the policy of the more decisive sectors of American production.[75]

Portfolio managers, like workers, essentially treated corporations as sources of income, content to cash their pay/dividend checks and showing no interest in usurping the prerogatives of management. Within the financial community, this practice became known as the "Wall Street Rule." Institutions would purchase stock for themselves or for those who had entrusted them with their capital according to the same economic criteria used by any individual. If the performance of the company was disappointing, the stock would be sold. Hurst noted as recently as 1970:

As the number of institutional investors increased, some prophets said that these investors, moved by their stakes and informed by their expertise, would begin to play in earnest the supervisory roles of the legendary stockholder. But throughout the 1960's the record showed little to bear out the prophecies.[76]

To equate Campaign GM with the Communist Manifesto would be an exaggeration: institutional investors did not suddenly become "class conscious." However, the analogy to the activities of workers remains useful: it would be more accurate to describe them as developing trade union consciousness. Institutional investors did not seek to overthrow the authority of management; rather they constituted themselves as a quasi-interest group, prepared to apply a limited amount of pressure on management under a limited range of circumstances. Thus, a survey of 196 institutions conducted by the Ford Foundation in 1971 revealed that forty-nine had recently reviewed, or were currently reviewing, the social aspects of their investment policy; forty-six were considering proxies relating to social and political issues on their merits; twenty-six were prepared to communicate directly with management to express their rules on corporate social performance; and, finally, twenty-seven acknowledged that they had established special procedural mechanisms that took social factors into account in their investment process.[77]

## UNIVERSITIES AND FOUNDATIONS

The institutions that played the pioneering role in using the proxy mechanism to scrutinize the policies of corporate managers were in the nonprofit sector. Although foundations and universities own slightly less than 5 percent of the private sector's equity, they, along with the church, initially proved most responsive to the appeals of shareholder activists. In the case of the universities and the churches, the initial impetus for the blending of investor and citizen roles came from within their own constituencies. More fundamentally, it has flowed from the contradictions inherent in their very social role. On one hand, they depend on the income from their securities to accomplish their basic objectives. Yet, on the other, the goals that justify their existence in society are frequently subverted by the activities of the corporations from whose profits they receive much of their support.

An official report submitted to Harvard University in 1971 clearly articulated this dilemma. It recommended that the university "should strive fundamentally for maximum return. [This is] a matter of sheer necessity in this era of spiraling costs."[78] It also, however, concluded that "once the University has taken a particular corporate plunge, choice in a sense becomes inescapable . . . like any other institutional investor . . . [the university] may properly, and sometimes should, attempt to influence management in directions that are considered to be socially desirable."[79] Accordingly, it "should vote its stock on occasion in favor of change for the symbolic effect of a great university's taking a position on a social problem."[80] Yale's president Kingman Brewster similarly referred to "the terrible tension at the moment between the imperative of university neutrality and the imperative of university morality."[81] The development of the public interest proxy contest, while exacerbating this dilemma, also provided a way it could be resolved. Unlike socially oriented investment and divestment, selectively voting proxies against management does not appear to demand any financial sacrifice for an investor.

The most influential analysis of the investor role of universities was published in a 190-page report to Yale University that appeared in 1972. *The Ethical Investor: Universities and Corporate Responsibility* represented the combined efforts of representatives of the university's law and divinity schools. It followed a year-long seminar established explicitly to explore this issue.[82] The report's central thesis was that corporations have a fundamental moral obligation to make "profits in such a way as to minimize social injury,"[83] and that the university, as a shareholder, has a "moral minimum" responsibility to prevent corporations from committing such "social injury."[84] While recognizing that "the university is an anomalous institution . . . [whose] special purpose and goals make it unusually fragile and vulnerable," it concluded that

the purposes and goals for which the university *is* organized—the criticism and transmission of ideas and methods—do make an institution within which individuals constantly make implicit and explicit judgments about normative issues with unusual care and precision and, thus presumably, competence.[85]

Twelve out of the twenty-eight major universities surveyed by the Ford Foundation in 1971 indicated general agreement with these principles. Mark Marlow, chairman of Wesleyan University's subcommittee on the social implications of investment policy, noted that same year, "Five years ago, no institution would consider voting stockholders proxies. Heads are being turned and people are turning corners."[86]

By 1977, approximately thirty universities were regularly participating in corporate elections. They included Harvard, Yale, Wesleyan, Princeton, Dartmouth, Smith, Bryn Mawr, the University of Pennsylvania, Stanford, the University of Minnesota, and the University of Michigan. In the winter of 1977–78, the University of Minnesota became the first university to initiate a proxy proposal. While the trustees usually maintain final voting authority, most schools have established advisory committees consisting of representatives of students, faculty, the administration, and alumni to make recommendations about the voting of proxies to the university's investment committees. The influence of these committees varies: at some schools they are little more than window-dressing, while at other institutions their responsibilities are taken more seriously.[87] In addition, the $4.5 billion

College Retirement Equities Fund and Teachers Insurance and Annuity Association, under the leadership of William C. Greenough, has taken the lead among pension funds in responding to the issues raised by public interest proxy proposals. Taking its voting responsibilities more seriously than any other institutional investor, the fund in 1977 voted against management recommendations twenty-one times.[88]

Foundations have also proven relatively responsive to the principle of "institutional citizenship." One of them, the Field Foundation, has actually been the only other secular institutional investor to initiate proxy proposals.[89] Fifteen foundations, including the Ford Foundation, the Carnegie Foundation, the Russell Sage Foundation, and the Rockefeller Foundation, officially take cognizance of the social policies of the corporations of which they are part owners. In order to assess their effort to "harmonize charitable and investment objectives,"[90] the trustees of the Ford Foundation asked two lawyers to survey current practices of corporate social responsibility and to indicate the range of options available to the nation's largest foundation. Their report, *Corporate Social Responsibility and the Institutional Investor*, appeared in 1973. Roger Kennedy, who as chief financial officer of the foundation played an important role in defining Ford's relationship to citizen challenges, notes:

The role is a classic one for us. As individual ownership has become less important, intermediaries—like foundations, endowments, and mutual funds—have become more important. That's what gives us our responsibility. We can't walk away from it.[91]

In 1974, the foundation supported twenty-nine resolutions opposed by management, abstained on six, and voted against seventeen. While universities and foundations have only voted in favor of a small proportion of public interest proxy resolutions, focusing exclusively on voting behavior is somewhat deceptive; the greater part of whatever impact they have had on management policies has taken place more informally. Thus, Roger Kennedy has become personally involved in a few issues of particular importance to him, largely involving the behavior of American corporations in Africa and Latin America. He has attempted to serve as a kind of intermediary between stockholder activists and the business community, translating the concerns of the former into language that the latter can understand and act upon. In another example, ACORN, a coalition of community organizations in Arkansas, in 1974 asked Harvard University to use its influence as the largest single shareholder of Middle South Utilities to pressure one of their subsidiaries, Arkansas Power and Light

Company, to install better pollution control equipment on a proposed power plant.[92] The farmers in the White Bluff area were concerned that the plant's sulfur dioxide emissions would damage their crops and livestock. The university commissioned a study evaluating the situation and then helped pressure both the company and the State Public Commission into reducing the plant's harmful effects. The chief organizer of ACORN recalled: "Bringing in Harvard and others obviously had the desired effect of upping the ante on the campaign, although it was not the primary reason for our eventually winning the campaign."[93]

### INVESTOR RESPONSIBILITY RESEARCH CENTER

In 1972, at the initiative of Stephen Farber, an advisor to the president of Harvard University, twenty major institutional investors established the Investor Responsibility Research Center (IRRC) in Washington, D.C. The establishment of IRRC both reflected and reinforced the interest of institutional investors, particularly those from the nonprofit sector, in monitoring public interest proxy contests. The immediate impetus behind its creation was the occupation of a building on the campus of Harvard University by a group of black students. They demanded that the university sell its stock in Gulf Oil in order to protest the company's presence in what was then Portuguese Angola. In addition, the number of public interest proxy proposals and the range of issues on which they focused had increased rapidly after 1970: in 1972, forty such proposals were submitted to stockholders for their approval. While Harvard had sent Farber to Angola to report on Gulf's role, the university could not very well conduct a similar investigation of each issue. Universities thus found themselves forced to make judgments on a wide range of extremely sensitive issues, with neither the time nor the resources to investigate the conflicting and contradictory claims of management and their student critics. Corporations also found themselves overwhelmed by requests for information from activists and were interested in the establishment of a central clearinghouse for questions about the social impact of their policies.

IRRC was established with a $160,000 grant from six foundations in order to provide "accurate and balanced" studies of the issues raised in public interest proxy proposals.[94] It does not make recommendations to its subscribers, but rather assists them in making more informed judgments. IRRC's reports on each stockholder proposal include a history of the issue, the respective positions of the corporation and its critics, and the likely implications of a vote both for and against management's recommendations. Each year IRRC publishes a lengthy special report that records the vote received by each public interest proxy proposal as well as the voting record of various institutions. (This is incomplete due to the reluctance of many institutions to make their decisions public.) IRRC also publishes a monthly newsletter that describes current developments in the area of corporate responsibility and, from time to time, issues detailed reports on subjects of particular interest to citizen activists and the corporations whose policies they are attempting to change.[95]

The initial reaction of shareholder activists to IRRC's establishment ranged from cautious approval to considerable skepticism. The Project On Corporate Responsibility, for example, saw it as a way of deflecting pressure away from university officials and questioned its claims of impartiality. They wrote Elliott Weiss, director of its seven-person staff:

We are troubled that IRRC will seek or tend to act as a middleman between shareholder proponents and institutional investors, thus limiting or eliminating the direct access of the advocates to those sought to be swayed. . . .

IRRC symbolizes $160,000 put up by institutions to study proxy issues proposed by organizations toward which the same institutions have over the years contributed nothing in resources and little by way of votes.[96]

A group involved in researching corporations, The Council on Economic Priorities, adopted a "wait and see" attitude.[97] Yet, on balance, over the last four years, IRRC appears to have considerably reinforced the effectiveness of stockholder challenges. As the "Congressional Record" of corporate elections, it has increased their visibility to business, the investment community, and to the public at large. Weiss remarked in late 1976:

IRRC has strengthened the ability of activists to directly challenge corporate activities. Formerly management could dismiss many of the activists as crazies. Our reports tend to substantiate many of the concerns of activist groups. Our objectivity gives the groups credibility.[98]

The second concern of the PCR proved better founded. Within two years, IRRC had become self-supporting. By 1974, its annual budget was $270,000 and the number of its institutional subscribers, each paying between $300 and $5,000 per year depending on the size of their portfolio, had increased to nearly one hundred. On the other hand, the PCR had folded partially through lack of funds. It remains one of the ironies of the public interest proxy phenomenon that the organizations and institutions whose continual annual submission of proxy proposals provides IRRC with its *raison d'être* remain in much more precarious financial positions than the center charged with evaluating their efforts.

Nearly half of the 102 current subscribers are either foundations or universities. The remainder are largely banks and trust companies, insurance companies, investment firms, and pension funds. Clearly, the nonprofit sector is represented disproportionately to its actual financial involvement in the securities markets. The contemporary importance of nonprofit institutions essentially reflects what has been one of the most important developments within the American political economy over the last four decades: the development of a series of major national institutions outside the direct purview of the corporation. These include, not coincidentially, the very institutions that have tended most frequently to vote against management, namely union pension funds (particularly those of public sector employees), foundations, and universities. The widespread ownership of stock by institutions throughout American society in the postwar period has thus proved a mixed blessing for corporate managers. On one hand, it makes the overwhelming majority of Americans—including those employed by nonprofit institutions—financially dependent on corporate growth and profits. On the other hand, thanks to the politicization of the shareholder role, the likelihood is greater that critics of business will find a sympathetic ear among shareholders.

## Institutional Investors: Profit

Churches, foundations, universities, and nonprofit sector pension funds, with few exceptions, virtually monopolized the scrutiny of management decisions by institutional shareholders during the three years following Campaign GM. Beginning in 1974, however, banks and insurance companies began to routinely violate the "Wall Street Rule." In an exhaustive, unpublished study of the behavior of institutional investors toward corporate management, written as a senior thesis at Harvard in 1976, Hugh Jeffrey Leonard concluded:

> . . . today institutional investors have attained a new and unprecedented level of interest in a wide range of social, political and business questions on which they are supposed to vote, and . . . this precludes adherence to the so-called Wall Street Rule of institutional non-involvement in all proxy voting matters. The philosophy of this rule . . . has been abandoned by virtually all institutional investors. . . .[99]

Institution did not, of course, cease to sell stock in those corporations whose performance they found disappointing. Rather they began to employ both mechanisms of influence—stock selection as well as proxy voting.

In 1975, only one of the 100 major institutional investors surveyed (25 of whom were large banks) indicated that it was their policy to vote automatically with management on all issues. A quarter of those surveyed, including 10 banks, reported that they had taken some new action during the previous year that increased the scrutiny of the social performance of management.[100] What had happened was that many profit-oriented institutional investors had begun to perceive that, at least in several critical areas, the conflict between behavior that corporate activists defined as "responsible" and corporate profits was often not as clear-cut as they had previously assumed. Four years after the Medical Committee for Human Rights had, tongue-in-cheek, urged Dow to cease manufacturing napalm because of its adverse effect on the company's long-term profits, a Statement of Principles of the Executive Committee of the Trust Division of the American Bankers Association declared:

The activity or inactivity of a portfolio in matters of social and environmental concern can have a substantial effect upon the economic well-being of the corporation, its earnings, and the long-term market performance of its securities. . . . The social and environmental issues on the agenda of corporate meetings should be thoroughly evaluated by the bank fiduciary. Based upon its study, the fiduciary properly may either vote or withhold its vote on such issues as on any other issue. . . . If the fiduciary believes that an issue raised and the corporation's response to it may have a substantial long-range impact upon the performance of the corporation's securities, it may be appropriate and in the best interest of the portfolio corporation for the fiduciary to discuss its beliefs with the corporation's executives.[101]

The senior vice-president for finance at Travelers Insurance Company responsible for management of a portfolio of over one billion dollars in common stock remarked, "If a company has a 'public be damned' attitude in this day and age, one could infer that management is not too sharp."[102]

By itself, the notion that the corporation's political and social environment was increasingly likely to affect its profits did not mandate any increased activism on the part of institutional managers. Quite the contrary: the idea that business should be sophisticated about its approach to a wide variety of societal concerns has historically been invoked as a defense of managerial prerogatives from the more narrowly focused economistic interests of shareholders. What prompted an increased interest in corporate conduct by institutional managers was their view—which essentially echoed that of the public—that these public responsibilities were being handled ineptly. The seventies thus witnessed a partial reversal of the historical relationship between shareholders and management. Formerly, the interests of the shareholders were assumed to be dominated by short-term considerations, while those of management were understood to be capable of taking a more long-term viewpoint, one which "balanced" the interests of shareholders against the corporation's other presumably more public-oriented constituencies.

Two developments undermined this relationship. First, the substantial growth of institutional investors in the sixties made the market for the securities in many large corporations increasingly illiquid: the "Wall Street Rule" had become irrelevant for many institutional investors, since their large holdings made the option of selling virtually impossible. At the same time that institutional investors were inadvertently acquiring a stake in the long-term future of the corporations in which their funds were invested, the growing spotlight on corporate economic performance—ironically encouraged by the investment patterns of the institutions themselves—had made management much more preoccupied with short-term considerations.

By a twist of circumstances that no one foresaw—least of all the institutions themselves—institutional investors found themselves, by default, placed in the role of guardians of the long-term profits and interests of the business system. By the mid-seventies, the portfolio managers of many financial institutions had come to the same conclusion that had originally animated the sponsors of Campaign GM: the current degree of managerial autonomy and freedom from outside scrutiny was in the best interest of neither business nor the society as a whole. They had simply come to that understanding from different starting points: the PCR used its somewhat artificial role as shareholder to raise public concerns, while the institutional investors used their quasi-public role to confront management with their interests as shareholders. One institutional investor summarized his understanding of the implications of this shift in the following terms:

It is no longer a question of this or that management doing something bad, it is a matter of general corporate morality. We must continue to rely on the capital markets, we have no viable alternative, so we feel it is our responsibility to our clients and our country to do whatever we can to bring the interests of business and the country into some sort of reconciliation. We believe that those who control a vast store of the country's capital [institutions] are slowly moving toward a consensus on this view, and that their unwillingness to give management the blanket approval it seeks is in everybody's best interests.[103]

Previously, institutions had been extremely reluctant to vote against management recommendations—viewing a vote on a proxy proposal as somewhat akin in spirit to a vote of confidence in the British House of Commons. They subsequently began to view proxy elections in somewhat less dramatic terms: to oppose the judgment of management with respect to a particular decision or issue did not necessarily imply a lack of faith in its ability to manage the corporation competently. This process was abetted by changes in the nature of the resolutions themselves: after 1972, a larger proportion began to address themselves to business decisions that were within the direct purview of management rather than symbolic of larger social ills. Their wording became more careful and their intent more sophisticated. (Many institutions, however, continue to vote against proxy proposals because they are poorly worded.)

The consequence of all these developments was that the proxy electoral process, originally taken most seriously by those institutional investors whose goals least complemented those of business, gradually became a mechanism for monitoring management by the traditionally most conservative of all institutions—banks and insurance companies. A number of the nation's major banks, including the Bank of America, First National City, Morgan Guaranty Trust, and insurance companies including Prudential, Travelers, and Equitable, established high-level committees to make recommendations about proxy proposals. Between 1973 and 1974, the number of banks responding to IRRC's annual survey of institutional voting patterns nearly doubled; by 1974, thirty-five banks and insurance companies had become subscribers to IRRC. The vote totals in support of public interest proxy resolutions since 1974 suggest that at least some financial institutions are, in fact, supporting proxy proposals dealing with social issues.[104]

Some institutional investors thus essentially began to undergo the same ideological metamorphosis that corporate management underwent at the turn of the century. They developed the equivalent of the doctrine of corporate social responsiblity. This did not lessen the commitment of portfolio managers to profit maximization any more than the managerial revolution made corporate executives less interested in profit around 1900. Rather, a minority of each group began to develop a somewhat more sophisicated notion of the social and political conditions that made economic accumulation possible.

To be sure, only a minority of the nation's financial institutions voted the stock they owned or controlled against management on public interest proxy issues, and fewer still publicized their negative votes; the actual degree of institutional support for shareholder social activism should not be exaggerated. However, in part due to the efforts of groups like the PCR, many have become more sensitive to social issues, and they often privately express their concerns to corporate managers. In 1975, for example, more than one-third of all institutions—both financial and nonprofit—polled by IRRC reported that they had either written letters or arranged meetings with corporate managements to question their political behavior. Indeed, the writing of letters to corporate officials criticizing or questioning their performance often has more impact than a vote in favor of a proxy resolution—particularly since the former may imply the threat of the latter.

Some of the flavor of the relationship many institutional investors have developed with corporate management is suggested in this dialogue from one of mystery writer Emma Latham's tales of corporate skullduggery, *A Place for Murder.* (Latham, the *nom de plume* of two women, writes social commentary as fiction.) The novel's detective/banker, John Putnam Thatcher, is instructing one of his subordinates about the junior executive's forthcoming personal attendance with the "proxies of the Sloan Guaranty Trust" at

what promised to be a very lively stockholders' meeting of a large automobile company several of whose executives had recently been discharged for taking payoffs from suppliers.

Latham writes:

"It never hurts to let them know we're keeping an eye on things," Thatcher pontificated.
"But how should I vote the things?" persisted Kenneth.
"For management, of course. But do it at the last possible moment. And look very, very grave."[105]

More significantly, having once accepted the principle that proxies should not automatically be voted in favor of management, many financial institutions began to apply it to those proxy proposals proposed by management itself. In 1975, these were most frequently "antitake-over" proposals. Faced by a decline in the price of their stock, many managements became concerned that their corporations were vulnerable to being raided. By proposing changes in the corporate charter such as electing directors on a staggered rather than an annual basis and increasing the percentage of shareholder votes required for mergers, they hoped to prevent the firms they managed from passing into the control of outsiders. Prior to the mid-seventies, it is likely that such proposals would have been automatically supported by institutional investors. Now, however, they were perceived as leading to the increasing insulation of management from the supervison of shareholders. This made many institutional managers uncomfortable. In 1975, more than 80 percent of the banking institutions polled reported to IRRC that they voted against at least one management proposal—usually one that sought to make take-overs more difficult. Corporate management took these signs of opposition very seriously and frequently contacted large institutions that had opposed them. One investor remarked, "Corporate management respects us, they know we're not just taking them for a lark or trying to pin them down as a 'scapegoat' for the system."[106]

## Watergate

The issue which, more than any other, established the legitimacy of shareholder activism was illegal corporate political participation.[107] "Watergate" was tailor-made for citizen challenges to business: what greater justification could there be for using mechanisms within the private sector's financial structure to make management decisions more accountable when the congressional hearings and the SEC investigations had demonstrated the wholesale ineffectiveness of government regulations? The Watergate revelations not only resulted in the most substantive changes in corporate governance; they also were the critical factor in altering the attitude of the investment community toward management. Watergate, in the words of the senior vice-president of one of the nation's largest insurance companies, had "shaken the very foundations of our previous trust in the managements of companies in which we invested."[108] At a conference held for institutional investors sponsored jointly by IRRC and the Center for the Study of Financial Institutions of the University of Pennsylvania Law School on the "Corporate Watergate," "an overwhelming majority" of the institutional investors who attended, most of whom represented profit-seeking institutions, said they were taking very seriously the conclusion of an IRRC study which had suggested:

. . . even if shareholders tell management they are willing to forego profits obtainable only through bribery or illegal activities, it is not clear that all corporations' management will avoid the activities. But if shareholders fail to speak out, or if they acquiesce in or actively support a continuation of conduct over the kind that has given rise to the current controversy, managements may well conclude that they have a license, at least from their shareholders, to continue engaging in illegal and questionable conduct which they believe will enhance their corporation's profits.[109]

The *Wall Street Journal* reported that the IRRC study "is, in itself, a reflection of the deepening concern among institutions over how to cope with the issue of questionable corporate activity."[110] IRRC's 1975 survey of institutional investors reported that "corporate political involvement was . . . the most significant issue of the proxy season."[111]

At the conference itself, several participants emphasized the importance of shareholder activism in helping the corporation develop new standards of conduct. Michael Klein, a Washington attorney whose firm had represented several corporations charged with failure to disclose political contributions, noted that "you people here, through the casting of votes and investment decision-making, have the power to bring to bear an influence which is particularly lacking in the current climate."[112] Louis Schwartz urged investors to help develop "creative tensions" in regard to corporate decision making:

Those who manage our major corporations are not less moral than the rest of us. But they operate at a point in our society where their choices are sharply limited by their circumstances. It is for this reason that we should attempt to change the climate in which they operate, using the whole range of social influences open to us.[113]

Closing the conference, SEC commissioner Sommer urged increased shareholder activism and corporate responsiveness:

I would like to see managements endorse some of the proposals which have been discussed here, and to say to shareholders: "This is a fine idea, and we endorse it, and we would like to see you, our shareholders, vote for it." Or, if there are defects in a resolution, I would like to see managements propose an alternative and explain to shareholders why its alternative is superior.[114]

### THE PROXY RESOLUTIONS

The subject of the participation of corporations in the governmental process first appeared on proxy resolutions in the spring of 1972—over a year before the abuses associated with Nixon's reelection campaign became public and indeed before most had taken place. The stockholders of Standard Oil of California and U.S. Steel were asked to instruct their managements to reaffirm the political nonpartisanship of the corporations by ceasing to use fund-raising techniques that pressured employees to favor one political party and to disclose all their political contributions. These proposals did surprisingly well: the one submitted to SoCal was supported by over 5 percent of the firm's shares voted and that to U.S. Steel by 6.7 percent of the votes cast. In the following two years—after the Watergate disclosures—corporate political conduct became a more prominent subject of proposals by shareholders. Fifteen proposals, including four submitted by the Project on Corporate Responsibility, were submitted to corporations on the subject of political activity in 1973; in 1974 and 1975, a total of sixty-eight resolutions were proposed dealing with this subject.

These resolutions had three primary objectives: to extend the letter of the law by prohibiting all campaign contributions as well as various legal, but questionable, practices that blurred the line between corporate and individual contributions; to affirm its spirit by forcing disclosure of all political contributions made directly or indirectly, by asking corporations publicly to declare "political nonpartisanship"; and thirdly, to punish those corporate officials responsible for past illegal behavior. The relatively high degree of shareholder support for these resolutions is particularly striking —especially since many of them were proposed not by organziations, but by individual shareholders. In 1974, half of these resolutions received at least 3 percent of the shares voted, while the resolutions submitted to RCA, SoCal, and U.S. Steel affirming the corporations' political nonpartisanship were supported by over 6 percent of the shares voted. In 1975, nineteen out of the twenty-two resolutions introduced for the first time received more than 3 percent of the votes cast; more than 10 percent of the shareholders of Twentieth Century Fox, General Public Utilities, and Pan American supported resolutions requesting management to make public all their previous political contributions. Of the eleven resolutions proposed for the second time, three received more than 6 percent of the shares voted. Of the twenty resolutions on corporate political activity voted on by share-holders in 1976, half were supported by at least 6 percent of the shares voted; one—a resolution asking General Public Utilities to disclose its political contributions—was supported by 18.82 percent of the shares voted.

The unusually high degree of shareholder support for resolutions in this area clearly reflects its broader importance: the role of the corporation in the governing process manages to bridge the distinction between share-holder and citizen roles. Reasonable people can disagree about whether or not the production of war materials or the living conditions of workers in South Africa are a legitimate part of the public's concern with corporate performance. But about the importance of public scrutiny of attempts to influence the state, there is no room for disagreement; they constitute an integral part of our definition of and requirement for a liberal, democratic society.

Those corporations that had already been convicted of illegal attempts to intervene in the political process found themselves particularly vulnerable to shareholder pressure. The legal issue having been disposed of through the state, the remaining problem was essentially one of law enforcement. Might concerned shareholders have an appropriate role to play in supplementing the obviously inadequate preventive measures enacted by both the corporate and public governments? Their legal and moral standing, in this instance, seemed unassailable: it was literally their money that had been squandered. Here was a unique instance in which the issue of the fiduciary responsibility of management—which formed one of the critical legal and moral underpinnings of the modern corporate structure— overlapped its social accountability. Management practices were revealed to be contrary to the interests of both the shareholders and the firm. It is in this sense that the events surrounding the corporate contribution to Watergate marked the coming of age of the politics of corporate accountability.

The reaction of the managements of the convicted corporations to public interest proxy proposals challenging their actions documents the changed status of the corporate activists within the governance of the firm; they now appeared in the role of the guardian of the interests of the corporation as well as the public. Of the five recipients of proxy proposals in this category filed in 1974, the management of only one firm, Phillips Petroleum, refused to concede any of its prerogatives to its shareholders. Management opposed a resolution sponsored by the Episcopal Church Committee on Shareholder Responsibility that would have required the board of directors to implement procedures to assure that there would be no occurrence of illegal political behavior on the grounds that such a procedure was unnecessary. By contrast, proponents of three resolutions designed to discipline the officers and directors of Goodyear for their illegal $40,000 contribution to the Nixon campaign agreed to withdraw them following an announcement at the shareholders' meeting by the firm's chairman, Russell D. Young, that he would pay the corporation's fine and legal expenses out of his personal funds. The management of Gulf Oil agreed to support a resolution requesting that Gulf discharge employees who make illegal contributions, while the management of the Minnesota Mining and Manufacturing Corporation (3M) took no position on a resolution to "deplore" the company's illegal contributions and request implementation of procedures to avoid recurrence; both resolutions then passed overwhelmingly. Due to inaccuracies in its proxy statements, Northrop was forced to postpone its annual meeting for three years following the conviction and fining of the firm and two of its officers less than a week before its 1974 meeting.

### SHAREHOLDER SUITS

The most dramatic and consequential shareholder participation in corporate governance took place through the vehicle of shareholder class action and shareholder derivative suits. The total number of shareholder suits filed increased substantially between 1970 and 1975.[115] Moreover, politically motivated shareholders began to use them as a vehicle to discipline corporate executives.

In the four years following the 1972 election, over 100 suits were filed by shareholders against management seeking restitution of damages for illegal political gifts at home and bribes abroad. To date, none have come to trial; they have all been settled or are in the process of being settled, usually on terms relatively favorable to the shareholders and public interest lawyers who brought them. The suits were filed under two doctrines: management violations of SEC disclosure requirements covering both proxy materials and financial records, and a traditional common law doctrine defining the fiduciary duty of the directors and officers to the company and its shareholders.[116] For the most part, these suits have aimed at the restoration of monetary damages to the company and the disciplining of its officials convicted of the illegal use of company funds; those brought by public interest lawyers have emphasized the adoption of policies designed to prevent future abuses.

The earliest suit was filed by the Project for Corporate Responsibility and a church group in 1974 against seven directors of Gulf Oil and lobbyist Claude Wild.[117] It followed Gulf's admission that it had donated $125,000 of corporate funds to the Nixon reelection campaign. Under the terms of the settlement—reached before the full dimensions of Gulf's generosity became public—Wild agreed to reimburse the company $25,000, and furthermore, the firm agreed not to rehire Wild except on an emergency basis that would require the approval of both the board and the plaintiffs' counsel. Subsequently, more than eight shareholder suits were filed against Gulf Oil by a variety of individual shareholders and counter-corporate activists. Eight of the suits were finally settled in 1976. Under the terms of the settlement, six former Gulf officials forfeited a total of $2 million in unawarded incentives, compensation, stock, and stock options. Dorsey, the company's former chairman, personally lost $1,250,000 as a result of the shareholder suit. While these financial penalties far exceeded those imposed on any other corporate officials, the company did agree to pay its officers' legal expenses and did not require any reimbursement from them for the more than $4 million distributed to U.S. politicians.

Five former officials of 3M agreed to repay the company a total of $475,000 while Mr. Spater, the president of American Airlines, agreed to pay the corporation he managed $75,000 plus interest over a four-year period in order to settle a shareholder suit. Several other actions followed a similar pattern: in each case the shareholder suits were initiated following the disclosure of illegal behavior, usually revealed by the investigations of the SEC. The suits themselves rarely uncovered significant new information about corporate misconduct and for the most part resulted in a transfer of sums from individual executives to the coffers of the firm.

In three cases, however, shareholder pressure markedly departed from this pattern. At least on the surface, these represent a significant and possibly far-reaching change in the balance of power between dissident share-holders and management. Between 1974 and 1976, the Center of Law in the Public Interest, a Los Angeles–based public interest law firm partially funded by the Ford Foundation, filed and settled its shareholder suits against Northrop and Phillips Petroleum.[118] The suit against Northrop brought to light a slush fund totaling over $1.1 million including a previously disclosed $150,000 donation to the Nixon reelection campaign. In addition to monetary damages, the settlement included significant structural changes in the firm's governance. Most importantly, Northrop agreed to add four new, independent outside directors subject to court approval and to reconstitute its executive committee so that five of its six members would be from outside the firm. In the future, 60 percent of the firm's directors would be outsiders, and both the nominating committee and the audit committee would consist exclusively of outside directors. Finally, Thomas Jones, the firm's chairman, chief executive officer, and president, agreed to give up the office of president within eighteen months; earlier it was announced that Jones, in addition to paying the fines and restoring the corporate funds appropriated illegally, would reimburse Northrop an additional $50,000. Jones's total out-of-pocket expenses, including legal fees, are estimated at over $400,000 as a result of the shareholder suit.

The Northrop settlement attracted considerable publicity. Coming just four years after Campaign GM had first raised the issue of the relationship between the accountability of directors and corporate social performance, it indicated a substantial shift in public and legal opinion. Federal District Judge Warren Ferguson, who approved the settlement, called it a "landmark in corporate reform," while a professor of corporate law at UCLA termed it "unusual, a backlash of Watergate."[119]

Its actual significance remains, however, a bit more ambiguous. In July of 1975, Jones resigned as chairman following a report of the committee of outside directors charging him with a heavy share of the responsibility for ". . . irregularities and improprieties."[120] He was, however, retained as chief executive officer, a post he continues to hold. The firm's shareholders' meeting, finally held in 1976, revolved around Jones's prediction that Northrop's revenues would "be significantly more than 1 billion dollars."[121] While stating that the recent past "had been painful—to me personally, to my fellow workers and to you as shareholders,"[122] he noted that the "improved legal and financial review and controls" would avoid similar transgressions in the future and told reporters that he intended to stay at Northrop for the next ten years. Two shareholders who rose to praise Jones's leadership drew enthusiastic applause, and the firm's owners overwhelmingly defeated a proposal that would have required the company to adopt stricter rules defining its nonpartisanship.

In 1976, a similar, though less drastic, settlement was reached between the Center of Law in the Public Interest and Phillips Petroleum. It changed the balance of the board of directors to at least 60 percent outsiders and shifted control of the company's nominating and audit committees to independent outsiders. The firm's chairman and chief executive officer, William Keeler, was not affected by the settlement, although he had been personally involved in transporting funds between Switzerland and the United States. He did, however, agree to reimburse the company $82,000. One of the center's attorneys stated that:

We believe this case to be the most positive resolution of any of the corporations that have been involved with either illegal campaign contributions or questionable overseas payments.[123]

The *New York Times* noted:

Business observers said that they felt that today's settlement could have a significant impact in terms of compelling companies to act in a more forthright manner about their political involvements.[124]

At its 1976 shareholders' meeting, the firm reversed the position it had held for the previous two years and agreed to support a shareholder proposal requiring that employees who fail to comply with federal and state political contribution laws be subject to disciplinary action, including dismissal. The change in the company's bylaws, which was approved by the firm's shareholders, went beyond the settlement in one respect: it eliminated identification provisions for officers. An attorney for the sponsors of the church-sponsored resolution stated, "We feel like we got the major part of what we wanted accomplished."[125]

In January of 1976, the board of directors of Gulf voted to remove Robert Dorsey from his post as chairman and chief executive officer.[126] The prime forces behind this action were the Mellon family, concerned about the damage to the company's reputation as a result of the exposure of Gulf's $12 million worth of contributions to politicians in the United States and abroad. On the surface, this can scarcely be regarded as a victory for citizen activism; the Mellon family's assertion of its ownership rights and responsibilities vis-à-vis the corporation's officers scarcely represents the kind of shareholder democracy or management accountability that corporate activists have in mind. Moreover, the major force behind the corporation's disclosures was the SEC, not the actions of private citizens. Yet when seen in a somewhat broader context, Dorsey's removal cannot only be claimed as an indirect result of direct challenges by citizens, but it also dramatizes the erosion of dual standards of corporate and governmental accountability.

Nine months previous to the board's action, Gulf's board, under Dorsey's leadership, had appointed Sister Jane Scully, a Roman Catholic nun and president of Carlow College in Pittsburgh, to the firm's board of directors. Since 1970, Gulf had been under very bitter attack by the United Church of Christ and several other Catholic and Protestant church groups for its investments in Angola. It had also been criticized for the all-male composition of its board.

Scully's appointment was initially greeted with some astonishment by church activists since they had never heard of her. They saw the addition of a new board member as an attempt on the part of the corporation to placate its critics—without actually compromising any of its prerogatives. Unlike Leon Sullivan, Scully did not publicly dissent from any of the corporation's decisions. Nor did she become identified with any particular social issue. She did, however, appreciate the social forces that had led to the creation of her own role.[127] It was, therefore, rather fitting—and particularly ironic from Dorsey's point of view—that it was Scully's vote against Dorsey which proved to be decisive in the board's deliberations.

It does not seem coincidental that the unprecedented removal of a corporate chief executive officer for political or social reasons, as opposed to strictly economic transgressions, took place only eighteen months after the equally unprecedented removal of the nation's president; Dorsey is Nixon's counterpart within the business system. And if both Dorsey's and Nixon's fates were equally unprecedents, their removals were also equally torturous. It took Gulf's board two and one-half years to decide to remove

Dorsey; the equivalent deliberations of the political process occupied about one and one-half years.

## The SEC

Aside from the increased willingness of institutional investors to question corporate decisions, the most important factor that has altered the balance of power between management and shareholders, including socially oriented ones, has been the liberalization of the rules governing the submission of proxy proposals. The SEC revised its rules in 1972 and again in 1976. The result has been to make the public interest proxy proposal a permanent part of the government of the contemporary corporation.

In 1971, the commission appointed Peter Romeo, a twenty-nine-year-old lawyer and accountant, to supervise the flow of proxy proposals that were generated in response to the liberalization of the SEC's rules governing the submission of proxy proposals. A year later, Romeo was named as a special counsel in the Division of Finance. His responsibility was to decide which proxy proposals submitted by shareholders could be legitimately excluded from the corporation's proxy statement. Although Romeo's rulings were technically only advisory opinions, they were generally regarded by both shareholders and management as binding; since the Dow case, there have been no judicial rulings on the issue.

Overall, Romeo's decisions have been almost evenly divided between management and activist shareholders. While Romeo claims to be "even-handed," the practical effect of his rulings has been to strengthen the prerogatives of shareholders—including politically oriented ones—and to reduce the autonomy of companies.[128] Prior to Campaign GM, the commission's decisions were virtually automatically in favor of management. A "neutral stance" thus shifts the balance of power away from management. In addition, since most socially oriented shareholder proposals are not submitted by individuals or groups sophisticated in corporate law, many violate the letter, while adhering to the spirit, of the commission's rules. In these cases, Romeo often suggests changes in the wording that would make the proposals acceptable—in effect, giving shareholder activists free legal advice.

On balance, management has been more unhappy with the SEC's interpretations of Rule 14a since 1970 than have shareholder activists. In 1974, *Dun's* reported that "Companies . . . tend to feel that while the SEC insists on full technical compliance with its complex proxy regulations, it leans over backward to favor the shareholders."[129] The following public statement by the corporate secretary of General Telephone and Electronics is unusual only in its frankness: "I wish you fellows in the media would do something about getting the SEC to put a stop to all this nonsense. Stockholders are fed up with it, and management is fed up with it."[130] Many managements feared that the liberalizing of Rule 14a would mean that the corporation's proxy machinery and annual meeting could be used to air social and political issues that concerned only an infinitessimally small minority of shareholders. Union Carbide, for example, wrote the SEC that:

. . . a problem that is of growing concern to most stockholders . . . is the increasingly common practice of individuals or groups having special interests —not related to the general welfare of either the corporation or the majority of its stockholders in their status as stockholders—obtaining an unfair share of the attention of management and shareholders. . . . Their primary purpose (of purchasing a few shares of stock) is to obtain a forum for airing their views on a frequently narrow subject. Most such proposals are supported by the votes of only a tiny percentage of stockholders at the meeting.[131]

Many corporations were also upset by the expense of including politically motivated proposals on proxy statements. Finally, several corporations resented the laxity with which the SEC interpreted its regulation allowing firms to exclude "substantially the same proposal," if it had previously received less than the requisite number of votes. Thus, in 1973 through 1976, IBM received proposals from church groups affecting its operations in South Africa. None received the support of at least 3 percent of the shareholders, but the commission refused to allow IBM to exclude any of them. It chose to define "substantially the same" as "virtually identical," and thus, because the specific content of the proposals varied from year to year (one requested information, while another asked IBM to establish a special committee), each was considered a new proposal.

In 1972, the commission issued its first revision since the Dow case of Sections 14a and 23a of the Securities Exchange Act of 1934. In order to curb some of the abuses of the proxy mechanism that had arisen since its use in 1970 and 1971, one new provision required that any security holder submitting a proposal must avow his "good faith" intention of personally attending the shareholders' meetings.[132] This was designed to prevent repetition of an incident which occurred in 1971 when a young lawyer purchased one share of stock in each of thirty corporations and then proceeded to submit to them more than 200 proposals covering a wide range of social and political issues. The commission argued that this imposed needless expenses on the other security holders. The second major revision limited to 200 words the length of supporting statements submitted by shareholders.

In the third, and most important, change, the SEC decided to revise the "general cause" test. Under the codification of proxy rules issued in 1952, the commission ruled that management could refuse to admit a proposal if it was "submitted by the security holder . . . primarily for the purpose of promoting general economic, political, racial, religious, social or similar causes."[133] In 1972, the commission substituted a more objective standard. It ruled that regardless of the intention of the shareholder, a proxy proposal needed to be "not significantly related to the business of the issuer or . . . not within the control of the issuer" to be legally excluded.[134] This ruling, in effect, gave shareholders the right to use the proxy process to raise social issues—so long as there was a discernible relationship between those issues and the business of the corporation.

In 1976, the SEC, after considerably more experience with public interest proxy proposals, decided to revise Rule 14a–8 again.[135] In July, the SEC announced a lengthy series of changes and invited comments from interested parties, and on November 22, 1976, the commission formally issued its revisions in time for the 1977 proxy season.[136] The practical effect on the new rules was to maintain and slightly broaden shareholder access to the corporate proxy machinery. Both the thrust and the tone of the new rules made clear the commission's judgment that increased shareholder participation in corporate decision making was consistent with the intent of the Securities and Exchange Act. In light of the business community's strong recommendation that the activities of politically oriented investors be significantly curtailed, the revisions, on balance, represented a positive development for the corporate accountability movement: the preservation of the status quo recognized the legitimacy of shareholder activism.

The commission's most important rules fell into three categories. The first focused on the "ordinary business" provision. Under this rule, in 1976 the commission had permitted the managements of two utilities to exclude shareholder resolutions questioning plans to build nuclear plants on the grounds that these decisions involved the "ordinary business" of the corporations. Shareholder activists strongly criticized the commission's ruling on the grounds that both the costs and environmental safety implications of the plants' construction made them not simply "ordinary." Romeo admitted that his rulings were "very difficult," and added that the commission's staff privately believed that the nuclear plants did, indeed, represent important business decisions on which shareholders should have the right to express opinions.[137] But he noted that the SEC rule did not distinguish between big and small business decisions. In its July 1976 proposals, the SEC replaced the "ordinary business" grounds for exclusion with a more narrow phrase: "a routine, day-to-day matter relating to the ordinary business operations" of the company.[138] While the commission finally decided to maintain the old wording, it did announce that in the future it would interpret the rule more flexibly. Its release stated:

[T]he term "ordinary business operations" has been deemed on occasion to include certain matters which have significant policy, economic or other implications inherent in them. For instance, a proposal that a utility company not construct a proposed nuclear power plant has in the past been considered excludable. . . . In retrospect, however, it seems apparent that the economic and safety considerations attendant to nuclear power plants are of such magnitude that a determination whether to construct one is not an "ordinary" business matter. Accordingly, proposals of that nature, as well as others that have major implications, will in the future be considered beyond the realm of an issuer's ordinary business operations, and future interpretative letters of the commission's staff will reflect that view.[139]

Under Rule 14a–8, a corporation could also exclude a proposal if it dealt with a matter "not significantly related" to the corporation's business. Formally, the commission had defined this standard quite specifically: the issue had to affect at least 1 percent of the corporation's total sales or earnings. Under this criterion, several corporations had been able to exclude proposals relating to the Arab boycott after proving that their involvements in the Middle East fell below the requisite levels. The American Society of Corporate Secretaries urged the commission to make the exclusion even broader and allow resolutions to be excluded that did not deal with matters of economic significance to the corporation. The commission again decided to maintain its earlier rule, but, as in the case of the "ordinary business" rule, also indicated that its interpretations would be more flexible in the future. It argued, "There are many instances in which the matter involved in a proposal is significant to [a corporation's] business, even though such significance is not apparent from an economic viewpoint."[140]

In its initial recommendations, the commission, to the delight of business and the chagrin of the activists, broadened the "substantially the same proposal" rule to read "deals with substantially the same subject matter."[141] In its November 1976 rule, the commission again decided against a change. It indicated that it would be sensitive to abuses of the rule, but felt that its proposed revision would unduly constrain shareholder participation in corporate decision making. It also noted the difficulty of objectively defining the phrase "substantially related."

The commission did adopt a few procedural changes that somewhat tightened access to the corporate proxy machinery. It lengthened the time during which proposals must be received by the corporation from seventy to ninety days prior to the anniversary of the mailing date of the previous year's proxy materials, forbade a shareholder from submitting more than two proposals to one corporation during the same year, and reduced the maximum length of each proposal. While shareholder activists by no means were completely satisfied with the commission's rulings, their comments on the SEC's initial recommendations were considerably more favorable than those of spokesmen for corporate interests. The gap between the commission's final rulings and those advocated by the American Society of Corporate Secretaries is revealed by the following recommendations by the society that the SEC ignored:

—allow only those who have held stock in a corporation for at least one year to submit proposals;
—allow corporations to set "reasonable qualification limitations" on who can sponsor proposals (and stipulate that limitations which allow 75 per cent of a corporation's security holders to sponsor proposals "shall be deemed reasonable");
—set an econmic test for determining when a proposal is significantly related to a corporation's business;
—state that a proposal can be omitted on grounds it is not within a corporation's control if "the underlying objective [of the proposal] is beyond the [corporation's] power directly to effectuate"; and
—raise the vote needed to make a proposal eligible for reconsideration to 6 per cent the first year, 10 per cent the second year and 15 per cent thereafter.[142]

## The Proxy Proposal

As a result of both the SEC's proxy rules and the interest of institutional investors in public interest proxy contests, the proxy proposal has become the mainstay of citizen participation in corporate deliberations. Even when other strategies for challenging corporations are employed, they are almost invariably accompanied by a proxy proposal; many groups regard the filing of proxy resolutions as a particularly effective means of making sure that management at least publicly acknowledges issues raised by their complaints. The proposals also continue to attract press coverage year after year.[143] The number of public interest proxy resolutions filed has gradually, though not steadily, increased since 1972; that year a total of thirty-seven resolutions was submitted for shareholder approval; and a year later a total of fifty-eight was submitted.[144] In 1974, the number of resolutions increased substantially—to 105. The following year the total declined somewhat; 85 were introduced. In 1976, 118 resolutions were introduced and in 1977, 180.

More than two-thirds of the public interest resolutions filed between 1972 and 1977 dealt with one of two issues: foreign trade or investment policies and business political activity, both foreign and domestic. The three other most frequently raised issues were the rights of women including equal employment as well as sexism in advertising, corporate governance, and environmental impact. All but a handful of resolutions raised these concerns by asking for either additional disclosure of the firm's social impact or for a statement of corporate policy.

The majority of the proxy statements have been filed by groups with a religious or ethnic identification—including various Protestant denominations affiliated with the National Council of Churches, a number of Catholic orders, and the American Jewish Congress. Nearly 200 have been filed by individuals. Public interest proxies tend to be disproportionately directed toward larger and more visible firms. While less than 200 corporations—out of the nearly 2,000 eligible—have received any public interest proxy proposals, a handful of firms have received several. Standard Oil of California heads the list with twenty-one, followed by Exxon with sixteen, Gulf with ten, and IBM and Phillips with nine each.

No public interest proxy proposal opposed by management has ever passed and none is likely to do so. Nevertheless, the degree of shareholder support for public interest proxy proposals increased significantly between 1970 and 1975. "Campaign GM" was unable to receive the support of 3 percent of the voted GM shares on any of the resolutions it submitted in 1970 and 1971. What makes the 3 percent total significant is that it is the degree of support a proposal must receive to make it eligible for resubmission the following year; if a resolution is introduced a second time, it must receive the support of 6 percent of the shares voted to be resubmitted. A resolution can thereafter be submitted indefinitely, providing it receives the support of at least 10 percent of the shares voted each year. The eligibility of shareholder proposals for resubmission provides a convenient bench mark by which the amount of shareholder support can be charted over time and is taken extremely seriously by both activists and management.

In 1973, seven public interest resolutions received the support of at least 3 percent of the shares voted. In 1974, a total of thirty-one were eligible for resubmission, including two which successfully met the 6 percent standard. In 1975, shareholder resolutions received significantly more shareholder support: forty-six of the sixty-six resolutions voted upon by shareholders received more than 3 percent of the votes cast. In addition, five out of the seventeen resolutions requiring the support of 6 percent of the shares voted received it. A year later in 1976, the level of shareholder support was somewhat lower; only slightly more than half the resolutions voted upon received more than 3 percent of the votes cast. However, nine resolutions obtained the 6 percent level of support they required to become automatically eligible for resubmission. In 1977, sixty-seven resolutions voted upon received more than 3 percent of the votes cast; a total of sixty were eligible for resubmission.

Overall, shareholder opposition to the political and social policies of management was highest in 1975, reflecting the impact of the scandals associated with the Nixon reelection effort. In that year the average level of support for public interest proposals was 6.15 percent of the shares voted. Support dropped to 4.34 percent in 1976 and increased to 5.67 percent in 1977.

The highest total of votes in favor of proxy resolutions opposed by management provides another index of the degree of shareholder interest in the public interest proxy mechanism. In 1973, the resolution that received the most support was one submitted by the Project on Corporate Responsibility to Levi-Strauss. It proposed a procedure through which shareholders could submit candidates to the board of directors. It was supported by 9.48 percent of the shares voted. No proposal did as well in 1974, although two received 7 percent or more. These totals were achieved on a resolution to Continental Oil asking it to withdraw from Namibia and one submitted to Phillips "deploring" its illegal campaign contributions. In 1975, two resolutions received over 15 percent of the shares voted. Both were proposed by individuals: one requested Twentieth Century Fox to report its political contributions (17.61 percent), while another, to the Dreyfus Fund, asked the mutual fund to disclose how it voted its stocks on shareholder resolutions (21 percent). A year later, five resolutions opposed by management were supported by at least 15 percent of the shares voted. The two with the largest voted totals—37.2 and 35.1 percent—were addressed to the Dreyfus Fund. They asked it to disclose its thirty largest shareholders and its proxy voting record. The three others were submitted to two utilities, General Public Utilities and Consolidated Edison. General Public Utilities was asked to make public its political contributions, while Con Ed received two resolutions, one calling for the disclosure of the names and fees paid to their outside counsel and the other for the disclosure of the firm's thirty largest shareholders. In 1977, ten resolutions were supported by more than 10 percent of the shares voted. In addition, 27.84 percent of the shares voted by the stockholders of Eastern Airlines supported a resolution asking the corporation to affirm its political nonpartisanship, while a resolution asking Textron's management to disclose its foreign military sales received 14.53 percent of the shares voted.

While there is no reason to assume that the degree of shareholder support will increase steadily, it is likely to at least maintain roughly the levels reached between 1974 and 1977. Shareholder activism is clearly not a function of bull markets and affluent institutional investors: it has become part of our system. As Roger Kennedy concluded in 1975:

We are watching the growth of a new dynamic relationship between management and stockholders, shrouded a little by the substitution of the pension or mutual fund for the stock broker as the chief intermediary between the two . . .[145]

Although the resurgence of shareholder activism has been dominated by groups and individuals advocating positions on the liberal end of the political spectrum, it has also begun to acquire a broader political cast. In 1976, Accuracy in Media, a conservative organization, submitted resolutions to three television networks protesting their alleged liberal bias, and an individual, Carl Olsen, has used his role as a shareholder to challenge corporations involved in East-West trade. More significantly, in part inspired by the example of social activists, shareholders have also become more vocal and vigilant in defending their financial interests both through resolutions and suits.[146] In 1977, three stockholder resolutions that sought to restrict Chrysler's executive compensation practices—all opposed by management —received the support of 20 percent of the votes cast.[147] Shareholder resolutions have also been proposed that would require management to disclose the fees paid to law firms and to prepare a report to shareholders about corporate dividend policies. For over a generation, a handful of "corporate democrats," such as the Gilbert brothers and Wilma Soss, have closely monitored and frequently criticized management's accountability to shareholders. While attracting some publicity, they have not been taken very seriously. But since the mid-seventies their concerns no longer appear so eccentric.[148] Thus, while in the early seventies traditional shareholders often found themselves defending management against social critics, since 1973 they are as likely to find themselves also challenging management prerogatives—though for different motives.[149]

## Conclusion

Since 1970, the formal mechanisms of corporate governance have become revitalized, in part through the efforts of direct citizen pressures. Corporate law has increasingly come to reflect changes in the social environment of the corporation. By skillfully using both the proxy machinery and shareholder suits, critics of business have forced both management and institutional investors to consider—and at times act on—more public conceptions of the responsibilities and accountability of corporate management. While both these strategies required the approval of the SEC and the judiciary, much of their impact has been due to the extent to which the issues they raised reflected concerns that were shared by a broad segment of the investment community and the general public.

The questioning of the composition of the corporate board by Campaign GM followed by only one year the largest bankruptcy in the nation's history to date. Penn Central's collapse raised serious questions within the business community about the viability of the role of outside directors.[150] Many were not aware that the firm for whose governance they were legally responsible was on the verge of bankruptcy until after this fact was made public. In a similar parallel, the court-ordered changes in the composition and selection of Mattel's board of directors helped establish a precedent for the decisions in the Phillips and Northrop cases.[151] The "Corporate Watergate" that began to unfold in 1973 provided further evidence that boards of directors were in urgent need of reform—a viewpoint shared across the political spectrum. Many outside directors again discovered, much to their embarrassment, that they had been kept ignorant of a number of critical political decisions made by management. SEC's commissioner Sommer noted that the outside directors of many companies were "embarrassed and angered when they learned of the way in which the corporations on whose boards they served secured and maintained their business."[152]

Thus, the concerns of the corporation's social critics with the corporation's internal structure of authority has been paralleled by a growing interest in this issue on the part of management consultants, students of corporate law, the investment community, and even management itself.[153] Both Neil Jaccoby and Peter Drucker have publicly called for the revitalization of the corporate board, while the New York Stock Exchange has urged each of its 1,560 listed companies voluntarily to appoint audit committees composed exclusively of outside directors; more than two-thirds of the companies listed on the NYSE had appointed some form of audit committee by 1976. These reforms are not intended to increase the accountability of management to nonfinancial constituencies; efforts to do so are strongly opposed by virtually everyone outside of the corporate accountability movement on the grounds that the board would become dangerously fractionalized.[154] Both activists and those more sympathetic to the corporations do, however, share a common belief that the balance of power within the corporation has become skewed in favor of inside directors (directors who are also managers)—and that a stronger, independent, and more representative board is in the interest of both the corporation and the public.

Shareholder rights are also increasingly attracting the interest of public officials. In 1977, the SEC announced that, for the first time in its forty-three-year history, it had authorized its staff to conduct a broad reexamination of its proxy rules. The commission stated:

> In recent years, commentors have frequently raised questions relating to the extent to which shareholders are able to participate meaningfully in the affairs of the modern public corporation. These questions are based on a recognition that in many public corporations management, in part because of its access to the proxy machinery, is able to exercise control over the election of directors and thereby, in effect, be in a position to set corporate policy and to avoid effective oversight. A number of matters involving questionable and illegal corporate practices and other previously undisclosed conduct have served to focus attention on the subject of corporate accountability.[155]

Among the proposals that the commission plans to consider are:

—whether shareholders should be allowed to use the proxy machinery to nominate directors;
—whether corporations should be requested to disclose additional information about the quality of director nominees—including the process by which they were selected and the qualifications they must possess;
—whether corporations should be required to allow the proxy to be used to facilitate communication between shareholders;
—whether corporations should provide a mechanism to enable shareholders to comment on management proposals (only the reverse is true now);

—whether minimum federal standards for conduct by directors should be established;

—whether outside directors should be required to present their views to shareholders on issues relating to the performance of management;

—whether the control of the proxy machinery should be taken away from management.[156]

Several of these changes have been advocated by various public interest proxy resolutions that have been proposed, and defeated, since 1972.[157] It is likely that at least some will eventually be adopted by the Securities and Exchange Commission. While the resurgence of shareholder activism is not the primary factor behind the SEC's growing interest in the subject of shareholder rights and management responsibilities, the efforts of the corporation's social critics clearly played a role in bringing the issue of corporate governance before the political process. Those critical of the social performance of corporations have now become among the strongest supporters of public policies designed to strengthen shareholder participation.[158]

# CHAPTER

# IV

*Corporate Disclosure*

A SECOND central concern of corporate activists has been to make the public more knowledgeable of the social impact of corporations. The issue of disclosure is central to both the ideology and the practice of the politics of corporate accountability. Most public interest proxy resolutions challenge management's control of information; their immediate objective is to increase the public's awareness of the nonfinancial dimensions of the performance of business. Virtually every citizens' group has put a significant portion of its energies into researching and publicizing various aspects of corporate behavior. In addition, a number of citizen organizations have formed whose primary purpose is to uncover and publicize as much information as possible about the social impact of corporate policies. Their achievement has been an impressive one, and the public's knowledge of the nonfinancial aspects of business has significantly increased over the last decade. Thanks in part to their efforts, the issue of corporate disclosure has come before the political processes of both the private and public sectors.

This chapter traces four aspects of contemporary citizen pressures for increased disclosure by corporations. It begins by discussing citizen organizations who use research as their primary tactics for influencing corporate priorities, with particular emphasis on one of the earliest and most successful—the Council on Economic Priorities. The second section describes the corporate accountability movement's effort to use the framework of securities regulations to reduce the privacy of the corporation—a strategy that parallels the one pioneered by the Project on Corporate Responsibility (PCR). The last two sections offer two case studies of the politics of corporate disclosure. They examine its role in encouraging ethical investment and the efforts of the women's movement to press for increased disclosure as a way of influencing corporate employment policies.

## The Council on Economic Priorities

In his study *Exit, Voice and Loyalty*, Albert Hirschman describes two mechanisms for influencing the behavior of an institution: exit and voice.[1] Hirschman's analysis readily lends itself to an understanding of the diverse strategies of the corporate challenge movement. The notion of voice is clearly central to the public interest proxy contest: those dissatisfied with the corporation seek greater participation in its deliberations. The notion of accountability through participation underlay much of the ethos of the civil rights movement as well as the early years of the New Left. Both these traditions were reflected in Campaign GM. The rhetoric of the antiwar movement, on the other hand, was heavily influenced by the concept of exit: much of its politics revolved around disassociating its participants from the war effort and encouraging other individuals and institutions to do the same. While the civil rights activists wanted blacks to have the opportunity to participate in corporate activities on the basis of civil equality, the antiwar movement's most vivid confrontations with corporations revolved around the demand that they reduce their cooperation with the federal government. It is this latter concept of exit that underlay the original philosophy of the Council on Economic Priorities, an organization that was directly inspired by protests against the Vietnam War.

In late 1969, Alice Tepper Marlin, a financial analyst for a Boston investment firm, was asked by a local synagogue to prepare a list of companies that were not involved in the production of war materials.[2] The resulting "peace portfolio" was advertised in the *New York Times* and over 600 individuals and organizations requested additional information. The *Wall Street Journal* and the Associated Press reported the story, and according to Marlin, "the idea just snowballed from there."[3] Marlin, who had been previously active in the McCarthy campaign, was impressed by the fact that, with all the extensive research on corporations by the investment community, no centralized source of information existed to guide the investment choices of socially concerned investors. Assisted by a private loan of $30,000, the Council on Economic Priorities was created as an educational, nonprofit organization. Its original staff consisted of six "research associates" with policy decisions made by a thirteen-member board of directors, including the economist Robert Heilbroner and the environmentalist Hazel Henderson.

Like the PCR, the council had an original approach to the issue of corporate responsibility. Economic rather than legal in conception, CEP attempted to politicize the investor role and thus make it a vehicle for nongovernmental public pressures on business. While the project sought to revive practices and principles of shareholder participation that had become moribund, the council's approach was to capitalize on that aspect of securities law that remained operable: the regulations governing the disclosure of relevant information about corporate performance to the investment community and, by extension, the public. While those sympathetic to business disagree as to whether shareholders should have additional power to participate in business policy decisions, there does exist a consensus, based on the principle of the market, that investors are entitled to as much knowledge about corporations as they need to make an intelligent decision about the appropriate allocation of their resources. The investor role thus carries with it a built-in bias in favor of corporate disclosure and, equally important, is associated with mechanisms for the careful and continuous scrutiny of corporations by the interested public. It is this relationship that CEP has attempted to use to improve the social performance of corporations.

CEP has been dubbed the "Dun and Bradstreet of Social Responsibility."[4] By design, it functions in a manner analogous to the research unit of a brokerage firm or institutional investor. Its methodology is mostly comparative. The council focuses on a particular industry and then ranks the behavior of the firms within that industry in terms of a specific dimension of their social impact. The council has concentrated on four areas: equal employment, the environment, business and the military, and business and foreign operations. These parameters were originally chosen because data were available, they were neglected by other groups, and they involved problems that corporations had created and had the potential to solve. CEP defined its goal as making "social responsibility become an additional standard by which corporate practices are evaluated and exposed to the investing public."[5]

CEP differentiates itself from all but a few other citizen groups by its professed objectivity. Each of its studies is presented without any editorial comment. Marlin told an interviewer from a management/investment relations newsletter produced by Georgeson and Company:

. . . we believe the facts speak for themselves. There is no reason to assume that the Council's reports will be any less objective than annual reports, investment newsletters and other generally accepted analyses of company financial performance. The Council fully realizes that its credibility, and therefore success as an organization, is largely dependent upon objectivity in both its research and presentation.[6]

The council's objectivity and neutrality are not simply a tactic; by comparing firms within a particular industry, they are measuring corporations in terms of what the best performing firm had been able to achieve. Its studies have thus both highlighted the inadequacies of corporate performance in a variety of critical areas of public impact, as well as given a great deal of highly credible public relations value to the firms that have done well. The methodology of its studies has also enabled it to avoid too close a public identification with more activist and militant groups. The result is that CEP probably enjoys the greatest degree of "respectability" of any group that can be considered part of the corporate accountability movement. How can it be accused of being "antibusiness" when corporations are simply being judged by the standards of their peers?

CEP originally saw its prime consitituency as the investment community. Its studies would enable investors—both individual and institutional—to allocate their capital in a way that would reward firms whose social and political policies were most in accordance with their values. Managers would thereby have the most familiar of incentives to behave more responsibly: the financial marketplace. Through the council's systematic research, the tools for ethical investing would become universally available. The principle behind consumer boycotts would be transferred to the capital market. Thus, *Science* magazine editorialized:

Now a great supplement to the consumer advocacy movement, the Council on Economic Priorities, is setting out to show that facts, if furnished to the right people, can help re-direct the priorities of corporate America.[7]

However, this expectation has not materialized in the way the council originally intended. Rather, the council's studies have been most frequently used by investors interested in CEP's data not because of their social commitments but because of the growing financial implications of government regulation. Thus, *Paper Profits*, CEP's first comparative industry study, attracted particular interest in the investment community through an analysis of its data by two financial analysts.[8] Comparing the environmental performance and profitability of seventeen of the companies studied by CEP, Bragdon and Marlin revealed that the "cleanest" companies were usually the most profitable, while the major polluters had relatively poor earnings. They concluded that a good environmental record is a sign of good management: executives sensitive enough to anticipate pollution control problems were also the kind of enlightened managers who normally produced high profits. This finding received about as much public attention as the original report, carrying with it the comforting conclusion that "nice guys can finish first." Several Wall Street firms incorporated material from the council's study of the pollution control record of the paper industry in their regular investment reports.

The council's main leverage on business, however, has been through the press rather than through the investment community. CEP has focused the attention of the public on corporate social performance; its studies have had minimal impact on influencing the flow of their capital. In addition to moving discussions of social issues from the general audience pages of the paper to the business section, the council has also moved discussions of corporate accomplishments and shortcomings from the business section to the front page. In expanding the number of constituencies interested in business performance, it has helped broaden the nature of the public's concerns and expectations of business.

As in the case of the PCR, the council received considerable press attention during its first year.[9] This was due both to the novelty of its approach and the professional competency of its initial studies. The council was also aided by the press's interest in the personality of its founder. Magazines as diverse as *Time, Playboy*, and *Vogue* featured stories about Marlin, the twenty-nine-year-old "pretty Wellesley graduate" and "crusading citizen" whose new approach was going to make American corporations behave more responsibly.[10] In addition, CEP's emphasis on the preparation of research studies has lent itself extremely well to a long-term, mutually beneficial relationship with the press; in a sense, what CEP has done is to institutionalize investigative reporting. Seven years after its founding, the releases that accompany each new report continue to receive extensive coverage in both the national press as well as in the newspapers from communities where spotlighted companies are located.[11]

CEP is now one of the oldest organizations created as a result of public interest in direct challenges to corporations. It has steadily grown in size and scope. Its budget has grown from $30,000 in 1969 to $485,000 in 1977; its total staff is currently about twenty. About 30 percent of its income comes from corporations who subscribe to CEP's studies: approximately 100 profit-making institutions pay CEP between $450 and $1,000 a year. The rest of its funds comes from either individual and nonprofit institutional subscribers or from contributions by foundations or individuals. CEP has been particularly successful in receiving foundation support; more than thirty foundations had contributed to its efforts, largely in the form of unspecified grants. Currently the council has approximately 2,000 subscribers to its newsletter.

IMPACT

In the course of its research, CEP found that in many instances corporations had no idea about the social conduct of their competitors and were ignorant of the degree to which both they and their competitors were employing the best available technology. One staff member noted:

We're an information providing group. We're constantly surprised that people in an industry don't know more about the issues and alternative solutions available on topics such as pollution control. It's pretty dramatic to show a company that some of its competitors are doing a better job at being socially responsible. We hope that corporations will compete for better social performance, just as they have competed for better financial performance.[12]

An important role of CEP has been to educate the business community about itself and thus raise its expectations. In addition, CEP's comparative methodology is also designed to create peer pressure within the business community. Marlin noted:

Alinsky had a big personal impact on me when we got started. One of the things he stressed was the importance of peer groups and peer pressure. What we try to do is to deal with businessmen directly, to divide the business community and thus create a setting in which publicity and peer pressure can have a big impact.[13]

The attempt to change corporate conduct by dividing the "establishment" was, of course, also used by the antiwar movement and Campaign GM; the council has refined it considerably by focusing on intraindustry differences.

CEP's first study released during the "Cambodia Spring" of 1970, *Efficiency in Death: The Manufacturers of Anti-Personnel Weapons*, listed the 105 U.S. corporations that had been involved in the production of these weapons during the previous five years.[14] This did little to take the public pressure off Honeywell, which, in fact, was the largest supplier, but it did reveal the participation of several firms not normally associated with military production, including the Bulova Watch Company, Motorola, and Zenith Radio. The study, whose release coincided with the high point of popular agitation over the Vietnam War, provided for the first time reliable documentation on the actual extent of corporate involvement in one aspect of the war effort. By focusing on antipersonnel weapons, then the subject of a nationwide protest, the council saw itself as providing both investors and consumers opposed to the war with an additional opportunity to express their political and moral beliefs—and in so doing reduce the degree of business's support for the military effort. The study's findings were the basis for a campaign by a group called Another Mother for Peace, which featured a speech by Bess Meyerson informing American consumers that they "didn't have to buy war." A flood of letters from consumers to Whirlpool saying they were buying appliances made by other companies because they did not want to patronize a firm making antipersonnel weapons did help convince Whirlpool to cease producing them.

*Paper Profits,* the CEP's exhaustively documented report on pollution control efforts by the twenty-four largest pulp and paper producers, established a new standard in the quality of corporate accountability research. The report disclosed that (with the exception of two companies, Owens-Illinois and Weyerhauser) the paper industry had been generally slow to install antipollution devices despite their availability; only 12 percent of the mills studied had adequate air and water pollution control equipment. CEP estimated that the industry would need to spend $750 million to bring it up to federal standards. Twenty-two of the twenty-four companies surveyed responded to the council's questionnaire. While the American Paper Institute called the report "one-sided" because it did not consider "the needs of individual communities" in the recession, it admitted that the report's net effect would be to help speed installation of pollution control equipment.[15] Council members believe that their report played an important role in increasing the pollution control expenditures of St. Regis and Crown Zellerbach, two companies whose previous efforts were particularly undistinguished.[16]

The council subsequently received additional publicity when it compared the environmental performance of several major corporations with the record revealed in their advertising; they were found to be negatively related.[17] More than half of the 280 pages of advertising costing about $6 million that firms placed in *Time, Newsweek,* and *Business Week* extolling their environmental performance were from the four industries with the worst pollution control records. The council also found clear evidence of what it regarded as distortion. One paper company, Potlach, featured a picture of a crystal-clear river to emphasize its commitment to clean water; the picture was actually taken several miles upstream from its plant. Similarly, the council singled out the International Paper Company's record. They wrote: "Its idea of responding to a [pollution] problem is to call in its public relations firm and have it taken care of by means of a large advertising and press release campaign."[18]

*The Price of Power,* CEP's study of the environmental record of fifteen investor-owned utility companies, focused more directly on government policy. One staffer noted:

Our major goal is to provide factual material for the debate between environmentalists and the utility companies. We want to de-mystify the issues, establish whether the companies are spending more on advertising than on clean-up and pollution, research and bring the facts to the public.[19]

The study consisted of a detailed analysis of the companies' 131 largest power plants. The council evaluated the environmental protection record of each plant in terms of the highest feasible standards of pollution control. They discovered that only 45 of the 125 fossil fuel plants in their study measured up to particulate state-of-the-art standards. The council received a grant from the Point Foundation to distribute copies to citizens and environmental groups throughout the United States. *The Price of Power* was successfully used by a number of the local groups to improve the environmental performance of utility companies. This has since become more systematic: the Environmental Policy Center, as well as other organizations, now regularly disseminates copies of the council's environmental studies throughout the United States.

The council continues to regularly publish studies in which the performance of corporations with respect to a particular issue are compared to others in their industry. These have included surveys of the pollution control efforts of the steel and petroleum refining industries and a study of the employment of women and minorities in the banking industry.[20] The latter report, which was updated three years after it originally appeared, helped influence the hiring priorities of the First Pennsylvania Bank; the Philadelphia-based bank showed substantial improvement in the follow-up study. In 1977, CEP published a *Pollution Audit* that summarized the rankings of firms in all its previous pollution control studies; it represents "the only major national effort to review corporate environment performance in a comparative and systematic fashion."[21]

In addition, CEP has published another group of studies that is more policy-oriented. In 1975 the council issued the first study that was focused directly on governmental performance. Titled *Leased and Lost*, it was an indictment of governmental policies regarding the leasing of coal land in the West. Copies were sent to local groups throughout the West, and its author, Jim Cannon, was sent on a personal speaking tour throughout the West to alert local activists with his findings. He argued that corporations were not at fault: abuses had arisen due to public mismanagement. Cannon worked with Senator Metcalf's staff to develop a new Mineral Leasing Act. A bill incorporating over half the council's recommendations and passed over a presidential veto, was considered a "major legislative victory" by CEP.[22] CEP also published a study of the operating efficiency of nuclear power plants that was heavily policy-oriented; it revealed that the plants were functioning far below their operating capacity and thus were less economical than their advocates contended.[23] Marlin notes, "Someone on our staff testifies at least once a month at a hearing in Washington or before a regulatory commission."[24]

It is difficult to generalize about CEP's relationship with the corporations it studies; their willingness to cooperate with CEP varies considerably. Indeed, one of the dimensions on which the council ranks corporations is in terms of their degree of cooperation with its research.[25] The initial reaction of most corporations is one of apprehension; they are afraid that CEP's studies will put them in an unfavorable light. Since each comparative study always reflects well on some firms—on occasion the very ones which were most concerned or uncooperative—the release of CEP's reports usually receives a mixed reception from business. When CEP has had the resources to return to a particular industry in order to update its findings, the numbers of firms willing to cooperate usually increases. On balance, most corporations have been both surprised and impressed by the technical competence of the council's research. Its credibility with the business community has gradually increased with the passage of time, and CEP is able to draw upon the advice and support of a large number of executives, some of whom help open doors to companies that have not yet been exposed to the council's sophisticated style of citizen pressure. On the other hand, some industries and some firms within particular industries refuse to cooperate with CEP at all, forcing the council's research staff to rely more heavily on government documents.

## Other Research Efforts

CEP is distinctive in terms of its visibility and the uniqueness of its approach to the problem of corporate accountability. It is, however, one among a large number of organizations that has surfaced over the last decade primarily devoted to researching the social and political impact of the modern corporation. While most of these groups define their goals in more explicitly political terms than the council, they themselves only infrequently lobby either the state or the corporation. Rather, they function largely as support groups providing information that assists the efforts of a wide variety of organizations, including trade unions, public interest lobbies, and community organizations, in their conflicts with corporations. The politics of these research groups, as well as the organizations that use their material, range broadly across the left-liberal political spectrum: some are interested in assisting foreign "anti-imperialist struggles" while others are concerned about high utility rates. Virtually all, however, share a belief that their effectiveness is largely contingent on the quantity and sophistication of their knowledge of business. As a result, there exists a considerable degree of informal sharing of information about corporations among organizations which, on the surface, appear to have little in common.

One group of research organizations is a spin-off of the left social movement of the sixties. Among the most important are the North American Congress on Latin America (NACLA) founded in 1965 and the National Action and Research on the Military-Industrial Complex. NARMIC is affiliated with the Quakers and played an active role in both the Honeywell Campaign and the campaign against the B–1 bomber. NACLA, which has offices in New York and Berkeley, is exclusively research-oriented. Most of its output consists of a monthly report that spotlights a particular aspect of the involvement of U.S. corporations in Latin America.[26] NACLA's studies, which are highly regarded even by those who do not share their political perspectives, are based largely on press clippings; its support comes from the sales of its literature, individual contributions, and some church sources. It also maintains extensive files available to the public on corporations. The Pacific Studies Center, in Palo Alto, is similar to NACLA except its focus is on the role of U.S. corporations in the Pacific. Others groups have a similar political slant, but monitor firms located within a particular geographical region in the United States. These include the Madison Area Committee on Southern Africa, New England Action Research on the Military Industrial Complex, and the Pacific Northwest Research Center. These groups publish material on locally based corporations and also encourage community pressures on them.

A second broad category of research organizations derives more from the corporate accountability campaigns of the seventies. While their research largely centers on corporations, their activities also include pressures on governmental authorities. The Institute for Southern Studies researches hiring practices, defense ties, and employment records of corporations in the South and publishes *Southern Exposure*. San Francisco Consumer Action—in addition to its lobbying for consumer protection legislation—published in 1973 a study called *Break the Banks: A Shopper's Guide to Banking Services*. The Center for New Corporate Priorities in Los Angeles has been examining the social impact of the Bank of America's lending policies in California since 1972. In March 1973,

Joanne Underwood, a former codirector of the CEP, established a group called Inform.[27] Funded by several large foundation grants, it has committed itself to four major studies of various aspects of the social impact of corporate policies. These include the consumer and environmental impact of the land sales and subdivision industry, the role of the energy industry in developing new energy resources, occupational health and safety in the nonferrous metals industry, and the publication of a pollution control manual for regulatory officials and managers in the private sector.[28]

Discovering the pattern of ownership and control of corporate securities has long been of interest to corporate reformers as well as to various government agencies. It has taken on renewed interest, particularly among citizen groups, with the development of public interest proxy contests. It is rather difficult to apply pressures on large individual and institutional stockholders if one does not know who they are. In 1975 an organization was established in New York with the sole objective of discovering, documenting, and publicizing the ownership and control of American corporations. To date, the Corporate Data Exchange has published detailed studies on two industries: transportation and agri-business. Like the council, the Data Project relies upon the marketing of its material to the business community, particularly the investment community, as an important source of funds. Michael Locker, the project's founder and formerly a staff member of NACLA, stated:

The level of understanding of the corporate structure is too low. Individual businessmen can only be made accountable if they become real human entities and not just a "street name." We see our role complementary to that of shareholder activists. Those filing shareholder resolutions can only devise a strategy to influence votes after they know who the shareholders really are.[29]

The exchange supplied the Amalgamated Clothing and Textile Workers Union with a stockholder profile of the J. P. Stevens Company and also furnished a list of the principal stockholders of the various manufacturers of infant formulas to several religious denominations.

Paralleling the studies of the Data Exchange, a number of public interest proxy resolutions themselves have focused on the issue of the disclosure of corporate ownership.[30] In 1976 three Catholic orders requested that Consolidated Edison of New York, Mobil Oil, and Exxon disclose their top thirty voting shareholders. Exxon agreed to ask all the institutions whose aggregate holdings placed them among the top thirty shareholders to specify their voting power. The resolution was withdrawn. Mobil declined to write its institutional investors, while Con Edison, after opposing the resolution (it received the support of 16 percent of the shares voted), agreed to follow Exxon's example. In 1977 similar requests were made to IBM and American Airlines.

### THE MOVEMENT'S SELF-CONSCIOUSNESS

One of the most important subjects of research has been the corporate accountability movement itself. In its first publication, issued in April of 1970, the Council on Economic Priorities briefly described four other citizen challenges.[31] This represented the first time citizen challenges to corporations had been labeled as a distinctive political phenomenon. That summer it published a twenty-page report based largely on press accounts that reported on all the corporate challenges that had taken place in the spring of 1970.[32] The ten conflicts it described dealt mostly with antiwar issues. Following that study, CEP decided to devote one annual issue of its bimonthly magazine, *Economic Priorities Report*, to summarizing citizen challenges to corporations during the previous year. The report, released each spring under the title *Minding the Corporate Conscience*, provided the most comprehensive account of political pressures on corporations during the four years it was issued. It described the nature of the organizations involved, their particular concerns, the range of tactics they employed, and their impact on corporate conduct. Most importantly, each survey listed the names and addresses of all citizen challenge organizations in order to promote direct communication among them.

It is difficult to evaluate the reports' impact on the consciousness of citizen challenge groups; when a letter was mailed by the author in 1975 to all groups listed in each of the four reports asking how they saw themselves in the context of the movement to politicize the corporation, many expressed surprise that they were, indeed, part of a larger political phenomenon. On the other hand, *Minding the Corporate Conscience* was one of CEP's most popular publications. In addition to recording the movement's history for posterity, it contributed to furnishing local groups with a sense that there were indeed other efforts paralleling their own all around the country—often focusing on quite narrow issues and isolated from the media and political centers of Washington and New York. Marlin considers one of CEP's most important contributions that "most public interest groups now focus a lot of their energies on corporations."[33] CEP's publication, along with the Investor Responsibility Research Center's *News for Investors* and the Interfaith Center's *The Corporate Examiner*, has greatly facilitated the dissemination of information about the plans, efforts, and accomplishments of the corporate accountability movement. In addition, a few groups have written case studies of citizen challenges, attempting to create a sort of citizens' counterpart to the studies prepared for the training of future executives by business school faculty, but these have had little circulation.[34]

The sharing of experiences among those groups and individuals at the center of the citizen challenge effort has also taken place on a more informal basis. For a time during the early seventies the living room of Marlin's New York apartment was an important meeting ground for the handful of individuals who helped forge the corporate challenge movement out of the social currents of the sixties. In addition to Marlin, they included Phil Moore of the Project on Corporate Responsibility, Mary Williams of the Council for Corporate Review, and various representatives of the National Council of Churches. A similar role on the West Coast was played by Mike Phillips of the Glide Foundation. In the fall of 1971, he invited twenty-two corporate activists from around the country to a weekend conference in order to introduce them to each other and to discuss the range of emerging strategies for challenging corporations. Phillips recalled, "It made people feel part of a community and gave them a sense of power as a group."[35]

## SEC

The importance of disclosure as a tactic for influencing the behavior of corporations led the corporate challenge movement to the Securities and Exchange Commission. In 1971 the National Resources Defense Council (NRDC) and the Project on Corporate Responsibility requested the SEC to require corporations to disclose their equal employment practices as well as any adverse environmental impact associated with their major activities or products. The SEC agreed to amend its reporting forms to require companies to disclose the economic effects of their compliance with environmental laws and regulations but refused to initiate rule-making proceedings on the broader issues raised by the petition. The commission's refusal was appealed to the D.C. District Court. In December 1974, Judge Richey ruled against the commission. He wrote:

There are many so-called "ethical investors" in this country who want to invest their assets in firms which are concerned about the acting on environmental problems of the nation. This attitude may be based purely upon a concern for the environment, but it may also proceed from the recognition that awareness of and sensitivity to environmental problems is the mark of intelligent management. Whatever their motive, this court is not prepared to say that they are not rational investors and that the information they seek is not material information within the meaning of the securities laws.[36]

The court ordered the SEC to resolve two factual issues: the extent of interest among "ethical investors" in the disclosure of information about environmental and equal employment policies and "the avenues open to such investors to eliminate corporate practices inimical to the environment and equal employment opportunity."[37] Thus, for the second time in five years, the federal courts had required a reluctant SEC to consider the needs of its new constituency—one whose existence was certainly not anticipated by the drafters of the Securities and Exchange Act of 1935 nor particularly welcomed by those mandated by Congress to administrate it.

The commission's nineteen days of public hearings in May of 1975 featured written and oral testimony by the entire corporate accountability movement; the hearings provided the movement with an opportunity to demonstrate its political existence and to demand that it be taken seriously with respect to public policy affecting the social control of the large business corporation. There is, of course, some irony in a group of organizations, many of whom were committed to the desirability and importance of regulatory mechanisms which bypassed the government, coming to Washington to participate in the rule-making decisions of a government regulatory agency. From one viewpoint the corporate challenge movement can be seen legitimately as the analogue of the public interest organizations that have surfaced as watchdogs for each government regulatory agency. Thus, the Civil Aeronautics Board has the Airline Consumer Actions Project (ACAP), while the Federal Communications Commission has the Association for Children's Broadcasting as well as the Media Access Project; now it was the SEC's turn to acquire a "public interest" shadow. Yet unlike the other relationships between regulatory agencies and the "guardian's guardians," corporate activists were not interested in monitoring the SEC. Such groups as the project, CEP, and the Interfaith Center were interested in the regulatory agency only insofar as it affected their access to corporations directly. A better analogy might be the relationship between labor organizations and the National Labor Relations Board. The SEC was entrusted with establishing the ground rules for citizen challenges to business in much the same way that the NLRB set the framework for union-management conflicts. For many groups, their presence at the hearings was their first formal participation in the governmental process.

By seeking to expand the SEC's mandate, corporate activists were not only attempting to extend the criteria by which citizens could legitimately judge corporate performance. They were also implicitly seeking to undermine the presupposition that the burden of decision as to what information about corporate performance should be made public rested with the corporation, not with the public. In effect, their petition attempted to legalize the inroads into corporate privacy that the public interest movement itself had painstakingly made over the previous five years. If they were successful, virtually nothing a corporation did would find itself immune from public scrutiny under the rather elastic term "social impact."

In March 1975, the NRDC established a Corporate Information Access Project to coordinate and encourage movement participation in the SEC's deliberations. In a letter to corporate activists, Glenn Stover, the project's director, noted, "The importance of this SEC proceeding and of substantial participation by people concerned about corporate responsibility cannot be overestimated."[38] Noting that the court's decision had directed the SEC to determine the actual extent of interest in socially responsible investment, Stover stressed the importance of maximum possible public participation: "The public's response to the SEC's invitation for comment will have a substantial impact on the SEC decision."[39]

A total of 402 individuals or organizations submitted either written or oral testimony before the SEC; 227 opposed "social" disclosure, while 175 favored it.[40] More than half of the institutions or organizations who offered their opinions were from the business community; with only two exceptions they strongly opposed any expansion of the disclosure requirements. (Several Wall Street executives, in fact, favored the proposed expansion of reporting requirements, but they felt under strong peer pressures not to make their views public.) Business spokesmen argued that actually there was relatively little investor interest in obtaining such information and that in any event most of the information was available elsewhere. Furthermore, many corporate representatives contended that the request for disclosure would consume a disproportionate amount of management resources. They suggested that the concept of an "ethical investor" was in danger of becoming a *"carte blanche"* for each individual citizen interested in any aspect of corporate performance: "The entire catalogue of the world's social problems would be grist for the ethical investor's mill."[41] Another asked rhetorically, "Ethical observers—whose ethics?"[42]

In addition to seventy-four individual investors, fifty-six representatives of corporate activist groups testified for the proposals. Their arguments represent a good summary of the underlying philosophy of the corporate accountability movement. One argument defended the extended disclosure requirements on the grounds that recent changes in the corporation's social and legal environment now made social performance an extremely relevant dimension of management performance. By their own public statements and actions, corporations, they asserted, had come to recognize the importance of social issues in the conduct of their business. In short, "social responsibility" had become an integral part of the functioning of the modern corporation: "An investor need not be especially 'ethical' to be interested in the degree to which corporations can be expected to continue to manufacture and sell free of interruption."[43]

A second set of arguments focused on the "rights" of shareholders, which were becoming revitalized by the growing politicization of the investor role. The critics argued that as owners of the company, shareholders were entitled to information about social performance as a matter of right and that, in addition, the availability of additional information would enable shareholders to make better investments: there was often a close relationship between responsiveness to changing social demands and competent management. Since these regulations frequently become more strict over time, compliance with the law had become an insufficient criterion on which to base investment decisions.

Thirdly, a number of institutional investors from churches, universities, and foundations contended that institutions have a fiduciary and moral obligation to participate in corporate governance and that this was difficult in the absence of additional information. Finally, several who testified cited the experiences of the movement itself: the extreme difficulty—both time-consuming and expensive—of getting information about social issues (Marlin, whose organization was formed exactly for this purpose, noted that "the vacuum of data in the social area is staggering")[44] and the impossibility of making realistic industry comparisons given the present amount of information.

If the very existence of the hearings testified to the existence of the corporate challenge movement, then the commission's decisions reflected its political and economic weakness.[45] The commission, in large measure, made its decision on the alleged basis of a lack of sufficient investor interest in social issues. It explicitly noted both the relatively small size of socially responsible investment mutual funds as well as the extremely small percentage—less than 1 percent—of the total shares represented at the hearings. It was particularly impressed by the lack of "broad participation [of] financial institutions in the proceedings."[46] While noting the existence of numerous "socially responsible" organizations of investors, the commission recognized, quite accurately, that the thrust of shareholder activism was directed at the voting of proxies—not the buying and selling of shares. The commission concluded that its

. . . experience over the years in proposing and framing disclosure requirements has not led it to question the basic decision of Congress that, insofar as investing is concerned, the primary interest of investors is economic . . . other motives are probably present . . . but the only common thread is the hope for a satisfactory return, and it is to this that a disclosure scheme intended to be useful to all must be primarily addressed.[47]

The commission did, however, agree to make an exception in the area of environmental expenditures in order to bring the SEC into compliance with the National Environmental Policy Act (NEPA) which directs all federal agencies to promote environmental protection to the "fullest extent possible." While rejecting the request that corporations be required to release environmental impact statements, the commission did propose to amend its reporting rules to require corporations to file any compliance reports indicating their failure to meet any governmental standards over the previous year. It also slightly expanded its requirement that corporations estimate the material effect of compliance with environmental protection regulations.

The commission's decision emphasized that it was the uniqueness of the letter and spirit of NEPA and the commission's need to comply with the court's decision that led it to alter its traditional conception of its responsibilities for the economic welfare of corporate shareholders. It refused to expand its disclosure requirements to cover equal opportunity policies because it saw no way of distinguishing equal employment "from among the myriad of other social matters in which investors may be interested in the absence of a specific mandate comparable to that of NEPA."[48] Indeed, to buttress its argument the commission listed over 100 different "social matters" in which "ethical" investors indicated interest during the hearings; the very diversity of the concerns of the corporate challenge movement evidently made the commission reluctant to legitimize any of them. Yet in the process of explaining why additional disclosure requirements would advance the cause of environmental protection and thus enable the SEC to comply with NEPA, the commission found itself echoing the rationale for corporate activism. After noting that the "effectiveness of these . . . tactics . . . does not readily lend itself to generalization," it went on to suggest that

disclosure to investors of information reflecting corporate compliance with existing environmental standards might have some indirect effect on corporate practices to the benefit of the environment.[49]

It concluded:

. . . the availability of such information may result in some investor or shareholder action. Participants in the proceeding pointed out that the submission of and voting on socially-oriented shareholder proposals has often caused a corporation to alter its behavior.[50]

The commission clearly appreciated the effectiveness of shareholder activism and its ability to advance public goals; it did not, however, define its mandate as enhancing that effectiveness.

A half a year later the SEC decided to drop the requirement that corporations disclose information about their violation of environmental regulations. The commission's decision did not damage corporate activism; it simply left their access where it had been before. NRDC appealed the SEC's decision in the U.S. Circuit Court for the District of Columbia which again supported the environmental group's claim. The court ordered the SEC to reconsider its ruling; the controversy continues.

ETHICAL INVESTMENT

In spite of the unwillingness of the SEC to force corporations to disclose more about their social performance, the level of public awareness of the behavior of individual corporations steadily increased throughout the late sixties. By the early seventies the dimensions of corporate conduct on which individuals of social conscience might want to express their judgment had expanded significantly beyond participation in the war in Vietnam. They had come to include the treatment of women and minorities, investment in the Third World, and, most importantly, thanks to "Earth Day" in the spring of 1970, the impact of the firm and its products on the physical environment.

The amount of information available about the behavior of specific corporations as well as the sudden increase of popular interest in corporate performance raised the possibility that ethical investing could become much more than a symbolic act: it could be generalized into a principle of corporate reform.

This expectation underlay the initial conception of the Council on Economic Priorities. In an interview conducted soon after CEP was founded, Marlin remarked:

. . . there can be little doubt that advising and informing these institutions of the opportunities for socially conscious investments can bring financial pressure to bear on corporations. . . . The Council is trying to foment a new market psychology which will provide corporate management with a rationale for their social responsibility . . . a corporation [should be] . . . aware that socially responsible behavior will attract the attention of investors.[51]

An editorial in the *Nation*, published shortly after the release of *Paper Profits*, revealed the extent to which this notion had caught the imagination of those on the left of the political spectrum. The weekly suggested that

> Surveys of this kind provide a new technique for public-spirited citizens, mutual funds, etc.—everybody with funds to invest—to work for the public good. Other things being equal, it is obviously in the public interest to reward the conscientious by investing in their securities and to punish those who are exclusively profit-minded.[52]

It confidently concluded: "Companies which persist in polluting air and water face a dim future."[53]

There was also another factor. CEP had sought to give individuals and institutions the opportunity to "vote" their political and social beliefs with their purchase of securities. The existence of socially oriented investors would, in turn, make it in the self-interest of the corporation to behave more responsibly; investor "social responsibility" would thus inexorably lead to corporate "social responsibility," even if—or to be more precise, because—managers remained exclusively oriented to the bottom line. The investor, however, like the voter, would not necessarily be maximizing his economic self-interest; for this arrangement to work he would have to be prepared to sacrifice some financial return. But what if "socially responsible" conduct turned out to be in the firm's self-interest as well? In view of the steady increase in federal regulations affecting a wide variety of corporate decisions, the boundaries of managerial discretion appeared to be rapidly narrowing. If the preferences of socially oriented investors were to eventually be enacted into law, then the trade-off between profits and responsible behavior on the part of the corporation would be minimized. These investors could then have the best of all possible worlds: they could simultaneously appease their consciences, use their capital to improve society, and earn a high rate of return on their investments.

The stage was now set for the effort to place "corporate social responsibility" on a sound commercial basis.[54] The concept of "ethical investing," or "stocks without sin" as one writer termed it, convincingly demonstrated the viability of the American business instinct; even public criticisms of corporate performance could become marketable. Adam Smith's promise of the identity of private greed and public welfare was revived, but with one difference: the intervention of socially sophisticated mutual funds managers would now be required. Accordingly, in 1971 at least six mutual funds were established with social objectives. Their introduction was widely reported in the financial press and generally greeted with considerable enthusiasm; now individual investors would become part of the effort to transform the behavior of American business. As the prospectus of one fund put it, "Private investment can be a positive force to enhance and encourage further social progress in America."[55]

The largest of the funds was established by the Dreyfus Corporation in the spring of 1972 with $26 million in assets—rather modest by Wall Street standards. It planned to invest at least two-thirds of its assets according to criteria quite similar to that of the council's studies. It would pick those firms which, by comparison with their counterparts, had acceptable records in four areas of social concern: pollution control, occupational health and safety, product purity and safety, and equal employment opportunities. Up to one-third of its assets would be invested in companies "that are doing breakthrough work in ways that will affect the quality of life in this country in the decade ahead."[56] Of the first 500 companies it studied, 103 made it to the eligible list; investments in those companies were then made according to traditional criteria. A former administrative assistant to Senator Edward Kennedy was hired to manage the Third Century Fund. It saw its initial market as nonprofit institutional investors. The fund denied an interest in pressuring corporations; it saw itself essentially as a commercial venture. Those who established the fund were confident that social and pecuniary objectives were mutually reinforcing. Its manager contended that "the managements who look after pollution control, consumer protection, and minority hiring are going to be the really profitable ones in the future."[57]

Other mutual funds were more oriented to individual investors. The Pax World Fund was established by two Methodist ministers in order to "contribute to world peace." It restricted its investments to those corporations less than 5 percent of whose sales derived from contracts with the Defense Department. The First Spectrum Fund was organized around the principle of avoiding any investment in corporations that the fund's managers had reason to believe were not in full compliance with existing laws and regulations governing protection of the environment, civil rights, and consumer protection.

### THE DIFFICULTIES

The most obvious problem of the funds was simply their inability to attract investors. The Dreyfus Fund failed to sell out its initial offering of 2.5 million shares; only 2.1 million were sold. Two and one-half years later, its initial capital of $24.3 million had been reduced to $19.4 million. The First Spectrum Fund's managers estimated that they would need assets of $15 million to generate enough management fees to cover their expenses and pay their salaries and between $50 and $100 million before corporations would take them seriously. Their assets never went much over

$600,000. Finally, it was dissolved in 1974. The other funds had equally undistinguished histories. Because of their small size, there is no evidence that they had any impact on corporate behavior.

Why did the funds fail to attract investors? First, they had the misfortune to be introduced into a bear market and thus found themselves the victims of declining investor interest in mutual funds in general. More importantly, as far as individual investors were concerned, there simply did not appear to be a market for social responsibility issues. Some people—their number is difficult to estimate—appeared willing to avoid the purchase or to sell the securities in a corporation that was deemed to be on the wrong side of an issue about which they felt very strongly. There is, however, a considerable difference between avoiding the stock of one or a few firms out of a strongly held social commitment such as took place during the Vietnam War and deliberately structuring one's investment portfolios to achieve various social objectives. With little exception, people purchase stock to make money, and even if they wish to consider social principles, they are unlikely to delegate that task. As Walter Goodman noted, "I don't know any investment advisor whom I would care to act in my behalf in any matter except making a profit—and I'm not sure about that."[58] Institutional investors, for the most part, also proved uninterested. If they were going to make investments on the basis of social criteria, they preferred to keep the prerogatives in their own hands rather than surrender control to mutual fund managers.

There was also a more fundamental problem: by what criteria could one reasonably decide which firms were socially responsible and which were not? In a highly influential article in *Harvard Business Review*, Malkiel and Quandt urged portfolio managers not to consider political and social issues when making investment decisions. They concluded that:

a case could be made for avoiding investment in virtually any company. . . . It is hard to imagine a company completely free of connections that might be considered objectionable on moral, political or social grounds by some member of the portfolio manager's constituency.[59]

Ethical investment was predicated on the assumption that somehow corporate social policies could be evaluated by the same objective, quantitative criteria with which one made economic decisions. But judging the social performance of an entire corporation, as contrasted to its behavior with respect to a particular issue, was actually more analogous to deciding which candidate to support: the decision was subject to a wide variety of overlapping and frequently conflicting considerations. Divestment or purchase was often too crude a lever. Should one purchase Xerox in recognition of the social usefulness of its product, as one Harvard study proposed, or sell it because of its investments in South Africa, as a Princeton student group suggested? U.S. Steel's pollution control record was one of the worst of any corporation in the United States. On the other hand, its mining safety record was one of the best in the industry. Should one buy it or sell it? (Ironically, when Milton Moskowitz, editor of *Business and Society* newsletter, published his list of the ten most socially responsible corporations in 1975, one of them was none other than Dow Chemical.)[60]

While an individual investor could, like a voter, in principle decide which issues were most important, this was much more difficult for an institution like a university that was composed of individuals with diverse social and political priorities and which also faced the problem of absorbing the possible costs associated with a "clear" portfolio.

Finally, the appeal of ethical investment was substantially diminished by the development of the public interest proxy contest. Voting proxies against management has two advantages over disinvestment as a strategy for influencing corporations: it is virtually costless and allows investors to focus on particular dimensions of corporate behavior. Moreover, some activists have argued that selling a company's stock is a one-shot action that is not suited to a controversy whose resolution may take years: after you sell, what do you do for an encore? One activist criticized it as a "head in the sand approach"; its consequence would be that those firms whose social conduct was most in need of citizen scrutiny would receive it least. Proxy voting, on the other hand, allows politically motivated shareholders to raise issues at annual meetings and vote against management year after year. Tim Smith, the director of a coalition of Protestant and Catholic organizations particularly interested in corporate investment in South Africa, has reported that some executives, annoyed and frustrated by the continuous pressure they have received from church groups, have actually encouraged their dissident shareholders to sell their shares rather than continue to publicly oppose management policies. As Smith noted in 1972:

the churches are beginning to say that . . . if they own stock in a company like Gulf Oil Corp., they will challenge that corporation. And, in fact, they may do more, they may be able to create more pressure by running an on-going campaign against the Gulf Oil Corp. instead of selling stock. That has been the logic up to now. This creates much more pressure on a company than divestment.[61]

But while ethical investing has not become as important as some of its earlier enthusiasts anticipated, it has by no means disappeared as a strategy. It has, however, been exclusively used to punish firms rather than reward them. Pressures for divestment have most often been raised in connection with issues of corporate conduct that have a particularly strong moral dimension. As it developed during the war in Vietnam, its original spirit was akin to that of draft and tax resistance; one disassociated oneself from the prosecution of the war by refusing to lend one's resources—both financial and personal—to the private and public institutions responsible for its continuation. More recently it has been raised in connection with corporate investments in South Africa, particularly by students demanding that their university sell their stock in companies doing business in South Africa as a way of politically protesting apartheid and demonstrating their refusal to financially benefit from it.

The list of actual divestments is not a large one. During the sixties, a few universities sold their stocks in banks participating in the 1960 loan agreement with the South African government, and others divested their stock in the Gulf Oil Corporation. Columbia University sold all its holdings in GM and Gulf because of their involvement in South Africa. In 1972, the Church of the Brethren sold all its stock in companies involved in the production of weapons. A year later, the Board of National Ministries of the American Baptist Churches sold its 21,000 shares of stock in United Aircraft to protest that company's continued military production. In 1974, the Phillips-Van Heusen Pension and Retirement Fund sold its holdings in ITT because of that firm's irresponsible behavior concerning political contributions and intervention in the political process, both domestically and internationally. Three years later, the University of Massachusetts and the Oregon Board of Higher Education decided to divest their portfolios of all companies with investments in South Africa, while Smith College sold its 42,000 shares of Firestone Tire and Rubber because the company had not satisfactorily responded to their inquiries about its role in South Africa. Amherst College indicated that it would consider selling stock in any firm that had not signed a pledge to prohibit racial discrimination, while the University of Wisconsin announced a similar policy. Hampshire College, a small private college in New England, actually divested its entire portfolio, pending its analysis of what constituted an ethical investment policy. Divestment, however, remains seriously limited as a strategy for pressuring corporations because of the potential financial costs associated with it. Moreover, under certain conditions portfolio selection on the basis of social or moral criteria may also violate the fiduciary duty of trustees—though the courts have yet to address this issue.

## The Women's Movement

At a shareholder's meeting in 1970 the women's movement began to bring its demands before the corporation.[62] A spokesperson for the Women's Liberation Front told the president of Columbia Broadcasting at the company's annual meeting in San Francisco:

> CBS abuses women. . . . You use our bodies to sell products. We won't be put on the market. You blackmail us with the fear of being unloved if we do not buy. . . .
> Your meeting here is perverse and ugly. You talked about how much money you made. . . . You assume no responsibility in terms of human values, only in terms of profit. . . . You brag that six hours of every day is spent mostly by women watching television: mind-coddling, dull, alienated, and you should be ashamed of yourselves.[63]

While the issue of the image of women in advertising continues to be raised in proxy resolutions, most of the pressure of the women's movement on business has focused on corporate employment practices. Pressuring corporations to disclose their employment practices has been a central part of their strategy.

A good deal of the impetus for the recent challenges to business originates in the case brought against AT&T in September 1970 by Equal Employment Opportunity Commission (EEOC), National Organization of Women (NOW), and the NAACP. Although this was basically a governmental action, NOW's participation in this suit created a momentum for citizen pressures. "NOW women, for example, picketed Bell installations, testified against Bell at FCC hearings across the country, and attacked the company's policies in speeches and in the press."[64] NOW's primary concerns were: (1) to do away with classifying jobs on the basis of sex and (2) to force AT&T to pay women and minorities the opportunity cost of the wages they lost because they thought company policy prevented them from seeking promotions. In January 1973, AT&T signed a consent decree in which it agreed (1) to pay $15 million in restitution and equal pay claims, (2) to provide 36,000 workers with $23 million in higher pay and adjusted pay schedules, and (3) to set up goals and timetables to bring more women and minority group men into its better-paying craft jobs and management jobs.[65]

NOW subsequently began to explore ways in which it could directly help enforce compliance with the consent decree. Noting that 37 percent of AT&T's shareholders were female, NOW contended that "by uniting their proxy statements, Bell's proverbial 'widows and orphans' could become an effective lobby for change."[66] In 1971, NOW published a pamphlet entitled the "Handbook for the Corporate Suffragette." It stressed that women must begin to exercise the power given to them through stock ownership:

Women have, until now, been reluctant to use the power that is theirs. One of these powers is that of shareholders in America's corporations, large and small. NOW recognizes that herein lies one of the means for women achieving control over their destiny in society. When women have their full voice in the management of their corporations and a greater say in how their money will be invested, full and equal opportunities for women in this society will come closer to being a reality.[67]

The purpose of the pamphlet was to make women aware of their rights to attend annual meetings, submit shareholder resolutions, vote shares, and inspect corporate records. The ultimate purpose of these tactics was to bring pressure to bear on top-level management to be responsive to the demands of women. "As women shareholders we must see that oppression of women employees of America's corporations is ended; that women be placed in all levels of management; that discriminatory employment practices be stopped; and that the needs of all women employees be met."[68]

Just as Campaign GM had attempted to persuade GM's shareholders to relate to the auto manufacturer in their role as citizens, so NOW wanted the majority of investors to become conscious of their sexual identity. Adopting the litany of "socially responsible" investors, NOW argued that in the long run there was no tension between the financial and social interests of female shareholders:

A well-managed corporation not only yields profits for its shareholders, it provides fair employment practices for all employees, it is responsive to consumer needs and concerns, it advertises its products without exploitation of any class of persons, and it operates for the benefit of the whole community.[69]

Direct pressure on corporations has come also from the Interfaith Committee on Social Responsibility in Investment. In 1973 the coalition of church groups decided at a long-range planning conference that equal employment opportunity was to have top priority for the coming year. Its principal strategy was to propose proxy resolutions that required corporations to disclose the composition of their labor force by race, sex, and job category. By forcing corporations to make public this data, it hoped to increase public pressure on them. Once a firm begins to disclose figures on equal employment opportunity (EEO), "public and shareholder concern about EEO and the corporation's progress will be emphasized."[70] Armed with the data, communities could then monitor the progress of the corporation and put public pressure on recalcitrant firms to improve their performance. Corporations with progressive records could be commended while those who refused to disclose data on their employment practices would be regarded as having something to hide and thus pressure further. The task force anticipated that this movement for public accountability and disclosure would have a domino effect: "the more corporations that 'come out,' the more corporations will feel pressure to do so."[71] In a sense, the idea behind the church's disclosure resolutions was similar to the principle that underlay the Council on Economic Priorities' comparative studies.

The resolutions filed by participants in the Interfaith Committee on Social Responsibility in Investments in 1974 requested that corporations publish the following in their next annual report: (1) employment data for the past three years by race, sex, and job classification (such as is required by the EEO-1 form); (2) data indicating the total number of males and females in the standard job categories; (3) a statement of the corporation's policy with regard to equal employment opportunity; (4) the affirmative action guidelines they will use to implement this policy; (5) an explanation of the problems they have encountered in their attempt to implement their policy (as well as the achievements). They also requested that these data be published for three years following the initial report and that affirmative action plans and EEO-1 data for the past three years on local facilities be made available to individual shareholders upon request.

The Interfaith EEO Task Force meeting developed several explicit criteria for selecting "target companies" with whom they would file disclosure resolutions. First, they were interested in companies that would either be responsive to the resolution or would feel vulnerable and thus be compelled to act. Second, they gave priority to those companies with whom the church had a particular relationship (for example, the United Presbyterian Church, U.S.A., had studied Kraftco at length, and the United Church of Christ had had previous discussions with Proctor and Gamble). Third, they decided to emphasize companies that the EEOC was currently investigating, including General Motors, General Electric, and Ford. Finally, they reasoned that several companies who had recently released extensive data on their employment practices in South Africa would find it difficult to argue against the release of the same kind of data in the United States.

After sending letters to more than fifty corporations asking for statistics and explanations of their equal employment practices, the church project submitted in February 1974 the EEO disclosure resolution to Farah Manufacturing, Ford, General Motors, General Electric, Goodyear, IBM,

Kraftco, Polaroid, Sears Roebuck, and Xerox. The Glide Foundation in San Francisco filed similar proposals with American Home Products, Celanese, Souther Co., and Southern California Edison. In addition, Joan Hull, a group manager of Celanese corporation and a member of NOW who is generally regarded as "the heroine of the shareholder proposal movement,"[72] submitted three proposals to Celanese and Gulf. They required the corporation to (1) amend the corporation's bylaws to allow for the nomination of women to the board of directors in proportion to the number of women shareholders; (2) report to shareholders on employment practices regarding women and minorities; and (3) institute cumulative voting for directors.

In 1975 resolutions for EEO disclosure became more specific and more sophisticated. The Unitarian Universalist Association asked Minnesota Mining and Manufacturing Corporation (3M) not only for the disclosure of consolidated statistics filed for the past three years with the EEOC, but they also requested a summary and status report of all complaints filed by the EEOC, other agencies, or courts alleging discrimination by the corporation in hiring or employment practices on the basis of race or sex, as well as an assessment of potential financial damages resulting from such complaints. After the Unitarians threatened 3M with litigation because of a misleading argument in management's rebuttal to their proxy, management agreed to provide most of the information a few days before the annual meeting.

A year later EEO disclosure resolutions were filed with Avon, Celanese, Chrysler, Gillette, Meredi, and Warner-Lambert. They were similar to those filed in previous years, but again asked for more detail. For example, Joan Hull asked Celanese for a detailed report on the hiring and promotion progress of women on the staff of the legal and personnel departments and chief operating officers. She also asked for a report on the legal expenses Celanese paid out in 1975 to claimants because of sex and discrimination practices. Hull argued, "Shareholders have a right to prior knowledge of any potential liability their corporation has so they can make intelligent investment decisions."[73] This resolution was supported by 5 percent of the shares voted, making it the only resolution affecting women eligible for resubmission in 1977.

Overall, the campaign for the disclosure by corporations of their treatment of women and minorities has been quite successful. Prior to 1974 virtually no major corporation had released to the public its "EEO–1" data. In 1974 nine of the seventeen equal employment disclosure resolutions were withdrawn after management had agreed to supply the data collected. By January 1976, the church task force reported that approximately fifty major corporations had made EEO–1 type data public, largely in response to shareholder resolutions. What is less clear, however, is what effect this has had on company compliance. Evaluating the data is extremely difficult and time-consuming. Furthermore, the church and NOW have no independent way of checking the accuracy. As an IRRC report noted: "There is, in addition, one highly significant limitation which is common to all forms of equal employment information. None of the information can answer the question of whether a company is practicing illegal employment discrimination."[74] Elizabeth Forsling Harris, the former director of NOW's Stockholder Action Task Force, concluded:

I think it's one of the slowest ways of accomplishing equal employment, because of all the red tape involved. But I think it's an extremely effective way . . . in the education that is acquired . . . so, if you have the patience, it's a very effective device.[75]

## Conclusion

Increasing the public's knowledge and awareness of corporate policies is likely to remain a major concern of the corporate accountability movement.[76] Regardless of its substantive concerns, virtually every citizen pressure on corporations publicizes a report describing some aspect of corporate conduct and continually seeks to persuade management to furnish more information about its activities. Moreover, many challenges begin by asking management to investigate its own behavior. In a discussion paper on corporate disclosure written in 1977, Gordon Adams, the director of military research for the Council on Economic Priorities, argued, "Among the many routes for controlling corporate behavior, disclosure is one of the most fundamental."[77] Adams suggested that the ability of each of the corporation's constituencies to define and defend their interests vis-à-vis management was critically dependent on its awareness of business behavior. He concluded that "disclosure ought to be one of the priority activities of any coalition seeking greater corporate democracy and accountability."[78]

As with the issue of corporate governance, the role of public policy with respect to this dimension of corporate accountability is critical. While groups may successfully convince management to increase the amount and information they make available to their stockholders—and thus the public at large—citizen groups ultimately want the federal government to enact stricter reporting requirements for corporations so their effectiveness can increase. Public disclosure requirements are one of the most important ways in which the government can assist direct citizen pressures.

The importance of disclosure to the basic strategy and philosophy of the citizen challenge effort is emphasized by Donald Schwartz. Campaign GM's former counsel wrote:

> As notions of corporations expand to embrace a societal obligation, the universe of relevant information likewise expands. . . . one purpose of [increased] disclosure is to deter conduct by the corporation which, however profitable, may be injurious to certain segments of society. The full disclosure approach is intended to implement the ability of affected groups to help themselves protect their interests.[79]

Moreover, greater disclosure requirements are among "the least restrictive form of regulation."[80] Particularly when analyzed and publicized by citizen groups, they can help "act as a check on management and stimulate executives to higher ethical standards regarding public interest matters."[81]

The kinds of information that corporate reformers would like corporations to be required to make public are extremely broad, encompassing virtually every conceivable dimension of the actual and potential social impact of the large firm.[82] This includes the identity of the firm's principal beneficial owners, the impact of corporate activities on the environment, detailed corporate hiring policies and practices, corporate political contributions and activities, relationship with law firms, occupational health and safety records, and the extent and nature of government contracts. Reformers also want the corporation to disclose suits by the government for violation of regulatory laws. Because of the strategic position of banks in the economic system, citizen groups would like financial institutions to also disclose their holdings of stock, their voting arrangements with the stock's beneficial owners, and their votes on proxy proposals.[83] Many of these have been presented to corporations in various proxy resolutions;[84] all are likely to eventually come before the political process. The logical end of contemporary pressures for increased corporate disclosure would be legislation extending the Freedom of Information Act to corporations—another illustration of the growing similarity of public expectations for both business and government.

# CHAPTER

# V

---

*Corporate Conduct*
*Abroad*

**R**ELIGIOUS institutions and organizations of all three major American denominations played an important role in citizen challenges to corporations over the issue of the civil rights of black Americans and the American presence in Vietnam. With the emergence of interest in the more general issue of corporate accountability in 1969 and 1970, their contributions to the corporate challenge effort increased substantially. Their primary area of interest has been the behavior of American corporations outside the United States. Regarding corporate international trade and investment decisions as having important political and moral implications, they have pressured corporations to allocate their economic resources in accordance with principles other than that of profit maximization. This chapter traces the role of Protestant, Catholic, and Jewish organizations in the corporate challenge movement.

While religious and ethnic groups have been interested in a large list of international issues including the role of ITT and other firms in Chile, Ford's operations in the Philippines, overseas political contributions or questionable payments, and the effect of agri-business on world food supplies, this chapter focuses on the three issues in which their role has been most visible: (1) the activity of American-owned corporations in South Africa, which has been of primary concern to Protestant denominations; (2) the sale of infant formulas in Latin America, which was raised by a Catholic order; (3) corporate compliance with the Arab boycott of Israel, which was the focus of a major shareholder campaign by the American Jewish Congress.

## The Church as a Shareholder Activist

The social philosophy that underlies a major thrust of the politics of corporate accountability—namely, the responsibilities inherent in ownership—began to concern the National Council of Churches (NCC) nearly a quarter of a century before it became a political issue. In 1947, it established a unit on the Church and Economic Life to promote the ethical analysis of economic issues.[1] In 1963, the governing board of the National Council of Churches became the first organization to suggest publicly that equity relationships to corporations might be used to influence their social conduct. The general assembly of the NCC requested member churches to examine their investment portfolios to see if they included firms that practiced racial discrimination and to "remove such investments from enterprises which cannot be persuaded to cease and desist from practicing racial discrimination."[2] In 1966, the general board expanded the implications of this position, officially contending that "decision-makers in the private sector must accept accountability for the impact of their decisions on the whole society."[3] Anticipating the analysis of the Project on Corporate Responsibility, they contended that "persons in economic . . . power centers must be subject to . . . checks and balances"[4] similar to those in the political order. Two years later, the general board of the National Council of Churches issued a statement entitled "The Church as Purchaser of Goods and Services," which held that "the nature of the Church requires that as an economic institution it also consider the social impact of its . . . decisions in terms of justice and equity."[5] The statement included the first specific reference to church investments.

The church's interest in the issue of the social responsibility of the profit sector was largely an outgrowth of the concern of many in the church with the stewardship of its own considerable economic resources.[6] Churches are a significant economic institution in their own right: the total wealth of all churches has been estimated at over $160 billion—more than the combined assets of the ten largest industrial corporations in the United States. In terms of monies received and distributed yearly, churches are second only to the federal government. The holdings of corporate stock by religious institutions are estimated to be approximately $20 billion. The Episcopal churches, alone, have roughly $1 billion invested in corporate securities. The churches are not only among the wealthiest private, nonprofit institutions in the United States; they are also the ones whose legitimating principles are most likely to bring them into conflict with business. It is the centrality of their preoccupation with the relationship between individual and social morality that distinguishes religious institutions from the other institutional participants in challenges to corporations. Thus, the treasurer of the American Baptist Home Mission Societies recently wrote:

The shareholder responsibilities that go with stock ownership cannot be neglected by the church. If the church is indifferent to the responsibilities of ownership with respect to its own securities, can church members be expected to take seriously their responsibilities as stewards of their possessions?[7]

One of the first full-time participants in corporate challenges by the church, Frank White, drew out the political implications of this perspective:

The church's power is symbolic. Traditionally, the church has been seen as the one institution in our society that does deal with ethical and moral concerns, and even though the church is declining, there is still a remnant that bothers people. We know from talking with many people in the corporations that of all the institutions and individuals that bring social concerns out into the limelight, they most fear the church, because companies don't like to have the image of having to confront the church. The real power of the church is in consciousness raising and in embarrassing the corporation into doing what it ought to be doing.[8]

In addition, the church is itself a major institution with local and national structures, a professional staff, available funds, established organs of communication, and access to a defined constituency. Even though they are extremely fragmented, religious institutions are positioned to play an important role in the formation of public opinion.

Moreover, both the church and the corporation are among the world's most important transnational institutions. Citizen demands to business are almost exclusively an American phenomenon with the distinctive exception of challenges emanating through the Protestant churches. In three major Protestant countries, Canada, England, and the Netherlands, church groups have applied direct pressure on companies involved in South Africa. In addition, considerable sharing of information and boycotts of particular companies have been organized across national boundaries.[9]

As in the case of the university, the immediate impetus behind the church's involvement in the contemporary politics of corporate accountability was a direct challenge to its commitment to its professed values.[10] In 1969, James Forman issued a Black Manifesto, demanding reparations from the church to black Americans. While several churches in the New York City area literally closed the doors to his appeal, his dramatic gesture had the effect of forcing many of the more liberal members of the major Protestant denominations to critically reexamine the sources of the church's income and the use to which it was being put. They discovered, as had Alice Marlin of the Council on Economic Priorities, that their knowledge of American business was too limited to enable them to make such judgments.

Two years later, in an unrelated development, the Episcopal Diocese of Puerto Rico became concerned about the long-term economic and immediate environmental impact of proposed copper mining by Kennecott and

American Metal Climax on the island commonwealth. Fourteen representatives of six denominational investors that together held $7.5 million of the stock of the two companies traveled to San Juan to hold open hearings on the impact of the mining project on "the health and local well-being of the people of Puerto Rico" at the request of the local diocese.[11]

These hearings marked an important increase in sophistication in the church's attempt to relate its own ethical concerns to the policies of management. They indicated both the church's lack of faith in the ability and willingness of the government of Puerto Rico to protect the interests of its citizens and its concern that specific corporate decisions be debated and examined in a forum more public than the boardroom. Following the hearings, the churches recommended that the companies postpone the mining operations. To date, the Puerto Rican government has not granted the two companies the necessary permits.

Between 1969 and 1971, the governing bodies of four major Protestant denominations—the United Church of Christ, the Protestant Episcopal Church, the United Presbyterian Church in the USA, and the Lutheran Church—voted to establish committees or task forces to monitor the social implications of their investments.[12] In 1971, the Episcopal Church became the first clerical investor to file a shareholder resolution: it was addressed to the shareholders of GM and requested the company to cease its operations in the Republic of South Africa.

As a result of these developments the National Council of Churches authorized funds for the establishment of a center to "gather, store and disseminate information pertaining to the social impact of corporate America."[13] In 1971, the Corporate Information Center (CIC) was established in the council's offices in New York City with a staff of five. It was given responsibility for conducting research in five areas: social profiles of corporations, alternative investment opportunities, government policies toward business, current corporate challenges, and church economic research. CIC rapidly became the subject of considerable controversy within the church when it released its first analysis of church portfolios. The report, entitled "Church Investments, Technological Warfare and the Military-Industrial Complex," documented and criticized the extensive equity positions of the nation's ten major Protestant denominations in corporations that engaged in defense work.[14] The National Council of Churches was revealed to have stock in twenty-nine of the sixty largest defense contractors. The report was followed by a series of detailed "social profiles" of fifteen corporations, most directed at their involvement in southern Africa. The title of the first of them suggests the political thrust of CIC's analysis:: "Gulf Oil—Portuguese Ally in Angola."

The CIC, described in *Business Week* as a sort of "clerical Nader's Raiders," combined the activism of the Project on Corporate Responsibility with the range and depth of research characteristic of CEP and the Investor Responsibility Research Council.[15] Unlike these organizations, however, CIC had a defined constituency which it was dedicated to mobilizing. In order to provide its various clerical subscribers with as many options as possible for participation in corporate deliberations, it developed a wide repertoire of tactics. At the outset, divestment was the most widely discussed and advocated alternative. Thus, Horace Gale, the treasurer of the American Baptist Home Mission Societies, asked rhetorically in 1971:

How can the principles the church stands for . . . be justified if its portfolio includes the stocks of the top defense contractors; of companies which pollute the air and water . . . of those companies which provide token or no opportunity for minority groups . . . of companies which strip underdeveloped countries of their resources without adequate payment and/or use the cheap labor for exploitation?[16]

Echoing Gale's perspective, Frank White, CIC's first director, initially reported that one of his basic goals was to establish a comprehensive "social rating system" that could easily enable churches to determine which corporations deserved their investments.[17] While there have been a handful of cases of divestment by religious institutions over the last six years, churches have tended to place more emphasis on other strategies. These include shareholder resolutions, shareholder suits, public hearings, private meetings with management, letters to management, demonstrations, boycotts, leafleting plants' retail outlets, attendance at stockholder meetings, research and publications, and fact-finding trips.

The politics behind the interest of activists associated with the church in corporate responsibility range broadly. Several Protestant mission boards have provided funds for the North American Congress on Latin America, a research organization that defines its politics as anticapitalist and antiimperialist. On the other hand, one of the most active Protestant laymen is Robert Potter, the chairman of the Episcopal Church Committee on Social Criteria for Investments. Mr. Potter is a partner in the Wall Street law firm of Patterson, Belknap, and Webber and counts David Rockefeller as among his personal acquaintances. What animates most of the church's full-time staffs involved in corporate challenges is a combination of moral indignation—often well-grounded in scripture—and a contemporary variant of American populism. Indignation is most frequently invoked in connection with apartheid and the despoliation of the environment, while populism supplies much of the political rationalization for the church's involvement in proxy contests. The most comprehensive compilation of arguments in defense of shareholder activism by the church, *Corporate Responsibility and Religious Institutions*, makes frequent reference to two central assumptions of the politics of corporate accountability—the pervasive impact of corporate decisions and the institutionalized overlap of business and government:

Today, ordinary people are becoming conscious of the fact that a great deal of economic power, in the hands of a relatively small number of people, is influencing and making major decisions which negatively affect our lives. . . .

In many instances [corporate managers and government officials] . . . are either the same people who wear different hats at different times or in close relationship through the constant interplay of the various sectors of our society. There is more need for the generalist today than ever.[18]

Moreover, the populist argument has also been raised *within* the church in connection with the domination of church investment bodies by corporate executives and bankers.

The Reverend Howard Schomer, the director of a corporate social responsibility unit organized under the auspices of the United Church of Christ, has argued:

As shareholders, fractional owners of great corporations, the mainline Protestant churches are aware that how their invested money makes money is as definitely a moral matter as how they spend what it earns. They are determined to press business to do a more effective job of production for basic human need, with all stakeholders in the production process—capital, labor, management, consumers and the enabling political community—receiving a fair return for the value contributed. When any of these stakeholders is exploited or cheated, they are not merely indignant, but ready to propose a remedial action.[19]

Schomer added, "We never give up. We're fractional owners of more than 126 different corporations, and we're not about to accept any policies that contradict the policies of our church."[20]

In 1973, representatives of ten national Catholic orders and colleges established the National Catholic Coalition for Responsible Investment. Its most active regional coalition is in Milwaukee, where largely through the efforts of Brother Michael Crosby, the Corporate Responsibility Program of the Justice and Peace Center has been particularly active in challenging corporate investments in southern Africa.[21] In San Francisco, the Joint Strategy and Action Commission, an agency of ecumenical urban ministry, established a corporate responsibility project in 1974.[22] One of its primary purposes was to use the portfolios of Bay Area churches to apply pressure on Bay Area firms. Much of the energies of the Northern California Interfaith Committee on Corporate Responsibility has been focused on three issues: utility rates (PG&E), equal opportunity employment (directed to the region's fifty largest employers), and agri-business (Del Monte and Tenneco).

In 1974, the Corporate Information Center merged with the Interfaith Committee on Social Responsibility, an ad hoc group of several Protestant denominations and Catholic organizations that had been initially formed to investigate the copper mine proposed for Puerto Rico. The new organization was officially named the Interfaith Center on Corporate Responsibility (ICCR) and was made formally separate from the national council. The center, whose staff has remained at between six and twelve, is supported and responsible to 150 Catholic orders and fourteen Protestant denominations. Its purposes are essentially twofold: to help develop and coordinate the strategies of its member constituents and to conduct research on corporate social performance. To further the former end, five task forces have been created, each responsible for a particular issue of importance for clerical activists. They include economic and environmental justice, the status of women and minorities, transnational corporations, issues concerning southern Africa, and military production and sales.

In 1975, ICCR's annual budget was roughly $200,000, the majority supplied by the dues and contributions of member institutional agencies. Those contributing at least $1,000 per annum are eligible to send voting members to the center's governing board. In addition to its extensive production of lengthy and detailed research reports, the center distributes to its members a monthly newsletter, the *Corporate Examiner*, that summarizes current developments in citizen pressures on business from both within and outside the church. Each month the *Examiner* is supplemented by a four-page CIC brief that highlights in more detail a particular challenge, issue, corporation, or industry. In addition, the Interfaith Center maintains extensive files on both corporations and corporate challenge campaigns.

The task forces, usually meeting in New York, attempt to coordinate challenges falling within their particular issue areas. The actual process of initiating demands on corporations is quite decentralized, reflecting the pattern of control over church investments. Although there is considerable overlap, most often a rough division of labor emerges each proxy season between national and local bodies and among the various denominations. The priorities of the center's membership vary considerably, depending on the political interests of the individuals involved, the pattern of equity holdings, and the specific history and geographic location of a particular agency or order board. Between 1974 and 1977, shareholder resolutions were proposed by more than 100 individual church units.

## Southern Africa

The preponderance of the church's challenges to corporations has focused on the presence and conduct of American-owned corporations in the underdeveloped world. This is largely a function of the church's missionary activities, which both predated and accompanied the internationalization of American business. The particular region that has most concerned the American church organizations has been southern Africa. Since 1966, churches, along with civil rights activists, have made the involvement of foreign corporations in Namibia, Angola, Mozambique, Rhodesia, and the Republic of South Africa the issue that has most frequently and continuously appeared on the corporate accountability agenda. In contrast to challenges to corporations in most other areas, political actors concerned with this issue have disproportionately focused their energies on the corporation. Rather than supplementing pressures to the state, in many respects it has replaced them. Between 1965 and 1975, the corporation was the primary arena for most of the political controversy that took place in the United States concerning the future of southern Africa. Indeed, in an unusual reversal of roles, those politicians who have been most interested in these issues have prominently supported nongovernmental challenges to the corporation.

The most important explanation for this rather unusual situation is that the issue of U.S. involvement in southern Africa has had relatively low public visibility prior to the Carter administration; save for brief intervals, it has not been before the governmental process. This, in turn, is a function of the fact that U.S. policy toward southern Africa has not been primarily made by the American government. In sharp contrast to most other points of tension within the less-developed world, the American government has until recently actually made relatively few policy decisions that could have become the subject of political controversy. To an unusual extent, decisions about the U.S. role in this part of Africa have been private ones;

other than the churches, it is the corporation that has been the major American presence in southern Africa. Potter has noted:

I think one of the reasons corporate responsibility groups have opted for pressuring business rather than government is the feeling that business is the acting process in the national picture in many areas. For instance, I think it would be arguable that United States foreign policy vis-à-vis South Africa is the $100 billion that is invested in South Africa by American corporations as opposed to what the President might say in the White House.[23]

## The Republic of South Africa

BANK LOANS

Conflicts between corporate activists and corporations over economic relations in the Republic of South Africa have revolved around four issues: bank loans, trade of specific products, corporate employment policies, and withdrawal of investments.

Bank loans to the South African government were first a focus of controversy in the mid-sixties. When the issue surfaced again in 1973, the church had replaced the civil rights movement as the most important source of citizen pressure.[24] In July 1973, the Corporate Information Center obtained confidential internal documents from sources within a U.S.-based multinational banking firm that revealed that a group of forty banks from the U.S., Europe, and Canada had loaned over $210 million to the South African government and its agencies since 1970. Representatives of the bank confirmed the veracity of the corporate challenge movement's "Pentagon Papers" (they actually became known as "The Frankfurt Documents") at a meeting in New York City. The CIC regarded the unusual secrecy of the loans as a confirmation of the effectiveness of citizen protests during the late sixties. None of the ten banks involved had participated in the earlier loan agreement; with the exception of Wells Fargo, they were relatively small, regional financial institutions.

Intensive local efforts were immediately organized by local church groups to terminate the loans. These turned out to be remarkably successful; many of the banks were simply not aware of the political consequences of their actions. Within a year, seven of the banks had either disposed of their loans or, more importantly, had publicly pledged not to make future loans to the South African government. Ernest Arbuckle, the chairman of Wells Fargo, wrote to ICCR, "The concern about the South African situation shown by your organization is understood and shared by us." He said that his bank was "not contemplating additional loans to South Africa."[25] The agreements did not, of course, cover loans to companies that invested in South Africa. Wells Fargo subsequently did make loans to the South African government through an international consortium.

In 1976, several days of riots and demonstrations by black students in Soweto reduced the rate of foreign and domestic investment, again causing the South African government to substantially increase its foreign borrowing.[26] In the spring of 1977, resolutions were submitted to the shareholders of First National City Bank, one of the principal organizers of the new loans, as well as to Continental Illinois, First Chicago, Manufacturers Hanover, and Morgan Guaranty Trust, asking them to establish a policy prohibiting further loans to the South African government. They argued that "it is [not] an overstatement to say that U.S. bank loans subsidize South Africa's military capability and thus are a direct source of machinery for oppression of the black majority."[27] While these resolutions were opposed by the banks' managements, Wells Fargo announced that it would no longer lend to the South African government. Several other banks, including the Central National Bank of Chicago and the First Pennsylvania Bank of Philadelphia, stated that they would no longer participate in any loans to the South African Republic. The First National City Bank also announced that it would no longer make loans to the South African government or to government-owned enterprises.

Chase's chairman, David Rockefeller, responded to questioning from representatives of church groups at the bank's 1977 stockholder meeting by announcing that, in accordance with the bank's recently adopted code of ethics, Chase would not make loans "that, in our judgment, tend to support the apartheid policies of the South African government or reinforce discriminatory business practices."[28] Chase, in fact, turned down a loan to purchase new buses for travel between Soweto and Johannesburg because it did not want to endorse discriminatory transportation and residence patterns. It also indicated it would not lend to Newmont Mining because of that company's poor employment record in Namibia. Morgan Guaranty Trust and the Bank of America, on the other hand, refused to consider any limitations on their loans in South Africa.

As of 1977, the overall availability of bank funds to South Africa had not actually been reduced. Rather, many banks concerned about the effects of adverse publicity and chanting pickets had instead attempted to reduce the visibility of their loans. One American banker noted, "United States institutions are trying to avoid 'press risk.' They don't want to have their names in headlines in the *New York Times* or the *Wall Street Journal*, because they aren't willing to be seen as supportive of the 'South African Regime.' "[29] This ploy however, appeared to have little success. In the spring of 1977, more than 150 private individuals, several members of Congress, and a number of church groups formed an *ad hoc* committee to oppose bank loans to South Africa. Adopting the same strategy that had met with some success a decade earlier, they launched a nationwide effort to encourage individuals and institutions to withdraw their deposits from forty-seven U.S. banks, including Bank of America, First National City Bank, and Chase Manhattan Bank. An attempt was also begun to encourage Americans to boycott the sale of South Africa gold coins. After the offices of Merrill Lynch were picketed in six cities, the nation's largest brokerage firm agreed to discontinue the sale of Krugerrands, though it denied that the demonstrations were a factor.

TRADE

The commercial relations of IBM and Polaroid with the Republic of South Africa have also become political issues as a result of the efforts of clerical and black groups. In 1963, the United Nations passed a resolution supported by the United States calling for an arms embargo against South Africa. Seven years later, the United Nations, with the United States abstaining, expanded the embargo by calling on member states to prohibit "investments in or technical assistance for the manufacture of arms and ammunition, aircraft . . . and other military vehicles."[30] Church organizations contended that the contemporary military importance of computers made IBM's sales to the South African government in violation of the U.N. resolution.[31] In November 1974, the National Council of Churches conducted two days of hearings on IBM's role in South Africa. The focus was on the legality and morality of computer sales to the South African government. Representatives of the church organizations who testified expressed concern that the computers were being used to increase the efficiency of the South African passbook system and that it could be used to develop South Africa's nuclear capacity. Several witnesses also argued that IBM's willingness to sell computers to the South African government directly contributed to the strengthening of the government's capacities for domestic repression; far from being simply a neutral, commercial act, the distribution and use of computers had important political consequences.

Twenty persons, representing the major religious and secular organizations in the United States interested in the politics of southern Africa and including two official representatives of IBM, testified at the hearings; a

125-page transcript was subsequently published and distributed by the National Council of Churches. W. E. Burdick, an IBM vice-president, told the church panelists why the company did business in South Africa:

First, IBM is perfectly willing to do business where the United States Government lets us. We don't make U.S. foreign policy. As you know, the State Department's position is that U.S. companies should remain in South Africa and it is encouraging business there to improve pay scales and working conditions. Second, IBM is in South Africa because it makes good business sense. . . . Third, IBM has found that it can supply dignified employment for all its South African employees. We provide . . . equal pay for equal work.[32]

Burdick stated that the hearing was IBM's fourth major effort in three years to be responsive to the National Council of Churches, and that in view of the superior quality of IBM's employment program in South Africa, "the hearing was counter-productive."[33] On the issue of computer sales, IBM's representatives explained that it had sold the government only standard commercial data processing products and that it was simply not feasible to monitor their use. While conceding that its presence in some ways did support the government of South Africa, the company disclaimed any responsibility for the maintenance of apartheid: "No political ideology that we know of is dependent on data processing equipment . . . apartheid was instituted before the advent of the computers."[34] IBM's chairman, Frank Cary, subsequently stated that if they had to make the decision all over again, they would not invest in South Africa, but that once committed, they had obligations to their employees and customers and that, on balance, IBM's presence was a force for good. IBM's management also did not think the South African government would tolerate the computer firm's presence if it refused to sell to it, and that if IBM withdrew, it would be replaced by a foreign computer company.

Representatives of the thirteen denominations that conducted the hearings, collectively holding about 130,000 shares of IBM stock, were not convinced by IBM's presentation. Their report concluded that whatever benefits IBM provided for its 149 black employees were more than balanced by its unwillingness to assume responsibility for the use of its technology. They argued that IBM's defense that its activities did not violate U.S. law represented "a serious abrogation of moral responsibility . . . no company can ethically argue that its only responsibility is to act in a way that doesn't infringe U.S. law."[35] Following the hearings, fourteen Catholic and Protestant groups holding nearly $9 million worth of stock cosponsored a shareholders resolution asking the company to end the sale, lease, or service of computers to the government of South Africa. IBM's chairman met personally with its sponsors on six different occasions prior to the shareholders meeting, although the company refused to change its policy. A number of congressmen and black leaders, while disagreeing among themselves as to the appropriateness of U.S. investment in South Africa per se, supported the church's position on this particular issue.

Polaroid took a position quite different from that of IBM.[36] In 1969, a small number of the firm's black employees joined together in a militant group called Polaroid Revolutionary Workers Movement (PRWM) and distributed leaflets charging, "Polaroid Imprisons Black People in 60 Seconds." They contended that Polaroid products were being used in South Africa's identification card system and called for an international boycott. In October 1970, the "corporation with a conscience," as Polaroid called itself, issued a statement denying that the firm's identification equipment was being used in the passbook program. Furthermore, it instructed its local distributor to halt the sale to the South African government of any products, including film, which might be used in the identification program. The firm's director of community relations declared at the same church-sponsored hearings at which IBM testified:

> We have a responsibility for the ultimate use of our product . . . In response to the charge [(by PRWM)] we articulated a very strict policy of refusing to do business directly with the South African government . . . We as a corporation will not sell our products in instances where its use constitutes a potential abridgement of human freedom.[37]

He went on to cite a number of instances where Polaroid had refused sales to American political authorities on the basis of its disagreement with their intended use. Polaroid also became one of the first American corporations to publicly condemn the apartheid system and, after a visit to South Africa by a group of employees, instituted a widely publicized "experiment" aimed at upgrading the working conditions of black employees. In 1977, an employee of Frank and Hirsch, Polaroid's South African distributor, revealed to Paul Irish, a staff member of the American Committee on Africa, that Polaroid film was in fact being secretly sold to the South African agency that issues passbooks for non-whites—a clear violation of the company's policy. Polaroid immediately announced that it was terminating all its shipments to South Africa—becoming the first American corporation to end its economic involvement in South Africa because of citizen pressures.

Unions have also been concerned with the issue of trade with South Africa. In 1973, the Southern Company signed a contract to purchase 2.3 million tons of coal from the Republic of South Africa. The company contended that it was unable to find domestic sources of supply at a reasonable price to meet Florida's air pollution standards. Five hundred mine workers throughout Alabama took a day off from work to picket the Southern Company's 1974 annual shareholders meeting in Birmingham. They carried signs that read, "Stop Southern Company Imperialism" and "No Slave Coal."[38] The workers, supported by the United Mine Workers, opposed the import on both economic and moral grounds. They argued that South Africa forces blacks to work as slave labor, paying them little more than $3 a day, and that American workers could not compete with such labor. UMW President Arnold Miller stated that there was adequate coal in the United States, "if utilities will pay the price," and added that "it is an outrage that coal is being imported from a foreign country more than 9,000 miles away, when there are billions of tons of 10w-sulfur coal underground in the United States."[39]

In 1973, the Interfaith Center on Corporate Responsibility filed a shareholders resolution asking the Southern Company to establish a policy prohibiting the import of coal from South Africa until that nation should end its racial policies. One church official referred to Southern's purchase as akin to "making a deal with the Mafia." Church representatives contended that the imports were "morally incompatible" with the Southern Company's stated commitment to comply with the provisions of the equal employment opportunity laws and that South Africa's coal, while the world's cheapest in monetary terms, was, in fact, "the world's most expensive coal when measured in terms of human dignity and equal rights."[40] The company responded that mining safety conditions in South Africa were comparable to those in the United States and that it was not responsible for the labor practices of its suppliers. The resolution was submitted again in 1976 and 1977. Although the company did not renew its contract with its South African supplier in 1975, it opposed the proposed restriction on the grounds that "business considerations dictate that subsidiaries be free to acquire needed coal supplies when necessary."[41]

INVESTMENT AND EMPLOYMENT

The two issues that have dominated corporate-citizen conflicts over the American presence in southern Africa have been the withdrawal of American investments and the employment practices of American subsidiaries. In 1971, the first of a continuous stream of shareholder resolutions dealing with these issues was filed. The Episcopal Church, on behalf of its Domestic and Foreign Missionary Society, submitted a resolution to the shareholders of General Motors calling for it to terminate its manufacturing facilities in South Africa. The initiators of the resolution did not think it likely GM could be pressured to leave South Africa and that even if it did, the apartheid system would remain. Their immediate objective was "to get social issues into the board room."[42] They hoped that through the public challenge, the corporation's management would become more sensitive to the politics of the South African government and act to help bring about changes in its policies. The church group also anticipated that the publicity surrounding the first use of the proxy mechanism to raise the issue of corporate policies in South Africa might discourage other firms from investing there.

The appearance of an Episcopal bishop at a General Motors shareholders meeting to challenge the investment policies of its managers represented an almost classic confrontation of cloth versus corporation. It also gave the conflict the aura of an "intraclass" struggle. No corporate activist could have been more identified with the social background of the nation's corporate leadership than Bishop Hines; 21 percent of the nation's chief corporate executive officers are Episcopalians. A postmortem on the meeting concluded:

The special courtesy extended Bishop Hines demonstrates both the power and the liability of the Church in these matters; power in that it can command attention when it has a message and danger in that courtesy and attention may often hide a basic lack of responsiveness to the issue.[43]

Hines's public criticism of GM's presence in South Africa—he told the assembled shareholders: "There has been no indication that American business presence has been a liberating force."—predictably aroused considerable controversy within his church.[44] Half of the vestries who took a position on the proxy proposal opposed its introduction, as did a majority of the letters addressed to the bishop. It also produced a broader backlash. On the November 17 edition of NET's "American Dream Machine," former Nixon aide and author of the "Southern Strategy," Kevin Phillips attacked the participation of the Episcopal and Presbyterian churches at the annual meetings of GM and Gulf. While criticizing the involvement of all nonprofit institutions, including churches, universities, and foundations, in the corporate social responsibility movement, he contended that the churches were the "most controversial operators, using the tax shelter of religion—and the self-interpreted moral dictates of Christianity—to enter the realm of pressure group politics."[45]

The 1971 meeting was also the first attended by the Reverend Leon Sullivan in his role as a GM board member. In an unprecedented public display of board disunity on a corporate social policy, the black minister requested the floor in order to speak in favor of GM's withdrawal from South Africa. Sullivan's presentation was the most dramatic moment of the meeting, which also featured a presentation by Campaign GM's Round II. He asserted that apartheid was being underwritten by American corporations and that "American industry can't morally continue to do business in a country that so blatantly and ruthlessly and clearly maintains such dehumanizing practices against such large numbers of people."[46]

That same year, sixteen representatives of major Protestant denominations undertook a seventeen-day fact-finding trip to South Africa in order to enable the church community to define its position on corporate involvement in South Africa. On their return, representatives of various units of six major Protestant denominations formed a project on U.S. investments in southern Africa in order to file disclosure resolutions asking firms to reveal the full facts of their involvement in the region. In 1973, CIC released a 242-page report on corporate involvement in southern Africa.[47] It presented detailed profiles of the largest U.S. corporations in southern Africa, including their relationship to the local government, employment policies, position on investment in the white-dominated region, and willingness to release information about their presence there in response to CIC's inquiries. The report contended, contrary to the claims of U.S. corporations, that South African law does not prohibit equal pay for equal work: "Most companies would be free under the law to advance their non-white employees and train them for better jobs at a much faster rate than they are doing."[48] On the basis of personal visits to the facilities of eleven U.S. companies, the church team concluded that

American companies are not more enlightened in employment practices nor in their sensitivity to the South African situation than are companies from other foreign countries. [Most do not give] equal pay for equal work.[49]

Over the last five years, citizen pressure on corporations with investments in South Africa has primarily focused on the treatment of black employees. Some critics of apartheid, including Leon Sullivan, black Congressman Diggs from Detroit, and author Alan Paton, have come out against withdrawal, instead suggesting that the interests of South Africa's black majority may be best served if foreign investors act as an internal force for reform. While the official position of most church groups favors total withdrawal, many of the actual efforts of the Church Project on U.S. Investments in Southern Africa have concentrated on pressuring American firms into upgrading the conditions of black workers. Their primary means for achieving this goal has been the submission of shareholder resolutions requesting full disclosure of personnel policies practiced in the African subcontinent.

Between 1972 and 1977, shareholder resolutions were proposed by various church missions and boards to more than two dozen corporations.[50] A number of firms proved responsive to the church's request for more information. Whereas in 1972 Mobil was the only company to provide the data on its employment practices requested by the church, the following year ten other firms reponded to the church group's satisfaction: Burroughs, Caterpillar, Eastman Kodak, Ford, GM, Gulf, ITT, Texaco, 3M, and Xerox. They were joined in 1974 by Chrysler, Colgate-Palmolive, John Deere, Gillette, International Harvester, Pfizer, and Weyerhauser. Between 1973 and 1974, a total of sixteen companies voluntarily agreed to disclose the information requested by the church project, and the shareholder resolutions were accordingly withdrawn. All told, twenty companies have prepared special reports on their investments in the Republic of South Africa, and the chief executives of GM, IBM, Ford, and Chrysler have paid personal visits to their South African subsidiaries. Chrysler, GM, and Union Carbide sent board members to South Africa in July of 1975, and Weyerhauser, Polaroid, and ITT established special review committees to examine company practices in this region. On the other hand, several other corporations, such as Englehard and Goodyear, do not appear to have made any response to the church's concerns.

Mobil, the largest U.S. investor in South Africa, developed a relatively good working relationship with its church critics. In January 1972, representatives of the World Ministries Board of the United Church of Christ, an African church agency that had been working in South Africa since 1835, suggested to Mobil's board chairman that it might be useful for the corporation to make a comprehensive study of its South African operations. The ministries board was not interested in a confrontation but in helping Mobil identify the problems that it was in a position to alleviate and to suggest possible solutions. Mobil's management, in turn, emphasized that it "in no way wanted to be seen in the public's eyes as doing battle with part of the Christian Church."[51] The corporation immediately sent its vice-president for public affairs on an inspection tour, and in December the board of directors itself met in South Africa for the first time in the thirty-year history of Mobil's operations there.

The company's report was released in July 1972. It was the most comprehensive study made by a U.S. firm on its South Africa operations. The United Church of Christ indicated it was "pleased with the clarity and comprehensiveness of the report," and suggested that it was an "example of the openness that should be common practices of U.S. business corporations."[52] It was not, however, enchanted with its contents; while Mobil's performance was well above average, 85 percent of its African employees were earning less than the $150 per month, considered a "bare living wage."[53] On the other hand, the report revealed that in the two years since the church's initial request for disclosure, the average minimum pay in the eight lowest wage categories has increased 57.75 percent, as compared with 13.2 percent in the two years previous to the church's request. In its analysis of the report, the CIC remarked, "It is interesting to note that recent pressure on the company might have been a factor" in the accelerated increase.[54]

The main impact of church pressures has been on corporate employment policies, encouraging a number of American-owned corporations to examine their role and performance in South Africa more carefully. Rather than assuming that economic growth will automatically improve the status of blacks, they have begun to reassess the social impact of their employment and purchasing policies. For example, Chase Manhattan, revising its earlier position that its relations to South Africa were "strictly economic" and hence "apolitical," told the CIC in 1972 that foreign investors

have both a chance and an obligation . . . to bring about improvements in the education, training and opportunities available to the non-white population. American investors, in particular, should bring to bear all the energy and imagination that have characterized their socially oriented activities at home.[55]

Ford, Mobil, Polaroid, and ITT have made similar commitments following requests for information by religious groups.[56] On an aggregate basis, the policies of American-owned firms in South Africa toward black employees remain indistinguishable from those of firms owned domestically. However, a lengthy study of the labor practices of U.S. corporations by the IRRC revealed that shareholder activism had an important impact on the practices of particular corporations. The report concluded:

In general, it seems clear, there was a significant linkage between expressions of investor interest in a company's South African operations and the surge in home office interest in those operations.

Both home office representatives and local managers reported that home office interest had a beneficial impact on the labor practices of companies in South Africa. . . . Representatives of most companies which have made progressive changes in the 1970s attribute at least some of the impetus for the changes to the interest expressed by the companies' shareholders.[57]

In 1976, domestic violence in South Africa changed the focus of citizen pressures back to the issue of corporate investment. The church-sponsored resolutions filed in 1976 and 1977 explicitly challenged the presence of American companies in South Africa. Ford Motor, General Electric, General Motors, Goodyear Tire and Rubber, Standard Oil of California, Tennaco, and Texaco were asked to terminate their operations in South Africa as expeditiously as possible, pending the commitment of the South African government to end apartheid. Kennecott Copper, Phelps Dodge, and Union Carbide received resolutions requesting that they not expand their operations in South Africa.

In 1977, the visibility of the involvement of American corporations in South Africa began to approach the level of the mid-sixties. University students, who had not shown any significant interest in the investment policies of their institutions for the previous five years, became concerned with the relationship between their universities and the American corporations conducting business in South Africa. Demonstrations and sit-ins took place at several campuses throughout the United States both to support the demand for the total withdrawal of American investment from South Africa and to urge adoption of the Sullivan principles. The campus demonstrations, which resulted in more than 700 arrests, echoed the campus protests against Dow Chemical a decade earlier. The specific focus of the rallies and sit-ins varied. Some urged the selling of the stock of any corporation that had facilities in South Africa, while others sought to pressure their universities to vote in favor of proxy resolutions requesting withdrawal.[58] In the city of Oakland and the state of California, the investment policies of public employee pension funds also became a center of controversy.[59] In addition, a handful of unions indicated they planned to end their pension fund investments in companies involved in South Africa.

As a response to the revival of public interest in the role of American companies in South Africa, twelve major U.S. corporations announced in February 1977 that they had agreed to support six principles aimed at ending "segregation" and "to promote fair employment practices"[60] in South Africa; within eight months they were joined by forty-two more firms.[61] The declarations were primarily inspired by the efforts of the Reverend Leon Sullivan, who, accompanied by the chairmen of the boards of GM and IBM, personally presented the statement of principles to the South African ambassador in Washington. Tim Smith, who had played the most active individual role in the church's efforts on this issue, was unimpressed. He stated:

In fact many of the signatories of the principles act in ways that directly assist and strengthen the power of South Africa's white rulers. Citibank has loaned $300 million directly to the South African government; IBM still provides computers to that government for any purpose, however repressive; Caltex and Mobil are major suppliers of oil to the South African military, and through South Africa they are the oil lifeline to Rhodesia; Union Carbide assists apartheid by investing in and on the borders of Bantustans; Caltex is in the midst of a $134 million expansion that acts as an economic vote of confidence in white South Africa's future. The list goes on.[62]

In 1977, faced with increasing racial unrest and reduced prospects for economic growth in South Africa, a number of corporations began to reconsider their financial involvement. General Motors, Control Data, and Ford announced that their future investment plans would be heavily influenced by prospects for the resolution of South Africa's racial tensions. Chrysler sold two-thirds of its South African subsidiary, and Weyerhauser withdrew completely. In addition, ITT sold its subsidiary to a local company, but retained a financial interest in it. These decisions were primarily motivated by an economic self-interest but were nonetheless welcomed by the church groups. On the other hand, Union Carbide, Caltex (jointly owned by Texaco and Standard Oil of California), and Phelps Dodge announced major expansions of their South Africa operations. The latter response was more typical, suggesting the controversy over U.S. corporate involvement in South Africa will be a continuing one.

RHODESIA

In 1976, the Center for Social Action of the United Church of Christ made public several documents it had received from a clandestine organization of white South Africans who oppose white supremacy in southern Africa. Based on more than a year of intensive research and the assistance of anonymous employees of Mobil, the documents disclosed that Mobil's wholly owned South African subsidiary had been supplying oil to Rhodesia in violation of American law. To circumvent the international embargo against Rhodesia, the company, along with Shell, British Petroleum, and Caltex, had established an elaborate and secret chain of bogus companies that disguised the illegal flow of oil. The center's report concluded that "with three U.S. citizens who are or have been directors of Mobil (South African) it is difficult to see how Mobil (U.S.A.) could be said not to know of the sanction-breaking activities of its U.S. subsidiary."[63]

Mobil was very embarrassed by the charges—which received considerable press attention—and particularly upset that the United Church of Christ had decided to release them through the People's Bicentennial Commission, a left-populist organization that had offered a reward of $10,000 for information leading to the conviction of a corporate executive.

The firm denied that it had "contravened U.S. restrictions on trade with Rhodesia" but did not dispute the authenticity of the documents.[64] The corporation sent a group of its top executives to South Africa to investigate the charges. It later reported that it was "unable to conduct any investigation in South Africa" because the country's official secrets act prohibited the disclosure of information related to the storage, distribution, and sale of petroleum products. The company claimed that it was caught "squarely between the U.S. government's attempts to enforce a boycott of Rhodesia and the equally determined efforts of the South African government to prevent any external or internal interference in the distribution of petroleum products."[65]

Mobil's testimony at the congressional hearings held on the controversy did not, however, weaken the credibility of the church's charges, and an investigation was begun by the Treasury Department.[66] The United Church of Christ filed a shareholder resolution in 1977 asking the board of directors to "take all measures necessary to insure that no Mobil products are supplied, directly or indirectly, to Rhodesia, and that no bulk sales of products are made to buyers who do not offer verifiable guarantee that said products are not destined for resale or transfer to Rhodesia."[67] The company opposed the resolution, contending that it had found no evidence that such sales were taking place.

NAMIBIA

The third region in southern Africa in which the role of U.S. corporations has been disputed through direct pressures on business has been Namibia.[68] Also known as Southwest Africa, Namibia is a former German colony with a total area of 317,000 square miles and a population of about 1 million. It is located on the west coast of Africa, bordering Angola, Zambia, southern Rhodesia, and South Africa. Since 1920, it has been administrated by the Republic of South Africa. Over the last decade, its sovereignty has been in dispute. In 1966 and again in 1967, the General Assembly ended South Africa's mandate and established a United Nations Council to administer the territory until independence. In May 1970, the U.S. State Department announced that the government would offer no protection to American investments acquired since the U.N. resolution. A year later the International Court of Justice rendered an advisory opinion confirming the General Assembly resolution and holding "that the continued presence of South Africa in Namibia [was] . . . illegal."[69] The U.N. Security Council subsequently adopted a resolution endorsing the advisory opinion. It declared that franchises or rights, etc., granted to companies by South Africa after October 1966 are "not subject to protection . . . against claims of a future lawful Government of Namibia."[70] Shortly thereafter, an unprecedented strike of 15,000 black workers broke out at the Tsumeb mine, protesting the South African government's policies toward migrant workers.

It was in this context that the Episcopal Churchmen for South Africa submitted a series of proxy resolutions to Newmont Mining and American Metal Climax (AMAX) (each owns 29 percent of the Tsumeb copper mine directly, and Newmont indirectly owns another 12 percent). It asked the firms to disclose the amounts paid as taxes to the South African government. A year later, resolutions were submitted to the two companies requesting them "not to conduct or be party to any operation in Namibia" and to wind up "present operations . . . in which it has an interest."[71] Both companies opposed both resolutions.

In 1973, a new tactic was tried. Eleven AMAX shareholders, all descendants of Max Schott, founder of Climax Molybdenum, one of the two firms that merged in 1957 to form AMAX, filed a shareholders derivative action suit against the directors of AMAX charging malfeasance in connection with a company that operates "illegally and immorally" in southern Africa.[72] While the plaintiffs defined their suit as essentially a moral one, its actual purpose was to force an American corporation to obey an international law.

Corporations criticized for their involvement in South Africa could legitimately defend their wage and investment policies as consistent with the broad dictates of American foreign policy as well as American and international law. But no such defense was possible for AMAX and Newmont. The black workers at Newmont's remote Tsumeb mine—hired on six, twelve, and eighteen-month contracts from their tribal homelands—worked under conditions of quasi-feudal servitude, housed in dormitories away from their families, with pay low even by South African standards. The colonial analogy was also suggestive in another sense. Since the government of South Africa did not legally possess sovereignty over the Tsumeb ore deposits, the American companies were appropriating them without even the nominal consent of the people to whom they belonged. It was a case of two multinational firms operating in the Third World without the rudiments of either equity or legality.

Moreover, according to a study by the CIC, Newmont and AMAX not only benefited from the legal status of Namibia, they helped perpetuate it. Since Tsumeb began production in 1948, it had paid more than $150 million in taxes to the South African government; its 1970 tax payment represented 8.6 percent of the territory's annual budget. When added to the more than $1 million annual exploration budget of the company, a powerful incentive for South Africa to defy the U.N. decision was created. The corporation's financial stakes were also considerable. The return on investment of Tsumeb between 1963 and 1970 averaged 31 percent.

In January 1975, as a response to church pressure, Newmont announced a worldwide equal opportunity employment policy. The firm stated that it would institute a 30 percent hike in the base pay of its employees in Namibia, develop a single-graded pay structure without reference to race, improve insurance and pension benefits, and consult a newly established black workers' representative council. Consequently, the United Church of Christ Board of World Ministries decided not to file their resolution. In 1977 (with the cooperation of Newmont), two high officials of the American Lutheran Church visited Namibia to investigate the conditions of the mining company's black employees (more than half of the residents of Namibia are Lutheran). They were impressed with the company's job training efforts and with its progress in constructing housing for 100 black families. But they were still concerned about the lack of information on changes in working conditions. Upon their return the United Church of Christ filed a shareholder resolution asking for a complete report on the wage discrepancy, training, and promotion of blacks since 1975. Urging Newmont's shareholders to approve the resolution—which management opposed—the president of the American Lutheran Church stated at the firm's shareholders meeting:

Tsumeb is training some black workers. Good. How many? For what positions? It has an advisory committee. How often does it meet? Is its advice heeded? The Resolution simply asks for an accounting. If it is not given, people will imagine the worst. Too much corporate corruption has been revealed in this country for even the fairest of companies to imagine that they can escape being tarred with the same brush—unless the facts are out on the table.

We urge Newmont Mining Corporation to say publicly what is going on. Say what the goals are for the short and for the long term, and how you hope to achieve those goals. That will keep you honest and it will keep us honest.

. . . We believe a complete report would show the necessity of a more aggressive corporate affirmative action program on behalf of non-white employees, but in any case the Resolution is a challenge to disclose fully the economic and social principles underlying this company's operations.[73]

The corporation's shareholders were not convinced. AMAX, on the other hand, issued a report on its Namibian mine operations that the churches found adequate, and they withdrew their resolution.

In addition to helping improve working conditions in the mines, citizen pressures also helped discourage additional investments in Namibia. Beginning in 1972, representatives of the Church Project on U.S. Investments in South Africa began pressuring five American oil companies—Continental Oil, Getty, Phillips, SoCal, and Texaco—to cease explorations off the coast of Namibia. They argued their case in large part on economic grounds: the ambiguous legal status of Namibia rendered additional foreign direct investment unusually hazardous. Not only was it in violation of international law and U.S. government policy, but the Council for Namibia —a quasi-government-in-exile—had declared that investment in Namibia without its approval was illegal and constituted virtual theft. Tim Smith, director of the ICCR, who participated in several lengthy conversations with the management of Continental Oil and Texaco, remarked:

It seems that the churches had done more homework on the implications of investing in Namibia than the companies themselves. Generally, the initial decisions by the five oil companies to explore for oil . . . had been taken without even a sketchy study of the country's political situation. Geological data had been the determining factor.[74]

In 1974, the church project's shareholder resolutions calling for withdrawal were submitted to four of the companies. By public interest proxy standards, two of the resolutions did unusually well. The one submitted to Continental received the support of 7.2 percent of the firm's shares voted— including the votes of the Ford and Carnegie foundations, Aetna Life Insurance, and Princeton, Harvard, and Yale; 4.9 percent of Phillips's shares were also voted against management on this issue. In October 1974, Continental Oil announced to the United Church of Christ that it would cease its explorations in the contested area. The Reverend Howard Schomer, who had led the church's negotiations with Continental, stated:

We wish to commend Continental Oil for this statesmanlike decision, and we recommend that its partners follow suit. . . . When the Namibian people win self-rule and the chance to develop their own resources, they will not forget which companies in their time of need recognized their inalienable rights.[75]

Within three months of Schomer's recommendation, the four remaining companies had followed Continental Oil's lead; no U.S. oil companies remain in Namibia. Clearly a number of factors encouraged the receptivity of the oil companies to the pressures of the church groups, including the decision of the U.S. government not to protect investments made subsequent to the International Court of Justice decision. Moreover, unlike the mineral companies, the oil corporations had relatively little invested. Smith concluded:

. . . clearly the points the churches brought to the companies' attention became factors they had to weigh in deciding whether or not to stay in Namibia. If the churches did nothing more than make management look at the realities of Southern Africa and examine their part in lending legitimacy to the occupation of Namibia, they would still have a significant accomplishment to their credit.[76]

ANGOLA

In 1969, a subsidiary of the Gulf Oil Corporation began producing oil in the Cabinda province of the Portuguese colony of Angola.[77] By 1974, Gulf had invested approximately $215 million in Angola, accounting for more than two-thirds of all American investment in Portuguese Africa. Between 1970 and 1974, Gulf's Cabinda operation was the focus of more intensive citizen pressure than any other aspect of the overseas operations of an American-owned corporation. A wide variety of political organizations, including New Left and radical black student groups, civil rights organizations, and several Protestant denominations, attempted to pressure Gulf to withdraw from Angola. Their tactics spanned virtually the entire repertoire of citizen pressures, involving participation and disruption of Gulf's shareholders meetings, shareholder resolutions, pressure on institutional investors, and an attempted boycott.

In 1970, Gulf's annual meeting in Pittsburgh was disrupted by an *ad hoc* coalition of local activists and representatives of two national radical organizations, the New Mobilization to End the War and the Committee of Returned Volunteers. Following the meeting, they marched into Gulf's downtown headquarters in Pittsburgh in order to further dramatize their solidarity with the guerrilla movements then fighting in Angola for independence from Portugal. Other than encouraging Gulf to move the location of its 1971 meeting to Atlanta, the Gulf Action Project had no real impact.

Of more long-term political consequence was a resolution passed at the 1970 annual meeting of the Ohio Conference of the United Church of Christ. The church had a long history of involvement in Angola: its missions, largely schools and hospitals, dated from the 1880s. The conference voted 223 to 84 to urge its 320,000 members to discontinue the use of Gulf products, turn in their Gulf credit cards, and vote their stock to change Gulf's African operations. More important, they formally urged Gulf "to withdraw immediately from any operation in Africa which contributes to the suppression and suffering of people."[78]

Gulf's reaction rescued the resolutions from obscurity. The oil company's president demanded "an immediate retraction of the resolution by the conference" and threatened to sue to "obtain redress from the damages done to Gulf Oil Corporation and to the reputation of its principal officers by the dissemination of the defamatory document."[79] Gulf's threatening of the church group received national press attention and proved highly embarrassing to the corporation. Several meetings were subsequently held between Gulf's officers and members of the United Church of Christ board of trustees, and a year later the conference reaffirmed its resolution; Gulf's suit never materialized.

In 1971, the Southern Africa Task Force of the United Presbyterian Church in the United States filed the first in a series of public interest proxy resolutions on Gulf's involvement in Angola. Three of the proposals submitted to Gulf's shareholders requested that the corporation make certain organizational changes that would enable its management and shareholders to scrutinize more carefully the company's relations with the Portuguese government. The final resolution was the most critical. It amended "The Corporation Charter to Exclude Investment in Colonial Africa."[80] The task force, in its supporting statements, sought to refute Gulf's contention that its investment was essentially a business decision that implied neither support nor opposition to continued Portuguese rule. They contended that "Gulf actively abets the maintenance of the last major colonial empire in Africa" by virtue of the income that it provides to Portuguese authorities; in 1972 this amounted to 11 percent of the Angolan budget. In addition, they argued that Gulf's discoveries constituted an incentive for the continued occupation of Angola by Portugal and that Gulf, through its close business ties to Portugal, had created a "natural vested interest in Portugal's colonial policy."[81] To emphasize its support for the rebellion in Angola, the Council for Christian Social Action publicly donated $500 at Gulf's shareholders meeting to the Reverend Andrew Young, who promised to give it to the Popular Movement for the Liberation of Angola (MPLA) through the World Council of Churches. Gulf replied that "it would be impossible to find sufficient reserves if we limited our search only to those nations with whose political philosophies we agree."[82] Furthermore, Gulf suggested that its presence made the citizens of Angola better off economically.

In the spring of 1972, the setting of the domestic conflict over Gulf's policies in Angola switched to the campuses. Extensive debate, largely inspired by the demand of black students that universities sell their stock in Gulf, took place at Columbia, Cornell, Harvard, Princeton, and Oberlin. Both Columbia and Cornell agreed to sell their holdings in Gulf—Cornell after the occupation of campus halls. The most important confrontation took place at Harvard. A year before, a group of black students—members of the Pan-African Liberation Committee (PALC)—had requested Harvard to sell its 683,000 shares of Gulf Oil. Shortly before Gulf's annual meeting, PALC took over Massachusetts Hall and the office of the president for one week. In a sixteen-page pamphlet entitled "Repression in South Africa," the committee declared:

The people of Angola and Mozambique have already made it clear that their freedom depends upon the complete withdrawal of the Portuguese government from their land. The lines are now firmly drawn. There is no middle ground: Blood must flow in the Portuguese colonies. How much blood must flow can only be determined by Harvard University and institutions like Harvard. Every dollar received by the Portuguese government means that the war must last a little longer and a few more people must die. Their blood will be on the hands of all those who equivocate on the issue of freedom.[83]

The university refused to sell its shares but did agree to abstain on a shareholder proposal by the Council for Christian Social Action of the United Church of Christ that asked Gulf to make fully public the details of its operations in the world's largest remaining colony. Robert Dorsey, Gulf's chairman, met personally with Harvard University officials, and pressure from Harvard's trustees is credited with forcing Gulf to agree to the requests for information contained in the church resolution, even though the proposal itself was predictably defeated by Gulf's shareholders. The university also sent Stephen Farber, an assistant to Harvard's president Derek Bok, on a four-week trip to Portugal and Africa. The Farber report expressed sympathy for Angolan independence, but concluded that divestment of Gulf by Harvard would be unlikely to further this end.

After their demonstration at Harvard, PALC attempted to organize a boycott of Gulf products in the black community. They reasoned that "Gulf is very vulnerable to attack by the masses of black people because Gulf presents their major products directly to the public as consumer items and adequate substitutes can be found."[84] Based upon their analysis of the geographic distribution of blacks and the percentages of black car ownership, they picked ten target states. A full-page ad was placed in *Ebony* listing fifty-six prominent black Americans who supported the boycott. PALC's effort supplemented that of the church-based Gulf Boycott Coalition, which, headquartered in Dayton, Ohio, had been undertaking a similar effort in the white community since 1971. A Gulf Boycott Committee was also established in London.

Although the extensive distribution of posters, bumper stickers, and leaflets that accompanied the boycott campaign marginally increased the public's awareness of Gulf's presence in Angola, the economic impact of the two boycott efforts appears to have been minimal. A handful of cities agreed to stop purchasing Gulf products, but within the black community the boycott was almost totally ineffectual. Not only did the high point of PALC's effort coincide with the gasoline shortage, but those most immediately injured by the boycott turned out to be the black owners of Gulf service stations.

Gulf's management and board, like that of Dow Chemical, reportedly devoted a considerable amount of time to analyzing the political and moral implications of the company's policies. They concluded "that Gulf's presence in Angola is in the best interests of the Angolan people and our shareholders."[85] An official of the company noted that while the critics "sit in parish headquarters and worry about world problems . . . stirring up these problems [Gulf was operating in] seventy free world countries."[86] He added that they were "guests of those governments and as a matter of policy and self-interest, we do not engage in public debate about their political systems. . . . As a legal corporate entity, an international company must remain politically neutral."[87]

Like other companies under intense and sustained citizen pressures, Gulf did become concerned about the boycott's impact on the company's "good name." Dorsey, along with several of the firm's top public relations executives, paid personal visits to Angola. The oil company also hired a black public relations firm in order to receive advice on advertising in black publications and donated $50,000 to the Southern Christian Leadership Conference. The donation prompted considerable controversy within the black community. Most important, Gulf officially declared that it would not invest in either South Africa or Mozambique.

The denouement of the controversy is replete with irony.[88] Following the overthrow of the Salazar dictatorship in Portugal, the new government moved to give independence to its African colonies. At the same time, Gulf began private negotiations with the leaders of the MPLA, which *de facto* controlled the land upon which Gulf's refinery was situated. The rebels assured Gulf that they had no present intention of expropriating its property; they just wanted to receive the royalty checks that had formerly gone to Lisbon. Gulf's management was more than happy to comply; they had indicated all along that they were indifferent as to who ruled Angola, and now they were able to demonstrate the consistency of their conviction. When asked how he felt about the MPLA's sudden acceptance of Gulf's presence in Angola after the guerrillas had encouraged a five-year international campaign against the oil company, a former leader of the Pan-African Liberation Committee stated that the government's decision caused him no difficulty: "We always saw our role as supporting the preferences of the Angolan people and if they now have decided that Gulf is in a position to be of use to them, we continue to respect their preferences."[89]

On the other hand, the U.S. government, which throughout the conflicts over Gulf's Angolan investment had officially remained neutral, was not as charitable. During the civil war that followed Portugal's withdrawal, Gulf found itself on the opposite side from that of the United States government. Dutifully Gulf was sending its royalty checks to the Soviet-supported MPLA, while the CIA was funding its Western-backed opponents. The company's payments, in fact, were larger than those of the CIA. Under pressure from the State Department, Gulf agreed to place its royalties in an escrow account for the duration of the conflict. Following the MPLA's victory, the payments were unfrozen, and Gulf resumed the payment of its royalties to the Republic of Angola.

## Infant Formulas

In 1975, church organizations introduced a new issue into the corporate political process: the marketing of infant formulas by American corporations in underdeveloped nations.[90]

Four years earlier an *ad hoc* working group of the U.N.'s Protein Advisory Group had observed that

The extensive introduction and indiscriminate promotion of expensive processed milk-based infant foods in some situations may constitute a grave threat to the nutritional status of the infants for whom they are intended. The sophisticated luxury and fashionable appeal of such products to the mother may lead to the undesirable effect of displacing the child from the breast, in circumstances where the mother may have no access to affordable alternative foods which can be given safely and without risk of alimentary infection and diarrheal disease.[91]

In 1974, the governing body of the World Health Organization passed a resolution noting "the mistaken idea caused by misleading sales promotion that breast feeding is inferior to feeding with manufactured breast-milk substitutes." It urged "member countries to review sales promotion activities on baby foods and to introduce appropriate remedial measures, including advertisement codes and legislation where necessary."[92] That same year, a British relief organization issued a report titled *The Babykillers*. It strongly criticized the promotional practices of formula producers from Switzerland and the United Kingdom. Among the practices it cited—and condemned—were media campaigns that created the impression that bottle feeding is superior, the use of "milk nurses"—sales persons dressed in white uniforms—to call on mothers and promote formula use, and the providing of free samples to doctors and hospitals.

What troubled these organizations was the nutritional implication of the dramatic reduction in breast feeding taking place in the underdeveloped world. Not only was human milk the ideal food for most infants, but due to poor hygiene standards, the inability of many mothers to read preparation instructions, and the relative high cost of formulas, infant malnutrition—already a serious problem—was increasing. A study by the Pan American Health Organization also reported a strong correlation between breast feeding and lower rates of death from diarrheal disease or nutritional deficiency. While the marketing of infant formulas was by no means the only cause of the decline in breast feeding, the promotional policies of private corporations appeared to be an important contributing factor.

Church groups associated with the Interfaith Center submitted proposals to American Home Products Corporation and Bristol-Myers in 1975 requesting data about their infant formula promotion practices. The proposal to American Home Products was withdrawn after the company agreed to include a statement about infant formula in its mailing to shareholders. Bristol-Myers recommended a vote against the resolution; 5.33 percent of the shares voted opposed management's position. Several institutional investors considered the issue the most important raised in 1975.[93] Following the annual meetings, representatives of the church, along with officials from the Ford and Rockefeller foundations, which had program interests relating to questions of infant nutrition in developing countries, met on several occasions with officials from the two corporations. In 1976 public interest proxy resolutions were proposed to both corporations, as well as to Abbott. After extended, "incredibly intensive" negotiations, American Home Products agreed to circulate a report to its shareholders that included much of the information requested by the resolution, and the proposal was withdrawn.[94] Abbott, in a report to shareholders, noted that

[the] charge that misleading public advertising of infant nutritionals [formula] has led to their use by some mothers who cannot afford them and who do not have access to the hygienic conditions under which infant formulas should be prepared . . . is not without some validity.[95]

Prior to its 1976 annual meeting, the corporation took a number of steps that seriously reduced the areas of disagreement between management and the church groups. A year later Abbott announced a major reform of its code of marketing ethics.

Bristol-Myers, however, proved more intransigent. The company did issue a special report about its infant formula marketing practices outside the United States, which it described as "totally responsive to the concerns expressed in both the 1975 and 1976 resolution."[96] However, both representatives of the Interfaith Center and Dr. John Knowles, president of the Rockefeller Foundation, found it unsatisfactory. Knowles, along with representatives of the Ford Foundation as well as the churches, met personally with Gavin MacBain, Bristol-Myers's chairman, to discuss the issue. Knowles questioned several aspects of the report and suggested that the company limit its sales to the developed nations, claiming that widespread poverty and the absence of a suitable home environment in developing countries made misuse of the formulas likely. The negotiations subsequently ceased, and a stockholders resolution was submitted to Bristol-Myers's shareholders by the United Church Board of World Ministers and the Sisters of the Precious Blood. It asked the corporation to issue a report describing

—Its operations that relate to the sale, manufacturing, packaging and distribution of infant formula, including data, by country, on market share, sales and earnings.

—Its infant formula promotional practices and advertising campaigns, including data on expenditures for different kinds of advertising and samples of promotional materials.

—Its latest research comparing infant formula and maternal milk and its plans to develop nutritional supplements for lactating mothers.[97]

Several institutions supported the resolutions, including two New York banks, Nationwide Insurance Company, Cornell University, and the Ford and Rockefeller foundations.

The resolution was supported by only 3.4 percent of the shares voted. However, following the 1976 meeting, the Sisters of the Precious Blood of Dayton, Ohio, filed a lawsuit against the company, charging it with lying to its stockholders about its sales of infant formulas in poor nations. In opposing the 1976 resolution, Bristol-Myers had denied in its proxy statement that its products were promoted "where chronic poverty or ignorance could lead to product misuse."[98] The Roman Catholic order demanded a new stockholder meeting to correct the alleged misstatements and an injunction barring further false statements. Accompanying their brief were affidavits from eighteen Third World countries documenting infant formula promotion and sales activity by Bristol-Myers. Supporting affidavits were also submitted by nine shareholders, including the Ford Foundation. The company termed the suit "grossly irresponsible" and stated:

Bristol-Myers believes its marketing policy is a correct one—to limit the sale of infant formula products to those countries where there is a substantial body of customers who can benefit from the products and afford to buy them; promote our products exclusively through professional medical personnel and not to market formula in those least-developed countries where chronic poverty or ignorance could lead to product misuse or harmful effects.[99]

On January 6, 1978, the lawsuit was settled out of court. The company agreed to mail to all stockholders a full statement of the church group's study of infant marketing practices and to cease promoting their use in hospitals, clinics, and doctors' offices. At the same time, the newly formed Infant Formula Action Coalition, a confederation of forty organizations throughout the United States, announced a boycott of Nestlé Corporation, a Swiss-based company that is the largest exporter of infant formulas, contending that "corporations [should] respect people above profit."[100]

## The Arab Boycott

In the winter of 1975–1976, the American Jewish Congress (AJC) announced that it was planning to submit proxy proposals to approximately 150 corporations requesting that they report to their shareholders their participation and policy toward the Arab boycott of Israel; it thus became the first Jewish organization to actively participate in the corporate accountability effort.[101] The AJC's decision to directly challenge the relationship of U.S. corporations to the nations in the Middle East was significant in two respects. First, it represented the largest shareholder campaign ever mounted. More importantly, it represented the first time that a mainstream liberal group, whose interest in business did not originate in the social movements of the sixties, attempted to use the proxy mechanism. It thus reinforced and reflected the increasing legitimacy of the movement for corporate accountability.

The AJC's action would have been inconceivable without the precedents established by the Project on Corporate Responsibility and, most immediately, the Interfaith Center on Corporate Responsibility. In preparation for his direct challenge, Will Maslow, the AJC's counsel and the campaign's director, consulted with both Tim Smith and Donald Schwartz. Following the 1976 spring round of meetings, he submitted an official statement to the Securities and Exchange Commission supporting rule changes that would liberalize shareholder access to the proxy machinery. In the statement, Maslow wrote that his sixty-year-old national membership organization "had substantial opportunity to experience first hand . . . the existing proxy rules."[102] He continued in language that was similar to that used by virtually all participants in the corporate accountability effort:

It is commonplace that business corporations . . . have become enormously powerful institutions in our society, exercising a pervasive influence on our way of life beyond the immediate concerns of their shareholders, employees and consumers. . . . The impact of their activities . . . inevitably give rise to moral and ethical issues concerning which shareholders have a legitimate concern.[103]

The American Jewish Congress decided to use the proxy route in order to achieve a variety of objectives. The first was an educational one, directed at both the business community and the general public. Submitting proxy resolutions was a way of forcing individual corporate executives and their firms to come to terms with the issue of their moral and legal responsibility for the continuation of the Arab boycott. Mobilizing the firm's shareholders was a way of making it more uncomfortable for those American firms who were in compliance; spotlighting the differing behavior of individual corporations was a way of "raising the ante."[104] In addition to raising the consciousness of the American business community, the congress wanted to use the publicity that accompanies shareholder challenges to make the issue of the compliance of American corporations with the Arab nations' boycott of Israel a more salient one, to shareholders—via the proxy statement—and to the American public as a whole—via press coverage. The congress recognized that monitoring the policy of each of several hundred corporations was far less efficient than seeking stricter enforcement of regulations by the government; the primary purpose of the shareholder effort was to help place the issue on the agenda of the governmental process, where it ultimately would be decided. Finally, as a membership organization, the AJC was particularly attracted by the use of the shareholder resolution as a vehicle for allowing its members, most of whom were relatively affluent and thus owned shares in various companies, to do something personally to affect an issue on which they had very strong views. Maslow wrote in a memo following the 1976 effort:

There is still plenty of room left for innovative action, when people care enough. Instead of leaving to lawyers, lobbyists and public relations men the defense of their rights, individuals were able by this project to utilize their resources in striking a blow at a hated adversary.[105]

The proxy challenge also reflected the fact that in the Middle East, as in southern Africa, the investment and trade decisions of American-owned corporations were viewed by various constituencies in the United States as fundamentally political. Indeed, the political impact of the trade and investment patterns of corporations in the Middle East on the political and military balance of power of the region was even more unequivocal than in southern Africa. In southern Africa, the role of American investment in supporting white rule was relatively indirect. In the Middle East, American corporations were consciously and systematically used by the Arab states to further their foreign policy aims—aims whose achievement would be facilitated by the isolation of the Israeli economy. In this sense, the direct use of American businesses to achieve political ends by Arab officials was perfectly complemented—and, the American Jewish community hoped, counterbalanced—by the pressures put on them directly by the American Jewish Congress in the United States.

The AJC did not want publicly to embarrass corporations because of their past deeds or misdeeds. Rather, it wanted assurances about their present and future policies. To achieve this end, the congress offered to withdraw its resolution if a company would meet two conditions:

(1) . . . write AJCongress explaining their business operations in the Mideast and the extent of their involvement, if any, in the Arab boycott
(2) . . . report to their shareholders a statement of future company policy on the Arab boycott which we would regard as meaningful and satisfactory.[106]

Between twenty-five and fifty corporations sent representatives to the congress's offices in New York to negotiate with the Jewish group. (One offered to provide a company jet to fly AJC officials to their headquarters —an offer which the congress declined.) Maslow and other AJC officials were struck by the unusually large number of Jewish executives who came to negotiate with them. They concluded that "our titans of industry were dredging the Executive Suite to find Jews," and made it clear to the companies that "such tokens were of no consequence to us and indeed were resented."[107]

AJC itself bought shares in six major companies that it judged particularly important. The remainder of the companies to whom resolutions were submitted were selected on the basis of the stocks held by 300 congress members who asked the AJC to submit shareholder resolutions in their name. One hundred and fifty-five corporations received resolutions. As a result of private negotiations, more than thirty corporations, including General Motors, General Foods, RCA, Xerox, Texaco, and Textron, gave the congress written assurances that they would refuse to submit to Arab boycott demands. They also agreed to circulate their policy to their shareholders. The resolutions were then withdrawn. Other companies were afraid that if they bargained with the AJC, "they would simply be laying the basis for an endless series of even more detailed reports." One corporate secretary commented, "Let's put the proposal in the proxy statement, vote it down at the meeting and be rid of it."[108]

Approximately seventy corporations did not include the congress's resolution on their proxy statements for one of three reasons: it was submitted too late, they had no business in Arab countries, and the issue of the Arab boycott was not "significantly related" to their business. The resolution was thus actually presented at the annual meeting and voted on by the shareholders of only thirty-two corporations. It did rather well. While the AJC received the support of over 5 percent of the shares voted—the number it had defined as constituting a "respectable" showing—in only eight firms, it received the 3 percent necessary for resubmission in twenty-one firms.

Maslow indicated that he was very pleased with the AJC's initial effort. He and the members of his organization who had attended various stockholders meetings felt that they were taken seriously by management. According to Maslow, "hundreds of thousands of shareholders" became aware of the Arab boycott of Israel.[109] While acknowledging that the only satisfactory resolution of the issue was for "federal legislation with teeth . . . that will absolutely forbid any American company to engage in any restrictive practice imposed by the Arab boycott," the AJC was pleased by the assurances of noncompliance received from several American firms.[110]

In 1977, with legislation still pending, the AJC decided to make its shareholder campaign more selective. It addressed resolutions to forty-four companies that it believed were substantially involved in the Middle East, including nine banks whom it wanted to discourage from processing letters of credit that contained boycott provisions. Six of the companies refused to include the resolution on their proxy statements on the grounds that they were "not significantly related to the companies' business." The American Jewish Congress appealed their refusal to the SEC. The commission's staff was undecided and polled the full commission, which divided evenly on the issue (the fifth commissionship was vacant). In an unprecedented action, the staff wrote to each company stating that the proposals had "implications beyond the ambit of the federal securities laws [and that it] is not in a position to express any view as to whether or not the proposal . . . may properly be omitted from the company's proxy material."[111] The practical effect of this stance was to require every company to whom the AJC had submitted a resolution to include it. This represented the first time the commission had allowed its decision on access to the proxy machinery to be influenced by the status of an issue before the governmental process, and it was severely criticized by several long-term observers of the SEC's administration of the proxy rules.

The American Jewish Congress was able to reach satisfactory agreements with eight companies. But the actual impact of these agreements remains unclear. While Maslow stated that seven of these companies had actually changed their policies, most of the companies disagreed. Dow Chemical and Chicago Bridge and Iron noted that all they had done was to rewrite their present policy in a form in which it could be distributed to shareholders. On the other hand, Bethlehem Steel remarked that "the resolution had a consciousness-raising effect and it made us more aware of new developments as we were formulating a position on boycott issues."[112] The AJC's resolutions came to a vote in twenty-six corporations and received more support than they had the previous year. The proxy proposals were supported by at least 3 percent of the shares voted—thus making them automatically eligible for resubmission—in twenty-one companies, and by over 6 percent in four. The overall vote totals averaged 4.65 percent, as contrasted with 4.21 percent in 1976.

Maslow indicated that he was "particularly pleased with the improvement in our voting record over last year" and "heartened" by the support of several major institutional investors including seven public employee pension funds. In the midst of the voting, legislation was enacted restricting the participation of American companies in the Arab boycott. Maslow indicated that "the millions of shares that were voted in support of our resolution helped create the national climate that resulted in overwhelming support in the House and Senate for strong antiboycott legislation."[113] If other membership organizations chose to adopt the AJC's strategy, there could be a substantial increase in popular participation in corporate electoral politics.

## Conclusion

The most distinctive aspect of citizen challenges to corporate trade and investment policies outside the United States lies in the extent to which they have created the most important forum for domestic discussions of the issues with which they have been concerned. The American Jewish Congress's effort is an exception to this pattern; like most of the efforts of the civil rights and antiwar movements, it addressed its demands simultaneously to decision makers in both the private and the public sectors. But while congressional hearings have been held on the role of American corporations in southern Africa and the marketing of infant formulas, prior to 1977 an adequate history of domestic conflict on these issues could be written by focusing almost exclusively on the private sector. The pressures directed against American firms doing business in Angola and South Africa were not primarily designed to influence public policy; those who participated in them believed that changing the policies of American corporations would itself have enormous political consequences.

Because they represent almost "pure" cases of citizen pressures, the conflicts described in this chapter make it possible to generalize about the impact of nongovernmental political pressure on business. Most obviously, no corporation was successfully pressured into doing anything costly to it. Gulf, the firm most financially dependent on the profits of its subsidiary in southern Africa, made no substantive concessions in response to citizen pressures. The oil companies who left Namibia did so primarily out of a concern for the future of their investments, not because of pressures from citizen groups. To the extent that the economic investment of American firms in South Africa declines in the future, that change will be due mostly to corporations' perception that growth rates in South Africa are likely to decline because of increases in racial tension. There has been some improvement in the wages paid to black workers in Namibia and South Africa by some firms, but when compared to the costs of withdrawal, the additional expenses involved appear rather marginal. It is also worth noting that Polaroid had no production facilities in South Africa, only a sales distributor. Not only were the company's total sales in South Africa less than $4 million, but there is nothing to prevent the South African government from purchasing Polaroid film from distributors in Europe.

On the other hand, an economic analysis by no means explains all corporate behavior. It does not account for the wide variety of corporate responses to increased information about personnel policies in South

Africa nor for whatever changes that took place in wage rates. As the IRRC study revealed, firms that have not been subject to domestic pressure pay lower wages than those that have, but even among those pressured by shareholders, the responses vary. It does not explain why Polaroid and Control Data were willing to assume responsibility for the purposes to which their products were put while IBM was not. Corporations also differed widely in their willingness to modify their marketing of infant formulas in less-developed nations and in their response to the AJC's requests.

We are left with the admittedly unsatisfying generalization that, when cost is held relatively constant, the responsiveness of corporations to citizen demands is largely idiosyncratic. This conclusion should not be surprising. We know that in the case of public policy issues there are often divisions within an industry that cannot be explained by their impact on the "bottom line." More broadly, some firms are well known for their relatively liberal political leanings, while others have a record of strong support for right-wing political causes. Similarly, some readily gave in to the blandishments of Richard Nixon's zealous fund raisers in 1972 while others stood firm. Corporations also vary in their political sensitivity to the concerns of their critics. At the margin, there is a considerable amount of corporate behavior that is a function of the personalities of its principal officers—particularly its chief executive officers—and more generally of its particular traditions or subculture.

Many of the demands raised by citizen groups are within the corporation's power to grant or refuse. When faced with a public interest proxy proposal, for example, management has four responses: it can recommend acceptance of the resolutions by the shareholders, negotiate a compromise with its proponents and thus have it voluntarily withdrawn, successfully oppose it and then declare a policy change that essentially does what the resolution requires, or simply steadfastly refuse any compromise. All these responses have at times been utilized; the self-interest of the firm can often be defined broadly enough to justify a variety of actions—"enlightened" as well as orthodox.

The controversy over the conduct of American-based corporations outside the United States also raises a series of extremely complex and critical issues. The position of most corporations has been relatively straightforward. They argue that it is impossible for them to fashion any criteria other than that of profit maximization as the basis for determining with whom they should enter into economic relationships. They are prepared, in principle, to accept political constraints on their investment decisions, but they insist that these constraints should come exclusively from the governments—not from private citizens. This argument has rich historical roots—a broader version of it was one of the earliest and most influential justifications for capitalism. As Samuel Johnson observed in his famous epigram, "There are few ways in which a man can be more innocently employed than in getting money."[114] During the seventeenth and eighteenth centuries, a large number of influential thinkers supported the emergent capitalist system precisely on these grounds. When compared to the passionate religious wars that were devastating Europe, a system that encouraged men to focus their attention on more mundane pecuniary pursuits promised a major improvement. Some of the contemporary defenders of the multinational corporation make a similar argument, namely that a world dominated by multinationals would be hard pressed to cause as much damage and sufferings over the next 400 years as the nation state has over the last 400.

This analysis, however, comes up against the reality of international economic behavior over the last centuries. Whatever its economic achievements, the influence of capitalism has certainly not been morally benign. Not only has it not made the world more rational and peaceful, but the pursuit of profits has also produced its share of social and political catastrophes.

The basis of the outlook of citizen critics of the conduct of American corporations abroad is summed up in this rhetorical question: even if it were legal under United States and German law, would you sell gas ovens to Hitler? If one is prepared to concede that, at least in principle, there are circumstances under which a firm should decline to make a legal profit, then the responsibility for either criticizing or defending each business decision on moral and political, as well as economic, grounds cannot be avoided.

What makes this issue so complex and frustrating to businessmen is that it is extremely difficult for anyone to formulate clear and consistent principles of appropriate corporate conduct. Both corporations and citizen groups have attempted to fashion general guidelines to govern the foreign relations of business, but they are riddled with inconsistencies. Corporations claim their investments are politically neutral, and yet they routinely attempt to directly influence the decisions of foreign governments. Church groups profess their commitment to human rights, and yet their actual efforts tend to focus on economic relations with only a relatively small proportion of the world's repressive regimes. The point is not that these political actors are hypocrites; it is rather that the complexity of international politics virtually dictates that each issue be argued on an *ad hoc* basis. The role and impact of American corporations in each country presents a unique situation and each controversy will ultimately be debated on its own terms, not on the basis of general principles. Governments, of course, have traditionally been forced to operate in the world on this basis; corporate executives are now finding themselves subject to the same dilemmas.

While it is ultimately U.S. government policy that will determine the presence and behavior of American corporations overseas, controversy over the conduct of American corporations abroad will continue to focus directly on the corporation. In part, this is a legacy of the role of the Vietnam War in increasing public awareness of the relationship between international politics and the behavior of American corporations. Not only does a significant body of left-liberal opinion perceive corporations as politically powerful international institutions, but equally importantly, they do not trust either the capability or the willingness of the American government to adequately supervise corporate conduct outside the United States.

Whatever the relevance to domestic American politics of the notion of the corporation as a private government, it certainly takes on added political significance when corporations are acting in an international setting. The power of the modern multinational corporation is frequently compared to that of the nation state not only by its adversaries but by its supporters as well. If any group of corporations appears to enjoy a degree of autonomy from both political authorities and competitive markets, it is certainly the multinationals.

Finally, while most criticisms of the behavior of corporations outside the United States have to date originated from the left of the political spectrum, this situation may well change in the future. For example, the substantial domestic opposition to commercial relations between the United States and the Soviet Union is likely to increasingly focus on the private sector. Indeed, there exist relatively few nations in the world whose economic growth and political stability are not viewed as contrary to human welfare by at least some groups of American citizens. Regardless of the official position of the United States government, they are liable to bring their grievances to the attention of corporate executives.

# CHAPTER

# VI

---

*Conclusion:*
*An Assessment of*
*Citizen Protests*

**W**HAT impact has the corporate accountability movement had either on the political system or on the corporation? How do businessmen view this new source of political pressure and how has their perception changed over the last decade? To what extent have the expectations of those who initiated the citizen challenges in the late sixties and early seventies been realized? How are we to assess the reforms offered by the corporate accountability movement?

## The Business Response

For the most part, corporations take citizen demands, particularly when expressed through stockholder resolutions, with increasing seriousness. The demands are regarded as a permanent, though not necessarily legitimate, part of the political and social environment of the modern firm.

This represents a considerable change from James Roche's speech before the Detroit Economics Club in 1971, in which he accused the Project on Corporate Responsibility of seeking to destroy the free enterprise system.[1] Few executives would now publicly respond as did Henry Ford in 1970 when asked if he thought the Episcopal Church was justified in praying for General Motors to leave South Africa. Ford replied, "I don't think it's any of their goddamn business. It's none of our business how South Africans run themselves."[2]

By any objective criteria—the willingness of management to voluntarily include public interest resolutions in their proxy statements, the number of resolutions withdrawn after satisfactory negotiations with politically oriented investors, and the frequency of meetings between chief executive officers and activists—the acceptance of citizen pressures by business has increased considerably. A survey of *Harvard Business Review* readers taken in 1976 reported that 62.4 percent of the respondents believed that "the polling of shareholder opinions on sensitive social issues" can have either "some" or "very positive impact."[3]

For those corporations that have been repeatedly challenged on a particular issue by the same organization over a period of years, corporate activists have come to occupy a role not dissimilar to that shared by trade union representatives; both agreements and disputes take place within the context of a "working relationship." Generally the more experience a corporation has with citizen demands, the less anxiety such demands provoke. Thus, Tim Smith of the Interfaith Center noted in 1977:

In the beginning we had most of our meetings with corporate public relations people. But now we find it easier to get through to the top man. . . . The rhetoric has changed dramatically. There is a growing tendency to give information when asked to review touchy questions.[4]

What accounts for this change? First, publicly held corporations tend to be very sensitive to any communication from their shareholders. One executive put it, "Anything from the stockholders, we have to take seriously."[5] AT&T's corporate secretary observed, "Even if a proposal does not carry in the voting, the size of the vote it gets can stimulate management to do something."[6] Viewed from the perspective of electoral politics, the votes gathered by shareholder activists appear rather inconsequential. However, when translated into the world of the corporation, 5 percent is a large number. A 5 percent decline in sales or the selling of 5 percent of a corporation's stock is economically very consequential. The process of historical expectations is also at work; having grown used to total shareholder acquiescence—save in the most extraordinary of circumstances—any lack of support is regarded as threatening.

In addition, shareholder activism makes the firm very vulnerable to bad public relations. What has induced a large number of firms to negotiate settlements with shareholder groups has simply been their concern about the publicity that shareholder public interest proposals receive.[7] During a period when management has been extremely sensitive to its public image, any possibility for avoiding adverse publicity cannot be dismissed. As a rule, executives try to avoid head-on confrontations with groups such as the church that can accomplish very little in the way of building public good will. Tim Smith reported that corporations hated to be seen as "doing battle with the church."[8] And Will Maslow of the American Jewish Congress observed:

# Conclusion: An Assessment of Citizen Protests

Billion dollar corporations are extremely sensitive to shareholder opinion. They do not wish to appear in an adversary position with the reputable and well-intentioned organizations offering such resolutions or to seem opposed to the good causes they are sponsoring. A stockholder's resolution seems a questioning of management wisdom, a rift in the happy family of shareholders.[9]

The offer to withdraw resolutions thus provides activists with one of their few pieces of leverage: they can offer to spare management the publicity associated with a confrontation with a citizens' organization and at the same time keep the annual meeting from being dominated by criticisms of the company's social performance. These provide important incentives for an "out of proxy" settlement. The last thing most corporations want is a story about criticism of their social performance on the front page of the *New York Times* or in a report of their annual meeting. Richard Hays of the American Society of Corporate Secretaries observes that increased willingness of corporations to agree to shareholder demands is partially due to the fact that "a number of companies aren't happy with the negative image that they are always against anything shareholders propose."[10] George W. Coombe, assistant general counsel for General Motors—who, in his former position as corporate secretary, handled the company's negotiations with Campaign GM—noted in 1975:

One thing that has helped considerably to quiet down the social issues is the pre-meeting dialogue. I have found most of the church people to be quite reasonable, once they understand what our problems are. Annual meetings, after all, are not the best forum for settling far-ranging disputes of this sort.[11]

The responses of General Motors, Exxon, and AT&T to shareholder proposals in 1977 dramatize some of the changes that have taken place in the six years since Campaign GM. A few years earlier a high official at GM had privately informed a church representative, "We cannot afford to support any resolution by a shareholder because it would show we are weak and willing to delegate management prerogatives." In 1977, however, two stockholder resolutions were voluntarily withdrawn by their church sponsors after GM agreed to meet their requests for additional information about the company's investments in Chile and South Africa. Exxon and AT&T went a step further. The world's largest energy corporation recommended that its shareholders support a resolution from the United Presbyterian Church asking for a report on its strip-mining activities. The last time the company supported a shareholder proposal was more than twenty years earlier—and that recommended that stockholders buy the company's products. AT&T, for the first time, also urged its shareholders to support a resolution requiring secret balloting at annual meetings—even though it had been defeated overwhelmingly on five previous occasions.[12]

Agreements reached privately with management provide perhaps the clearest index of the growing credibility of shareholder activists. Between 1974 and 1977, a total of ninety-eight shareholder resolutions were withdrawn by their proponents following negotiations with management. Equally significantly, the agreements reached in 1967–1977 were more likely to involve substantive changes in corporate policy—rather than simply additional disclosure.

ENLIGHTENED SELF-INTEREST

There are other factors aside from public relations to explain why at least some relatively "enlightened" executives have become more tolerant of direct political pressures. Most importantly, citizen challenges serve to reduce somewhat the chronic isolation of executives, putting them more closely in touch with the pressures and concerns of the "outside world." John D. deButts, the chairman of AT&T, told a meeting of the American Society of Corporate Secretaries in 1976:

. . . it's been a long time since we've had what I would call an uneventful meeting. . . .

Now you might expect me to deplore this development and the threat it poses to our ordered corporate ways. Actually, I do not. I do not because the annual meeting, contentious as it sometimes can be, provides an opportunity unique in the year's calendar, for management to respond, face to face, to the various constituencies to which it is in greater or lesser measure accountable. Striking a sound balance among the often competing interests of these constituencies— shareowners, customers, employees, the public at large—is the essence of the art of management. The Annual Meeting brings the entire process into dramatic focus.[13]

While their actual impact on corporate decisions is minimal, the increasing number of minority and women directors has also helped expose the corporation's top decision makers to a somewhat greater variety of perspectives.[14] Their very physical presence tends to encourage a greater awareness among the corporation's top officials and other board members of the impact of their policies on these groups. As Joan Ganz Cooney, president of the Children's Television Workshop and a member of the board of Xerox, First Pennsylvania Corporation, and Macy's Department Stores, put it: "My presence is a pressure."[15]

John Bunting, who appointed a black businessman, a black lawyer, a female television producer, and a college student to the board of the First Pennsylvania Banking and Trust Company, explains that his diverse new directors "influence me by their mere presence. The fact that I have a woman on my board reminds me of things that I should be paying attention to, even if she doesn't say a word. The same thing for Blacks." Bunting adds, "They have become management's 'window to the world.' "[16]

Patricia Harris, a black female lawyer who served on the boards of IBM, Chase Manhattan Bank, and Scott Paper Company prior to her appointment to Carter's cabinet similarly notes, "People who have always been in the power orbit . . . tend to get blinders."[17] The impact of the Reverend Leon Sullivan's public disagreement with his fellow board members on GM's investment in South Africa can also be seen in this context. Richard Gerstenberg, who succeeded James Roche as chairman of the board of GM, states, "We have some pretty good discussions at our board on the issues of our day. His [Sullivan's] presence has made us more conscious of some things than we might otherwise have been."[18]

Other corporate officials, particularly those responsible for negotiating with critics, have also noted that citizen challenges perform a useful service by forcing many important social and political problems to the attention of management. The Bank of America, as a response to its 1964 dispute with CORE, established two management committees with responsibility for researching and clarifying the bank's position with respect to citizen demands. These committees have not been dormant; the world's largest bank has been under virtually continuous citizen pressures since the mid-sixties on issues ranging from its lending policies in California to the presence of its branch in Saigon. James Langton, the bank's executive vice-president for social policy who has been responsible for negotiating with "third force" groups for over a decade, observes: "The protests have done a lot of good. They have forced issues to our attention that otherwise would be dormant and have taught us a lot about the complexity of many issues."[19] Langton's counterpart at Del Monte adds: "We are not perfect and these groups play a useful role by bringing our shortcomings to our attention."

The experiences of the American oil companies in Namibia are probably the most dramatic example of this informational exchange. The companies, acting on a straightforward economic calculus, were unaware of the tenuous legal foundations of their investment until the Interfaith Center brought it to the attention of the public. Critics of the role of U.S. corporations in South Africa discovered that most American executives were unaware of the working conditions of their employees; they had placed the management of their operations entirely in the hands of white natives. Similarly, the executives of the companies manufacturing infant formulas appear to be unaware of how their products were marketed in poor nations until this issue was raised through the efforts of various church groups and the Ford and Rockefeller foundations. In these last two cases, of course, it is likely that management would have preferred to remain ignorant of these aspects of their foreign operations. But activists raised issues with which the corporations will eventually have to deal, and it would be difficult to assert that continuing corporate ignorance served any useful purpose.

Even the act of preparing a rebuttal to citizen pressures can serve a useful management function; it often forces senior executives at least to think about the social and political dimensions of their profit-seeking efforts.[20] Indeed, one might argue that citizen groups have displayed a far greater sensitivity to changes in the relationship between economic and social issues than have most corporate executives. What is striking is how frequently social issues first raised by the corporation's critics have proven to be relevant to the long run economic welfare of the firm. For example, shareholder activists raised the issue of the composition and independence of the corporate board before it became an issue of widespread concern within the business community and urged the repudiation of the "Wall Street Rule" three years before the financial community began to recognize that rule's inadequacy. Moreover, because of the frequency with which citizen challenges anticipate the agenda of the governmental process, they offer businessmen a relatively inexpensive and highly reliable political forecasting tool. More often than not, the issues raised in proxy resolutions and consumer boycotts eventually become the subject of legislative proposals and administrative regulations—a dynamic of which some businessmen are very aware.

CONTINUED ANNOYANCE

Still, the willingness of management to take the concerns of citizen challenges seriously should not be exaggerated. Most businessmen continue to regard the entire phenomenon as tiresome and bewildering. As Richard Holton, former assistant secretary of commerce, noted in 1974:

In reading over the management responses . . . one has the impression that all too frequently when a proposal arrives in corporate headquarters, the scenario goes something like this: The proposal is turned over to the general counsel . . . [who] . . . seeks out some minor clause in the proposal that is unworkable or infeasible and recommends against the proposal because of this clause, rather than recognizing that the main thrust of the proposal may have merit. Or alternatively, the reaction may be that "this is already company policy and is therefore unnecessary."[21]

Businessmen particularly resent the tone in which demands raised by the church are made. An executive of a firm regarded by activists in the church as one of the more responsive privately labeled the activists "a pain in the ass." Another executive, who has negotiated extensively with clerical officials, said that he personally was very bothered by their "arrogance, singlemindedness and cavalier attitude toward the truth." A management consultant with a similar history of involvement in stockholder versus company confrontation told a reporter from *Dun's*:

I think the question of morality is ill-served by the church groups. After all, they have themselves shown a certain deviousness by, for example, suddenly acquiring two shares of stock in some companies and immediately sending in a 14-page proxy proposal. Moreover, they seem unwilling even to consider the cost of the morality they preach.[22]

Businessmen also tend to regard the choice of targets by activists as arbitrary. An acceptable history of the politics of citizen challenges could be written focusing on the experiences of a dozen large—and visible—corporations. Most of the principal targets of citizen challenges are among the fifty largest firms, including Exxon, General Motors, Mobil, SoCal, IBM, Gulf, ITT, U.S. Steel, Occidental Petroleum, Eastman Kodak, Rockwell International, Dow Chemical, and Boeing. Many executives do not believe that these firms have behaved less "responsibly" than others (often competitors) in whom activists have been less interested.

Finally, the diversity and complexity of corporate accountability movements is frustrating to executives who often find themselves subject to demands by groups about whom they know nothing. Most citizen challenges do not represent a clear constituency; it is difficult for executives to judge how seriously to take them. To help remedy this, the Public Affairs Council in 1971 published a small booklet called *The Challengers*.[23] It briefly profiled sixty organizations "dedicated to changing the private sector in America." The directory was updated in 1975 to reflect the shift from mass protests to "less visible but highly organized day-to-day work."[24] In 1977, the council published more detailed profiles of twenty-five groups, including their size, budget, scope, purposes, method of operation, funding history, effectiveness, and political orientation. Citizen pressures and the corporate response to them are also the subject of a number of case studies that are available for use by business school faculty, through the Inter-Collegiate Case Clearinghouse. In addition, IRRC performs a clearinghouse function for the business community, as does the Human Resources Network.

The problem with such research efforts is that different groups emphasize different issues at different times in different ways to different corporations. Although the American Society of Corporate Secretaries has served as a sort of "command post" for public interest proxy proposals, the sharing of experiences by corporate officials still tends to be sporadic. Corporations still typically deal with citizen pressures in isolation from each other; with the exception of the Sullivan principles—which were endorsed by more than fifty firms—businesses have not attempted to define common positions vis-à-vis citizen activists as they have with issues before the governmental process.[25]

### THE ANNUAL MEETING

What particularly upsets executives is the presence of protestors and critics at shareholder meetings. Even the relatively infrequent and innocuous appearance of "professional shareholders" or "shareholder democrats" in the fifties and early sixties—before the annual meeting became the setting for actual political conflict—disturbed business.* As *Fortune* editorialized in 1965:

There is no reason that management must tolerate all these obstructions to the proper conduct of company business . . . "Corporate democracy" derives from the hoary notion that the corporation is constructed on a model of a democratic political state, with the shareholders as the electorate and the board of directors the legislature. In fact, however, a corporation is not a republic in miniature. It is a business organization in which the owners—the shareholders—have some clear rights. But those rights are not analogous in any important way to the rights of citizens in a democracy, and the board of directors does not really resemble a legislative body.[26]

Or as the vice-president of one major corporation, whose responsibilities included preparation for the formal gathering of the firm's owners, put it: "I don't give a damn about the annual meeting. I'd like to see the thing abolished. The object of our meeting is to end it as fast as possible without making a fool of the chairman."[27] Given this perspective, the views of most executives toward political activists at the annual meeting are predictable. A study of corporate responses to political protests at annual meetings concluded:

* Ironically, it was management who pioneered the use of the annual meeting for purposes not related to the spirit of the securities law. During the thirty years following the Securities and Exchange Act, many corporations began to use the meetings as part of their marketing strategy. They reasoned that their stockholders, already predisposed to their corporation's welfare, would provide a receptive audience for the consumption of its products. Thus, the annual meeting of General Motors featured test drives in the firm's new sport cars, while the shareholders of National Dairy products were treated to pickles and cheese. The corporation's owners were treated like consumers long before public interest groups began trying to make shareholders into citizens.

# Conclusion: An Assessment of Citizen Protests

None of the companies responding to the inquiry was particularly happy about the prospect of having its stockholders' meeting used as a forum for reform. To the larger corporations, annual meetings are merely one feature (and a relatively ineffectual one, some executives say) of their investor relations programs —one of many channels of communication through which stockholders may question management and be kept informed about various aspects of the business.[28]

The annual meeting may well be the only time when the corporation's chief officers interact with the public in a physical environment that is not totally planned and controlled by them. True, the annual stockholders meeting is still a far cry from the proverbial New England town meeting. (A better analogy, and one that is more consistent with the constitutional origins of the corporation, might be the question period in the House of Commons.) On the other hand, it is the one time when corporate executives are a captive audience of their diverse publics; both the "corporation" and the "public" become, momentarily, real individuals, rather than abstractions. For one day a year, the individuals who manage the most hierarchical civilian institution in the United States are personally subject to the irreverence that pervades so many other aspects of American life.

Consider, for example, the tone of this dialogue between S. J. Ruskin, a shareholder from Los Angeles, and William Rockwell, president of the board of Rockwell International, at the corporation's 1976 meeting in Beverly Hills.[29] Ruskin wanted to know why the firm's business meeting and customer entertainment were done "down there in the Caribbean." Rockwell replied, "I think it's very convenient." Ruskin shot back: "Convenient to whom?" Rockwell's president replied: "Convenient to us."

The 1977 meeting of J. P. Stevens was the setting for a somewhat more serious dialogue. An employee asked the firm's president:

Mr. Finley, my name is Mary Frances Bradley. I'm one of your employees from the Statesboro plant. I'd like to ask you a question on salary. The proxy statement says you were paid $240,000 in 1975 and $380,000 in 1976. That's a 60 percent increase. The workers only got a 10 percent raise. Why?

FINLEY: Well, the best way I can explain it is that that was incentive compensation.

BRADLEY: Well, why don't we get it?[30]

What the political use of the annual meetings has done is to force corporate presidents and chairmen to respond to pointed—and at times angry—questions covering virtually every aspect of their social and political as well as economic policies during the preceding year. As a consequence, preparation for the annual meeting has become an increasingly burdensome, time-consuming, and nerve-racking task. As one investor relations specialist told *Forbes*: "Beneath their calm exteriors, most board chairmen are nervous as hell about going before their stockholders. You'd be surprised how much psychosomatic illness there is as meeting time approaches."[31]

Small wonder that many companies have sought to discourage the attendance of critics at shareholder meetings by scheduling their meetings on the same day (in 1976, for example, over 100 companies listed on the New York Stock Exchange held their meetings on April 27) and in relatively inaccessible locations. There is also some sentiment within the business community for actually abolishing the annual meeting—a measure that would be legal under the chartering law of Delaware, though not under the regulations of the New York Stock Exchange. To date, no major corporation has done so.[32]

## The Challenge of Corporate Accountability

In the final analysis, however, the reaction of corporate executives is likely to have only marginal impact on the future development of this third arena. American businessmen as a group have never been particularly receptive to challenges to their autonomy, and it is unlikely that the proportion of responsive executives has grown significantly over the last decade. A more important question is: what does the ten-year history of the corporate accountability movement indicate about the future of public control of the corporation in the United States?

Most obviously, the corporate challenge effort has failed to accomplish one of its principal initial objectives; it has not succeeded in becoming a popular political movement capable of mobilizing the populace against the abuse of corporate power. For a brief period between 1969 and 1971, there was a general mood of euphoria among many observers of corporate accountability movement politics. Marv Davidov, the director of the New Left's most serious effort to organize against business, the Honeywell Project, confidently predicted in 1970 that within two years, 50 to 100 other defense contractors would be the focus of similar efforts that same year. Hazel Henderson, a prominent writer on environmental affairs, predicted in *Nation* that:

this new "movement for corporate responsibility" whose goal is to politicize . . . the corporation, could become the most significant political development in the 1970's . . . open[ing] an almost untapped channel for organizing new constituents.[33]

Henderson expressed the aspirations of many frustrated with attempts to change government policies when she reported that "many . . . believe that the corporation may prove more responsive to political pressures than has formal government."[34] Nader prophesized that, through Campaign GM, people would begin to realize that

no street in any American city is safe from General Motors . . . The role of the individual share owner questioning the corporation in terms of social responsibility will increase . . . A whole new conception of citizenship—one including corporations—would come into being."[35]

There were two efforts to capitalize on the momentum generated by what many observers regarded as the concrete successes of Campaign GM and FIGHT. In order "to establish a constituency" and increase its "credibility clout"[36] in 1972, the Project on Corporate Responsibility decided to establish a Shareholder Joint Action Program. For an annual contribution averaging $25, the project would implement shareholder initiatives, particularly proxy challenges and litigation, on behalf of its membership. Interested individuals would supply the PCR with a list of the companies in which they held securities, and periodically communicate to it the kinds of social issues in which they were interested. On this basis the project would decide which companies to challenge and what demands to make to them.

The PCR's proposals were strikingly similar in principle to an organization that Saul Alinsky attempted to create as a result of his experiences with Eastman Kodak. Alinsky was confident that he had stumbled onto something important in 1968: "In all my wars with the establishment, I've never seen it so uptight. I knew there was dynamite in the proxy scare."[37] In order to build on his experiences with Kodak, Alinsky envisioned the creation of a national membership organization called "Proxies for People." Headquartered in either Chicago or New York, the organization would send out professional organizers to middle-class communities throughout the United States. The targets, issues, and policies would be selected by the national board, but the key to the strategy would be the active involvement of the membership of local chapters. They would meet to study corporate policies, make recommendations to the national organization, and select individuals who would personally attend shareholder meetings in their local areas.

Alinsky was critical of Campaign GM because "It's not doing anything to organize and involve people."[38] What intrigued him about the idea of "Proxies for People" was that it would be used as a device to organize the middle class. It appeared perfectly suited to precisely those people who, by virtue of their income and educational levels, composed the social base of the so-called conscience constituency. In contrast to much of the radical rhetoric of this period, it appealed not to people's guilt about their affluence, but rather to the potential access and influence that their economic standing gave them. Alinsky would use "People's Capitalism," the proverbial slogan of the New York Stock Exchange, to mobilize "the people." In the last chapter of *Rules for Radicals*, written shortly before his death, Alinsky predicted:

Proxies can be the mechanism by which these people [the middle class] can organize, and once they are organized they will re-enter the life of politics. Once organized around proxies they will have a reason to examine . . . various corporation policies and practices, both domestic and foreign, because now they can do something about them.[39]

In short, proxies were for Alinsky what the wage relationship was for Marx: a social relationship in terms of which people could define their common interests and challenge those who did not share them.

Neither the PCR nor Alinsky ever expected that their campaigns would actually win a majority against management. They were well aware that in a capitalist society, the wealthy, by definition, owned a disproportionate share of corporate stock. Rather, by mobilizing some significant fraction of the approximately 30 million Americans who owned stock—most of whom owned relatively few shares—they hoped to balance the inequality of wealth by the legitimacy that a democratic society attributes to sheer numbers. Acting collectively, citizens could acquire influence in corporate affairs disproportionate to their total individual wealth. It was this premise that presumably underlay the following Alinsky scenario:

I want to be able to move those stockholders meetings into Yankee Stadium—and this goes for all corporations. They will have their thousand or so stockholders there, and we'll have 75,000 people from Proxies for People. I want to see the chairman of the board—in front of the cameras and the mass media, with 75,000 people voting "aye" on one of our resolutions—announce that 98% of the stock is in his hands votes "nay," and they win. I want to see him look at 75,000 people and tell them that they haven't got a damn thing to say about it.[40]

Moreover, just as the power of institutional investors over management was ultimately based on the possibility of their divesting their shares in a particular corporation, so too would the influence of citizen investors derive in the final analysis from their ability to make their demands through the government.

In retrospect, it appears that the expectations of both the PCR and Alinsky were somewhat naive. Corporate accountability *per se* is too abstract an issue to capture the public's imagination. Moreover, except for the small minority of stock owners whose financial status would render them unlikely candidates to challenge corporate social policies, the shareholder role is not a particularly salient one; it is commonly seen as little more than a risky savings account. In addition, the number of individual shareholders has been steadily decreasing since 1971, and many of those who continue to own stock do so indirectly through mutual and pension funds. Mutual funds make the shareholder relationship even more nebulous; few holders are likely to have any idea about which companies they "own." Not only is the relationship of an employee or a retiree to a pension fund equally distant, but the beneficiaries of most union pension funds have little say as to how their stock is voted. Indeed, the trustee relationship even limits the voting rights of certain wealthy individuals.

Most importantly, even if large numbers of shareholders could be persuaded to take an interest in the social policies of their firms, they would probably be as likely to support management in order to protect their dividends as to vote in favor of public interest resolutions. The regular presence at shareholder meetings of sizable numbers of vocal supporters of management suggests that there is a promanagement constituency that includes many small shareholders.*

Moreover, the very emphasis on vote totals that informs most public interest proxy contests discourages the mobilization of individual shareholders. It is a far more efficient use of limited resources to concentrate on securing the support of institutional investors. Thus, although Campaign GM received its greatest support from small shareholders—an estimated 60,000 voted for at least one of its proposals—its emphasis on receiving at least 3 percent of the shares voted dictated its strategy of emphasizing institutional investors. To the extent that shareholder activists want to "win" in a numerical sense, they will be unlikely to emphasize popular participation.[41]

---

* The apparent identity of interests between most shareholders and management has tempted many corporations to seek to mobilize their shareholders to support public policies sympathetic to business. However, they have had no more success than public interest activists.

### THE POLITICIZATION OF THE CORPORATION

To the extent that citizen challenges have succeeded in mobilizing relatively sizable numbers of individuals—whether through the voting of proxies, attendance at annual meetings, support of consumer boycotts, or by involvement in demonstrations—for the most part they have done so in connection with a broader political effort. Popular participation in citizen pressures on business has occurred most often as a complement to the use of either one or both of the other principal mechanisms of public access to the firm—collective bargaining and state intervention. Thus, the greatest degree of popular involvement in citizen challenges occurred as a spin-off of the antiwar and civil rights movements—whose primary focus was the state. Similarly, shareholder meetings of several banks and utilities throughout the United States have been attended by relatively large numbers of people to protest their loan policies and rate structures. But these organizing efforts have taken place in connection with attempts to influence the government, particularly state legislatures and public utility commissions. With the exception of the early civil rights protests, virtually the only consumer boycotts that have apparently received widespread public support—and thus measurably affected company profits—have taken place as a supplement to union organizing drives. The successes of the United Farm Workers in organizing farm workers in Florida and California were largely made possible by one of the most extensive, well-organized, and lengthiest consumer boycotts in American history. A similar and equally successful nationwide consumer boycott was instrumental in forcing Farah Manufacturing Company to recognize the Amalgamated Clothing Workers Union.[42]

### THE ROLE OF UNIONS

Since pension funds own approximately 33 percent of the equity capital of major American companies, the role of the trade union movement is critical to an assessment of the degree of future public participation in citizen challenge efforts.[43] In 1977, J. P. Stevens became the first corporation in America to be pressured simultaneously from four directions: by the state through the National Labor Relations Board and the courts; by its employees through a strike; by consumers through one of the most extensive boycotts ever organized by the AFL-CIO; and by investors through the most elaborate and well-organized proxy challenges to which any corporation has ever been subjected on a social issue.[44] Five church organizations affiliated with the Interfaith Center filed two proxy resolutions. One asked for a written report to shareholders on the company's labor policies and practices, and the other requested the board of directors to disclose their equal employment practices. The Interfaith Center campaigned aggressively for the proposals, sending a four-page report to 8,000 specially selected Stevens shareholders. The company's annual meeting in New York was attended by a record 500 shareholders, many of whom were activists from church and labor groups. Among those who attended was Coretta King, who quoted her late husband's statement during the Montgomery bus boycott: "Our struggle is not toward putting the bus company out of business but putting justice in business."[45] Outside 3,500 people representing a broad cross section of the left-liberal community—not dissimilar in political composition to those who had opposed bank loans to South Africa a decade earlier—demonstrated. When the votes were tallied, the two resolutions were supported by 5.8 percent and 5.59 percent of the shares voted, impressive totals considering the fact that Stevens stock is closely held.

In addition, the union initiated a novel form of citizen pressure: it began a campaign to isolate J. P. Stevens from the business community by eliminating the interlocks between its board and that of other companies. The union organizer of the "corporate campaign" stated that his goal was "to display our power to Wall Street so they would know that any institution tied to J. P. Stevens would be held accountable. . . . No institution like J. P. Stevens can exist in a vacuum."[46] After considerable pressure, including a threatened withdrawal of union pension funds, James D. Finley, the chairman of J. P. Stevens, resigned from the board of Manufacturers Hanover Trust. Shortly afterward, David Mitchell, the chairman of Avon Products Inc., announced his resignation from the board of J. P. Stevens.

The union effort clearly represented a further stage in the politicization of the corporate board. Previously, activists had attempted to force corporations to add representatives of various constituencies to their boards; this was the first time they pressured particular board members to resign. The union's focus on financial intermediates as a means of challenging the policies of an industrial firm can also be seen as an extension of the strategy initially developed by Campaign GM's Round II. What is less clear, however, is whether the corporate campaign against J. P. Stevens signaled an increase of union involvement in the politics of corporate governance. On paper, the potential power of unions is impressive. Approximately one-fifth of private sector pension monies—amounting to between 50 and 60 billion dollars—are more or less effectively controlled by unions or their representatives. Another $140 billion are administered by trustees established by state and local governments. These figures hardly suggested the emergence of "pension-fund socialism," since most pension fund monies remain firmly under the control of the federal government or corporate managements. They are, however, significant. But with the exception of TIA-CREEF and a handful of locals in New York and California, unions to date have shown remarkably little interest in using their funds to influence corporate policies either by proxy voting or selective investment. Significantly, various unions threatened to withdraw their funds from the control of Manufacturers Hanover Trust, but they did not seek to influence the bank's voting of its proxies. There has been some interest in the voting of proxies by the boards that administer the pension monies of local government employees, but that too remains limited: only five public employee pension funds subscribe to IRRC and only one state—Minnesota— systematically considers social issues in its proxy voting decisions. As long as this pattern persists, citizen challenges are likely to remain more an embarrassment to business than a major focus of popular opposition to it.

## Constitutionalizing the Corporation

While the lack of widespread public participation has clearly limited the political impact of the corporate accountability effort, it has not proved a fatal handicap; indeed, many of the movement's most important effects on corporate policy and public opinion occurred after the atrophy of the social movements of the sixties. By any reasonable criteria the accomplishments of the relatively small number of individuals—numbering in the hundreds —who pioneered the creation of a third political arena for public pressures on the corporation, have been extremely impressive. In 1967, who would have thought that using annual shareholders meetings to raise criticism of the social and political impact of corporate policies would within a few years become the rule rather than the exception? Who, in 1969, would have predicted that the public interest proxy resolution proposed by an antiwar medical student would become a permanent part of the political and legal environment of the American corporation, used to address a broad array of issues by a wide variety of political factions? Who, looking at the level of shareholder support for Campaign GM in 1970 and 1971, would have imagined that within three years, a major proportion of public interest resolutions would either be voluntarily withdrawn by their participants or receive enough votes to make them automatically eligible for resubmission? And, as recently as 1970, who would have foreseen that this decade would witness the participation of institutional investors in the corporate electoral process?

By treating corporations as if they were governments, direct pressures on business have reflected and reinforced a relatively new and potentially important way of approaching the problem of corporate accountability. The logical extension of the politicization of the corporation is for the corporation's structure of authority to come to more closely resemble that of the government itself. The amount of government regulation of business is unlikely to diminish, but in the future it is likely to address itself not only to the substance of corporate policies, but to the processes by which those policies are made. Citizen challenges have already played a role in placing two related sets of issues on the agenda of the governmental process: the internal structure of authority of the investor-owned enterprise and the ability of citizens outside the corporation to scrutinize and question the deliberations of management. These concerns are reflected in the raising of issues such as the composition, authority, and selection of the board of directors, the responsibility of units within the firm for monitoring particular aspects of its social impact, the participation of shareholders in the formulation and discussion of corporate policies, and the degree of public access to information about business behavior.

Corporate activism also has been accompanied by a resurgence of interest among lawyers, economists, and political scientists in the relationship between the governance of the corporation and its social impact. Since 1970, a broad array of schemes have been proposed to make management more directly accountable to those whose stake in the corporation's performance is not primarily financial.[47] Among these suggestions are giving only one vote to each shareholder (a sort of application of the principle of *Baker* v. *Carr* to the private sector); granting standing to file a shareholder derivative suit to anyone adversely affected by management policies—not just shareholders; requiring cumulative voting; taking the control of the proxy machinery away from management; extending the ability of shareholders to initiate proposals; allowing shareholders' nominees for directors to be included in the corporate proxy statement; and adding society-oriented disclosure rules to the regulations of the SEC. Several of these reforms are included in the versions of federal chartering proposals advanced by critics of corporate social performance such as Ralph Nader and Donald Schwartz.[48]

There is also a growing interest among social critics of business in institutionalizing changes in the board room that would both better insure the financial integrity of the corporation and increase the likelihood that business decisions would be more responsive to those affected by them.[49]

John Kenneth Galbraith, Christopher Stone, and Robert Townsend have proposed that a certain number of directors of major corporations be chosen by the government. Others propose strengthening the independence and competency of the board without altering its selection procedures. For example, Schwartz wants all directors to serve full-time, while Nader would like to prohibit inside directors and make each director responsible for a particular aspect of social conduct. An important underlying goal of all these proposals is to somehow convert the board into a sort of internal regulatory agency, capable of helping both the public and the government more effectively monitor and intervene in corporate decisions.

What distinguishes these reforms from most of the scores of laws regulating business that have been enacted by the federal government since 1960 is that they address themselves not to the substantive impact of corporate decisions, but rather to the procedures by which these decisions are made. The strategy that informs them is a simple one; it is to strengthen the ability of those directly affected by corporate policies—acting either individually or collectively—to defend those interests that are inadequately protected by either the regulatory process or the marketplace. They attempt to give individuals both inside and outside the firm increased financial and legal resources in order to monitor and challenge corporate policies, without having to depend upon government officials. In a sense, they seek to apply the principle of checks and balances to the operations of the private sector. The proposed reforms represent a logical extension of the two central premises of citizen protests: the notion that the corporation has become a public institution and that the responsibility for making corporate decisions more accountable cannot be exclusively left to the government. They are an attempt to wrestle with the central dilemma that confronts contemporary critics of business: how do you increase public control of "big business" if you are equally suspicious of "big government"? As Ralph Nader told an interviewer in 1970,

I have a theory about power. If it is going to be responsible or extremely repressive, it has to be insecure, it has to have something to lose. That is why putting all economic power in the hands of the State would be disastrous, because it would not be insecure. No matter where [power] is located, it's going to be abused if the pathways are not open for a broader spectrum of values that have power behind them demanding recognition.[50]

A survey of 200 social activists reveals a similar perspective:

. . . attitudes in this study indicate the heavy premium social activists put on the establishment of new legislative machinery for giving "outside groups a more direct voice in helping to shape policy in the nation's boardrooms."

# Conclusion: An Assessment of Citizen Protests

The survey concluded, "What . . . they appear to want . . . is legislation which would enable themselves or others to make corporations more socially accountable through more direct disclosure of their operations and/or broader representation on boards of directors of appropriate outside interests." (Strikingly only 42 percent believe that "government regulation is the best way to make business more responsive to people's needs.")[51]

Donald Schwartz, Campaign GM's legal counsel, has clearly articulated the thinking behind this strategy. He told a conference at Berkeley on corporate responsibility that

[Contemporary reformers] ultimately desire to relocate the power more within individual hands, *since they believe that shifting the power to government hands is no shift at all.* The objective . . . is to reduce the size of corporations and government regulations alike and *strengthen the position of individual private citizens who will act directly—not through institutions*—against corporate abuse.[52] [emphasis added]

Phil Moore, one of the campaign's directors, added:

. . . most of all, we need a system of corporate governance . . . like our own [Constitution]—not one that solves problems, but that sets forth the process by which problems are solved. . . . In essence, the corporate constitution would open up the corporation to activism. It would create a system of access in which the anti-war activist, the Black activist, the environmental activist and the consumer activist could press their demands on the corporation.[53]

Thus, the principal way in which corporations and governments are becoming subject to similar standards is that both institutions are under pressure to allow the public a greater role in monitoring and participating in their deliberations. The suspicion of both private and public power has led contemporary reformers to seek to develop ways of increasing the vulnerability and scrutiny of decision makers in both sectors. This process is far more advanced in the public sector, particularly with respect to access to the regulatory agencies and the courts, but attention will increasingly focus on opening up the private sector. Those affected by the corporation in their roles as socially concerned investors and consumers are working for restraints on management prerogatives roughly similar to those that currently protect unionized workers.

## The Limitations of Corporate Accountability

All its brave rhetoric notwithstanding, the corporate accountability movement can hardly be regarded as a serious challenge to corporate authority in the United States. This is not primarily due to the lack of widespread participation in it by radicals and socialists—especially after 1970; that is a symptom rather than a cause.[54] Nor is it primarily a function of the extent to which the citizen challenge effort has become dominated by the use of the proxy mechanism. It is true that shareholder activism can be seen as a contemporary variant of nineteenth-century populism; for in both instances the preservation and expansion of private property rights are the basis of a challenge to the prerogatives of the corporation.

Yet this, too, is symptomatic. What is most striking about the corporate accountability movement is the modesty of its demands on business. This is most obviously true of the substantive issues that corporate activists have raised since 1970. Corporations could have yielded to virtually every demand without threatening either their profits or disturbing their power. The increased employment of women and minorities, the cessation of the production of particular weaponry, the disclosure of additional material about environmental impact, the willingness to lend money to inner city housing, the reform of the marketing of infant formulas in poor nations, the refusal to comply with the terms of the Arab boycott—these are hardly policies whose enactment would merit more than a footnote in the history of American business. Even the potentially most expensive demand—withdrawal of all investments from South Africa—would hardly cause more than a small ripple in most corporate balance sheets. Nader, who has closely followed the development of nongovernmental pressures on the corporation over the last decade, correctly observes:

The managers of the investor owned corporation have so many things to give. Corporations could go on meeting the demands of activists challenging them directly at the current rate forever and still their wealth and autonomy would remain essentially unaffected.[55]

Neil Chamberlain's perceptive analysis of the significance of the most visible dimension of citizen pressures can be generalized to most of the demands of the movement. He writes in *The Limits of Corporate Responsibility*:

## Conclusion: An Assessment of Citizen Protests

The consequence of adding a public forum aspect to the annual meeting is to "open" the corporate system to the realities of a society that has altered markedly since the days when statutory and common law established the present legal form. In so doing it does not meet, but in fact turns back, demands for broader participatory roles; it requires no sharing of power. The government of the corporation remains firmly in place. All that has happened is that it has become more public in its operations, more attuned to those voices that it has tended to ignore in the past. Management retains its centralized control by making modest and incremental adjustments in its practices and procedures to palliate those who call for more sweeping change.[56]

The efforts of the corporate accountability movement can be understood in the tradition described by Berle in *The Twentieth Century Capitalist Revolution*. Developed in Normandy, this custom provided that anyone who felt he had suffered an injury at the hands of his neighbors, feudal officials, or even the Duke himself, could cry, "Ha! Rollo!" The Duke would then be required to listen to his grievance and judge its merit "according to the law of God and good conscience."[57] In reality, citizen pressures have challenged the judgment of management, not its power.

The potential impact of the procedural reforms proposed by corporate reformers must also be viewed critically. Would improving opportunities for shareholder participation actually affect the kinds of social and political decisions made by corporate managements? Given the current distribution of stock ownership, one is entitled to be extremely skeptical. Even if shareholder activism were made easier, there is little reason to assume that the corporation's social critics could look forward to having any more direct impact on corporate policies than they have had in the past. The overwhelming majority of individual shareholders and institutional investors remain exclusively oriented to the bottom line. The kind of concessions management might be prompted to make to dissident shareholders have and will remain marginal.

The likely effect of the appointment by the government of "public" directors on the corporation's balance of power also appears rather minimal. Not only might their presence reduce the number of critical decisions made at board meetings—which are rather minimal in any event—but the danger of co-option is a real one. If officials in regulatory agencies responsible for the supervision of particular industries come to almost invariably share the perspectives of the industry they are responsible for regulating, what can we reasonably expect of officials responsible for monitoring the performance of just one firm? Leon Sullivan and Sister Scully notwithstanding, the performance to date of "public interest" directors is not a particularly encouraging one. None has developed an active political relationship with any of the corporation's constituencies. There is no question that the kinds of changes in the board room advocated by the corporation's social critics would complicate and, on occasion, actually modify the decisions of top management, but to expect any major change in corporate priorities is naive.

A similar analysis can be made of the effect of imposing increased disclosure requirements on corporations. The analogy between the impact of the mandatory disclosure of financial data and that of social data is a deceptive one. The first category of information goes to a small group of people who have a direct and unambiguous stake in its impact and who, most importantly, are readily able to translate it into a form that corporate executives take extremely seriously—the price of their stock. In contrast, reports of corporate social performance would presumably be for the benefit of the "public." It is true that public opinion can be an important political force, but there are limits to the public's attention span. How much more knowledge about the social conduct of the hundreds of corporations that dominate the American economy can the public be expected to absorb and act on politically? The public can react to occasional scandals, but can we really expect citizens to pay as close and continuous attention to reports of corporate social performance as the investment community does to that of corporate earnings?

This is not to say the increasing public access and scrutiny of the corporation will be without any impact; that conclusion is adequately refuted by the evidence presented in this book. Direct pressures on business can change corporate behavior, but they are capable of doing so primarily to the extent to which their demands on business expand or complement those required by law. The central premise of citizen activism—namely, that corporations have become, in effect, public institutions exercising a degree of power closely connected to or rivaling that of the state—is actually contradicted by the history of the corporate accountability movement itself. Paradoxically, its successes are due primarily not to the individual or collective efforts of citizens, but rather to the support of the state—the very institution whose alleged domination by business led to direct pressures in the first place.

Why has the corporate accountability movement been unable to offer an adequate vision of what "democratically accountable" corporations would look like? We come full circle: the limitations of citizen pressures on business are linked to their cause. The relative conservatism of the corporate accountability movement stems from its underlying ideology; the notion of the corporation as a governmental or public institution obscures more than it illuminates. The reason the efforts to apply to the corporation the same standards of public accountability that the modern democratic tradition applies to the state are doomed to frustration is because the two institutions are, in reality, fundamentally distinctive. The corporation is not simply another governmental or public institution; unlike the state, it confronts a set of constraints that are essentially economic in character. It is dependent for survival on its ability to accumulate capital in an extremely competitive domestic and international economic environment. As long as corporations remain dependent on private capital markets, there are real limits on their capability to consider nonpecuniary values in their decisions.

The notion of the corporation as a public institution or private government is both informative and misleading. It is informative in that it illuminates the extent to which the social impact of the corporation does resemble that of a government. But it is deceptive to the extent that it obscures the inability of the corporation to command compliance with its decisions. The reason that a corporation, unlike a democratically elected government, cannot be politically accountable to those affected by its decisions, is because the most important decisions made by any firm are out of the control of those who govern it; they are dictated by the imperatives of a market economy. As the range of responses to the demands raised by citizen pressures indicates, corporate managers are certainly not without discretion and many could act somewhat differently than they do. But the extent to which business executives could actually change the basic orientation of their companies is severely limited: corporate accountability is fundamentally limited by the inability of a privately owned firm to pursue objectives that are incompatible with long run profit maximization, however loosely that objective is defined: a politically accountable corporation in a capitalist system is a contradiction in terms.

There is a way in which corporations can be forced to make decisions not dominated by the logic of capital accumulation, but it cannot be achieved through "corporate accountability." It requires the direct intervention of the government. At best, corporate activists can supplement government regulation; what they cannot do is substitute for it. In the final analysis, who governs the corporation is less important than who controls the government. Moreover, in their intensive focus on the corporation—its structure, power, and conduct—corporate activists have paid insufficient attention to the dynamics, and difficulties, of the capitalist political-economic system within which it functions. The future of the corporation will be decisively influenced by the way in which the American political system deals with issues such as unemployment, inflation, resource scarcities, international competition, and uneven regional development. The corporate challenge movement has not and, indeed, cannot adequately address these fundamental issues because they can only be addressed through the governmental process.

## Conclusion

What, then, is the significance of the corporate accountability effort? What difference has it made? Clearly, what is least important about citizen pressures has been their direct, substantive effect on corporate decisions. These have been, and are likely to remain, marginal. Their impact on public policy has been more substantial. They have played a relatively important role both in bringing a number of issues before the political process, and in increasing the effectiveness of government controls over business. Their emergence means that the dynamics of government regulation of business can no longer be understood with exclusive reference to the governmental process.

Far more importantly, citizen challenges have helped increase the visibility and public scrutiny of corporate decisions. The business corporation is far less an abstraction than it was a decade ago. A significant number of interested publics have become more aware of the relationship between their political and social concerns and the specific policies of particular corporations. Those who exercise authority within the corporation are thus under far more scrutiny—by the government, the press, the public, as well as by institutional investors—than they were in the mid-sixties. In the course of treating the corporation as if it were a government, citizen pressures helped politicize the environment of the firm. Moreover, the form that pressures on business have assumed is itself of political significance; they are a reflection of widespread public mistrust of both business and government.

Finally, citizen pressures have increased the opportunities for the expression of public opposition to corporate policies. What is most important about the challenges to Kodak, Dow Chemical, Honeywell, Gulf, and General Motors is not their impact, but the fact that they occurred at all. Corporations can no longer depend upon the government to shield them from public hostility. Rather, to the extent that they make decisions that are widely regarded as having important political, social, and moral implications, they must now be prepared to directly confront substantial and prolonged public opposition—in all its diverse and novel forms. The most fundamental contribution of citizen pressures has been to link the corporation more closely with the vitality and turbulence of the democratic process. Ultimately, citzen protests have less to do with increasing corporate accountability than with preserving and strengthening democratic participation.

# Bibliographical Note

With the exception of Phillip Blumberg's "The Politicization of the Corporation," published in *The Business Lawyer* in July 1971, there has been no comprehensive scholarly treatment of direct political challenges to the corporation. Political scientists continue to reify the term "political," equating it with activity having to do with governments and thus, with relatively few exceptions, overlooking political pressures on other institutions. On the other hand, while law professors and students of management have written extensively on particular aspects of citizen pressures, they have made little effort to place their observations in an historical or theoretical framework.

This study is based primarily on five kinds of sources.

The most important source of information on citizen protests are two monthly periodicals: *The Corporate Examiner*, published since 1972 by the Interfaith Center on Corporate Responsibility, and *News for Investors*, published since 1974 by the Investor Responsibility Research Center. Between 1970 and 1974, the Council on Economic Priorities also published an annual summary of public pressures on business, entitled *Minding the Corporate Conscience* and since 1973, IRRC has published an annual report on the voting behavior of institutional investors. Both were extremely useful sources.

There have also been several case studies of various citizen challenges to business. The three editions of S. Prakash Sethi's *Up Against the Corporate Wall*, published in 1971, 1974, and 1977, contain a total of twenty-eight detailed case studies of direct pressures on business and the corporate response to them; an additional eight cases are on file at the Inter-Collegiate Case Clearinghouse at the Harvard Business School. Jesse E. Christman and High C. White of the National Industrial Mission of Detroit have written detailed accounts of three conflicts between citizen groups and business. These were made available through the Institute on the Church in Urban-Industrial Society in Chicago. Robert Heilbroner's edited collection of essays, *In the Name of Profit*, includes an account of the controversy over Dow Chemical's manufacture of napalm by Saul Friedman. *Minding the Corporate Conscience* by James Munves discusses the experiences of Honeywell, Gulf, and the Bank of America with citizen challenges. Individuals involved in the campaign against Gulf's presence in Angola, the 1967–1968 challenge to bank loans to the Republic of South Africa, Campaign GM, CAPUR, and the American Jewish Congress's criticisms of corporate compliance with the Arab boycott of Israel also have written detailed descriptions of their efforts. The availability of these studies considerably facilitated the preparation of this book.

A third important source is the material prepared and distributed by the activist organizations themselves. In the winter of 1974 the author mailed a letter to every organization and individual listed in the reports of the Investor Responsibility Research Center and the Council on Economic Priorities. A total of 150 letters were sent. The letter informed them of the preparation of this book and asked for a description and an assessment of their activities. A majority responded; their personal letters, press clippings, official replies from business, newsletters, internal memorandum, press releases, fliers, and pamphlets represent much of the primary source material for this study.

A fourth source of material is newspapers and magazines. Although direct pressures on business only received significant press attention between 1969 and 1971, a number of articles have appeared over the last decade in the *New York Times*, the *Wall Street Journal*, the *Nation*, *New Republic*, the *Progressive*, *Business Week*, *Forbes*, *Fortune*, as well as in various more specialized business publications, describing particular incidents. *Business and Society Review*, published quarterly since 1970, has been an especially useful source.

Finally, approximately thirty interviews were conducted, both in person and over the phone, with individuals involved with or knowledgeable about direct pressures on business. They included corporate activists, lawyers, journalists, foundation officials, government officials, and business executives. These were held after all other research was completed in order to clarify and illuminate published accounts. The interviews were conducted on the record and direct quotations from them are cited in the footnotes. On a few occasions, individuals requested that their name or that of their organization remain private. Their confidences have been respected; their statements are not footnoted.

# References

## CHAPTER 1

1. This has been true only since the 1930s. Prior to the New Deal the American Federation of Labor, under the leadership of Samuel Gompers, shied away from participation in the political process.

2. See "Black (Lists) and White," *New Republic*, October 26, 1968, pp. 7–8; and James W. Fraser, "The Campaign for Corporate Responsibility: An Honorable Tradition," *Corporate Examiner* 3, no. 8–9 (September 1974): 2.

3. Adolf A. Berle, Jr., and Gardiner C. Means, *The Modern Corporation and Private Property* (New York: Macmillan, 1932).

4. Robert Gordon, *Business Leadership in the Large Corporation* (Berkeley and Los Angeles: University of California Press, 1945); Walton Hamilton, *The Politics of Industry* (New York: Vintage Books, 1957); James March, "The Business Firm as a Political Coalition," *Journal of Politics*, November 1962; Richard Eells, *The Government of Corporations* (New York: Free Press of Glencoe, 1962); Peter Bachrach, *The Theory of Democratic Elitism* (Boston: Little, Brown & Co., 1967), especially chap. 7; Robert Dahl, "Governing the Giant Corporation," in *Corporate Power in America*, ed. Ralph Nader and Mark Green (New York: Grossman, 1973), pp. 10–24; Wolfgang Friedman, "Corporate Power—Government by Private Groups and the Law," *Columbia Law Review* 58 (February 1955): 155–86.

5. Eells, *The Government of Corporations*, pp. 10–11.

6. Dow Votaw, *Modern Corporations* (Englewood Cliffs, N.J.: Prentice-Hall, 1965), p. 87.

7. Earl Latham, "The Commonwealth of the Corporation," *Northwest University Law Review* 55 (March/April 1960): 33. For a similar argument see also Arthur Selwyn Miller, *The Supreme Court and American Capitalism* (New York: Free Press, 1968) and Philip Selznick, *Law, Society, and Industrial Justice* (New York: Russell Sage Foundation, 1969).

8. Robert Dahl, *After the Revolution* (New Haven: Yale University Press, 1970), pp. 120, 123; a similar argument was made earlier by Chayes. See Abram Chayes, "The Modern Corporation and the Rule of Law," in *The Corporation in Modern Society*, ed. Edward S. Mason (New York: Atheneum, 1966), pp. 25–45.

9. Lincoln Steffens, *Autobiography* (New York: Harcourt Brace & World, 1931), vol. 2, p. 408. Steffens writes:

> When he confessed under public cross-examination that he "worked for his own pocket all the time" he was denounced and politically doomed. But W. L. Strong, as a merchant, had done that all his life, and he was not condemned for making a profit. That was a matter of course in commerce.

See also p. 533.

10. Karen Orren, the only other political scientist to look at citizen pressure groups that focus on the corporation, draws a somewhat different conclusion. She writes:

> Perhaps nothing characterizes contemporary government as its active and intense intercourse with private interest groups; candidates are selected, policies framed and allocations allocated with an eye to group needs, demands and power. Corporate business, on the other hand, . . . is related to the public to whom it allocates its investments and products only in a manner which is general, diffuse, and legally insulated. ["Standing to Sue: Interest Group Conflict in the Federal Courts," *American Political Science Review* 70 (September 1976): 726.]

# References

This distinction is best understood as one of degree. The argument of this study is that the environment of the firm has come to more closely resemble that of the government; substantial differences of course remain.

For a conception of the corporation and its relationship to its environment that closely parallels the one offered in this study, see Charles G. Burck, "The Intricate Politics of the Corporation," *Fortune*, April 1975, pp. 109–112, 188–192.

11. Quoted in T. B. Bottomore, ed., *Karl Marx—Early Writings* (New York: McGraw-Hill, 1963), p. 13.

12. See Charles Peters and Taylor Branch, *Blowing the Whistle: Dissent in the Public Interest* (New York: Praeger Publishers, 1972).

13. The tension between legitimacy and accumulation is examined in James O'Conner, *The Fiscal Crisis of the State* (New York: St. Martin's Press, 1973) and Michel Crozier, Samuel P. Huntington, and Jodi Watanuki, *The Crisis of Democracy: Report on the Governability of Democracies to the Trilateral Commission* (New York: New York University Press, 1975). See especially the essay by Huntington in *The Crisis of Democracy*, pp. 59–118.

14. The influence of this literature is rapidly fading due to the resurgence of economic difficulties which seem to hark back to the social tensions of industrialism. A good example of its vision can be found in Peter Drucker, *The Age of Discontinuity: Guidelines to Our Changing Society* (New York: Harper & Row, 1969).

15. In 1973, 60 percent agreed with the proposition that "most elective officials are in politics for all they personally can get out of it for themselves." A total of 74 percent believed that "special interests get more from the government than the people do." And a 1973 survey taken regarding the influence of key groups on Washington decisions showed that 69 percent felt large corporations had a "great deal" of influence; 59 percent said the same for large financial institutions, while the "average" citizen was accorded only a 7 percent level of influence on Washington decision making.

See the Louis Harris & Associates study commissioned by the U.S. Senate Subcommittee on Intergovernmental Relations in 1974, "Confidence and Concern—Citizens View American Government," Timely Topics Roundtable (Cleveland: Regal Books, 1974). In 1966, those expressing a "great deal" of confidence in Congress stood at 42 percent, but this dropped to 16 percent by 1975; comparable figures, over the same period, for confidence in the executive branch of government show a drop from 43 to 15 percent. See speech by Louis Harris, "The Public Mood and Business: 1975," delivered in Boca Raton, Florida, on April 29, 1975, and reprinted by Louis Harris & Associates, Inc., New York.

An on-going poll conducted since 1958 by the Center for Political Studies at the University of Michigan asks "How much do you think we can trust the government in Washington to do what is right: just about always, most of the time, or only some of the time?" In 1966, 16.9 percent responded "just about always"; by 1972 this was down to 5.3 percent. While 28.2 percent answered "some of the time" in 1966, this response climbed to 44.3 percent in 1972. See Crozier, Huntington, and Watanuki, *The Crisis of Democracy*, table 4, p. 81, for a complete charting of the responses.

16. See John Kenneth Galbraith, *The New Industrial State* (Boston: Houghton Mifflin, 1967) and Galbraith, "On the Economic Image of Corporate Enterprise," in Nader and Green, *Corporate Power in America*, pp. 3–9.

17. Dahl, *After the Revolution* and "Governing the Giant Corporation," in Nader and Green, *Corporate Power in America*, pp. 10–24.

18. For an analysis of the distinctive pattern of American economic development that emphasizes the relative autonomy of the American business corporation, see David Vogel, "Why Businessmen Mistrust Their State: The Political Consciousness of American Corporate Executives," *British Journal of Political Science* 8, no. 1 (January 1978): 45–78.

19. "The Changing Fashion in Company Directors," *Business Week*, March 14, 1977, p. 32.

20. Michael L. Lovdal, Raymond A. Bauer, and Nancy H. Treverton, "Public Responsibility Committees of the Board," *Harvard Business Review*, May/June 1977, pp. 40–64, 178–81.

21. In an unpublished "Guide for Shareholder Activists," Phil Moore of the Project on Corporate Responsibility wrote:

> One shareholder can initiate actions which have far reaching effects. In a shareholder proxy contest, for instance, a single shareholder may force a corporation to communicate with millions of other shareholders, many of whom may have similar public concerns. . . . Indeed, for the price of one share of stock, one postage stamp, a couple of pieces of paper, and perhaps an hour of time, a shareholder may initiate a great public debate over issues of major public importance.

22. The phrase is from Adolf A. Berle, Jr., *The Twentieth-Century Capitalist Revolution* (New York: Harcourt Brace & World, 1954).

23. See, for example, Theodore Lowi, *The End of Liberalism* (New York: W. W. Norton, 1969); Grant McConnell, *Private Power and American Democracy* (New York: Vintage, 1970); Michael D. Reagan, *The Managed Economy* (New York: Oxford University Press, 1963); Robert Engler, *The Politics of Oil* (Chicago: University of Chicago Press, 1961).

24. See, for example, Walter Guzzardi, Jr., "Putting the Cuffs on Capitalism," *Fortune*, April 1975, pp. 104–07, 222; and Murray Weidenbaum, "The New Wave of Government Regulation of Business," *Business and Society Review* 15 (Fall 1975): 81–6.

25. For a summary of the role of the government in supporting the efforts of the public interest movement, see Lynn E. Cunningham, et al., *Strengthening Citizen Access and Governmental Accountability* (Washington, D.C.: Exploratory Project for Economic Alternatives, 1977); and R. A. Frank, J. N. Onek, and J. B. Steinberg, *Policy Participation in the Policy Formulation Process* (Washington, D.C.: Center for Law and Social Policy, 1977). For a more critical appraisal, see Richard B. Stewart, "The Reformation of American Administrative Law," *Harvard Law Review* 88, no. 8 (1975): 1669–1813.

## CHAPTER 2

1. Robert H. Brisbane, *Black Activism* (Valley Forge: Judson Press, 1974), pp. 21–72. Also see August Meier and Elliot Rudwick, *CORE: A Study in the Civil Rights Movement* (Urbana, Ill.: University of Illinois Press, 1975), pp. 101–24; "Races: The Revolution," *Time*, June 7, 1963, pp. 19–21; and "The Boycott Road to Rights," *Time*, June 7, 1962, p. 95.

2. Brisbane, *Black Activism*, p. 38.

3. Ibid., p. 39.

4. Ibid., p. 37.

5. Ibid., p. 43.

6. Ibid., p. 49.

7. Meier and Rudwick, *CORE*, p. 111.

8. Ibid., p. 122.

9. Brisbane, *Black Activism*, pp. 53–57, and Meier and Rudwick, *CORE*, pp. 134–44.

10. Marvin Rich, "CORE and Its Strategy," *Annals of the American Academy of Political and Social Science* 357 (January 1965): 113–18. The remainder of this paragraph is based on Meier and Rudwick, *CORE*, pp. 182–201, 233–36, and "The Boycott Road to Rights." See also, "Some New Tactics in Civil Rights: Push," *U.S. News and World Report*, March 16, 1964, p. 52.

11. This later tactic became an "official" part of American business life: in Arthur Hailey's *The Money Changers* (New York: Doubleday & Co., 1975), a fictional portrait of the contemporary banking industry, the girlfriend of the novel's hero is upset about the bank's decision to reduce its financial commitment to a low-income housing project. She conspires with community leaders to force the bank to reverse itself. A sympathetic municipal union distributes five dollars to each of several hundred residents of the project to enable them to open their own savings accounts. By prearrangement,

all converge on a single branch, effectively tying up virtually all its personnel for several hours. They then reappear in order to withdraw a small portion of their accounts. Needless to say, by the time several hundred minority members appear outside the door of a second branch, virtue triumphs: the bank renews its commitment and the community activist's lover subsequently becomes the bank's new president.

12. Meier and Rudwick, CORE, pp. 191–92.

13. Ibid.

14. This account is based on a case study by S. Prakash Sethi, "The Bank of America—CORE Disputes on Equal Employment Opportunity," *Up Against the Corporate Wall* (Englewood Cliffs, N.J.: Prentice-Hall, 1971), pp. 129–59.

15. Ibid., p. 130.

16. Ibid., pp. 148, 150.

17. Ibid., p. 141.

18. "Negro Leaders Tell Their Plans for '64," *U.S. News and World Report*, February 12, 1964, p. 76.

19. Sethi, *Up Against the Corporate Wall*, p. 140.

20. Adolf A. Berle, Jr., *The Twentieth-Century Capitalist Revolution* (New York: Harcourt Brace & World, 1954), p. 188.

21. See chapter 4 for a further discussion of this issue.

22. Meier and Rudwick, CORE, p. 229.

23. This section is based primarily on the following sources: S. Prakash Sethi, *Business Corporations and the Black Man: An Analysis of Social Conflict: The Kodak-FIGHT Controversy* (Scranton, Pa.: Chandler Publishing Company, 1970); "Eastman Kodak and FIGHT," a case prepared by Francis Sheridan under the direction of Professor Howard F. Bennett (Boston: Inter-Collegiate Case Clearinghouse, no. 9–412–068, 1967); "FIGHT and Eastman Kodak," a case prepared by Francis Sheridan under the direction of Professor Howard F. Bennett incorporating new material prepared by Linda Waters under the direction of Professor George C. Lodge (Boston: Inter-Collegiate Case Clearinghouse, no. 9–373–207, 1973); James Ridgeway, "Attack on Kodak," *New Republic*, January 21, 1967, pp. 13–14; and an interview with Ed Chambers.

24. Sheridan, "FIGHT and Eastman Kodak," p. 2.

25. Sethi, *Business Corporations and the Black Man*, p. 113.

26. Sheridan, "FIGHT and Eastman Kodak," p. 12.

27. Sethi, *Business Corporations and the Black Man*, p. 118.

28. Ibid., p. 21.

29. Ibid., p. 22.

30. Ibid.

31. Sheridan, "FIGHT and Eastman Kodak," p. 6.

32. Ibid., p. 118.

33. Sethi, *Business Corporations and the Black Man*, p. 79.

34. Sheridan, "FIGHT and Eastman Kodak," p. 9.

35. Sethi, *Business Corporations and the Black Man*, p. 33.

36. Ibid., p. 120.

37. Ibid., pp. 118–19.

38. Ridgeway, "Attack on Kodak," p. 12.

39. Sethi, *Business Corporations and the Black Man*, p. 37.

40. Saul D. Alinsky, *Rules for Radicals* (New York: Vintage Books, 1971), pp. 169, 173.

41. Sethi, *Business Corporations and the Black Man*, p. 39.

42. Ibid., p. 40.

43. As quoted in Sheridan, "FIGHT and Eastman Kodak," p. 11.

44. As quoted in Ibid., p. 13.

45. This account is based on the following sources: American Committee on Africa, "A Summary Report on the Bank Campaign Against the Consortium Loan to South Africa"; interview with Todd Gitlin; interview with George Houser; and "Banks and South Africa," *New Republic*, December 17, 1966, pp. 6–7.

46. Interview with George Houser.

47. American Committee on Africa, "A Summary Report," p. 3.

48. Ibid., p. 4.

49. Ibid., p. 1.

50. Ibid., p. 6.

51. This account of PUSH primarily draws from Barbara A. Reynolds, *Jesse Jackson: The Man, The Movement, The Myth* (Chicago: Nelson-Hall, 1975); and Robert Cassidy, "Jesse Jackson: Will Push Come To Shove?" *Business and Society Review/Innovation* 10 (Summer 1974), pp. 55–63. Also see Paul Delaney, "Operation PUSH Gains Strength in its Second Year," *New York Times*, June 2, 1973, p. 21.

52. Reynolds, *Jesse Jackson*, p. 109.

53. Ibid., p. 132.

54. Ibid., p. 137.

55. "The Sit-in at A&P Was No Tea Party," *Business Week*, February 6, 1971, p. 21.

56. Ibid.

57. Reynolds, *Jesse Jackson*, p. 151.

58. See Irving Kristol, "On Corporate Capitalism in America," *The Public Interest*, no. 41 (Fall 1975), p. 126.

59. See, for example, the special issue of *Fortune* magazine focusing on business and the urban crisis, *Fortune* 77, no. 1 (January 1968).

60. "The Port Huron Statement," quoted in Charles Perrow, *The Radical Attack on Business* (New York: Harcourt Brace Jovanovich, 1972), p. 14.

61. Todd Gitlin, "Power and the Myth of Progress," quoted in Perrow, *The Radical Attack*, p. 9.

62. Carl Oglesby, "Trapped in a System," in Perrow, *The Radical Attack*, p. 23.

63. This account is based primarily on two cases distributed by the Inter-Collegiate Case Clearinghouse, Boston: S. Prakash Sethi, "Dow Shalt Not Kill," 1970, no. 9–414–030; and Lawrence J. Lasser, "Dow Chemical Company," under the supervision of Professor George Albert Smith, Jr., 1968, revised 1971 by Barbara Pendergast and George C. Lodge, no. 9–312–029. It also draws upon Saul Friedman, "This Napalm Business," in Robert Heilbroner et al., eds., *In the Name of Profit* (New York: Doubleday & Co., 1972), pp. 128–53; and Ellis N. Brandt, "NAPALM—Public Relations Storm Center," *Public Relations Journal* (July 1968): pp. 12–15.

64. Brandt, "NAPALM," p. 12.

65. For a detailed account of this confrontation, see Kirkpatrick Sale, *SDS* (New York: Vintage Books, 1973), p. 374.

66. See Maurice Ford, "Dow at Harvard: The Right to Recruit on College Campuses," *New Republic*, November 11, 1967, pp. 11–13.

67. Lasser, "Dow Chemical Company," p. 9.

68. Brandt, "NAPALM," p. 13.

69. Sale, *SDS*, p. 382.

70. See George Wald, "Corporate Responsibility for War Crimes," *New York Review of Books*, July 2, 1970, pp. 4–6.

71. Sethi, "Dow Shalt Not Kill," p. 18.

72. Medical Committee for Human Rights v. SEC, 432 F 2d, 659 (DC Cir 1970), in Norman D. Lattin, Richard W. Jennings, and Richard M. Buxbaum, *Corporations—Cases and Materials*, 1975 Supplement (Chicago: Callaghan & Company, 1970).

73. Ibid. Young added the latter clause on the advice of his counsel in order to make the resolution qualify under SEC rules.

74. Ibid.

75. Ibid., p. 13. Both these arguments constituted legal grounds for the exclusion of shareholder proposals under the provisions of Rule 14a–8.

76. Sethi, "Dow Shalt Not Kill," p. 19.

77. Brandt, "NAPALM," p. 15.

78. Sethi, "Dow Shalt Not Kill," p. 20.

79. Ibid.

80. Ibid., p. 15.

81. Ibid., p. 13.

82. Ibid., p. 25. Also see "The Garbage Burner," *New Republic*, July 26, 1969, pp. 7–8.

# References

83. Brandt, "NAPALM," p. 14.
84. Lasser, "Dow Chemical Company," p. 15.
85. Friedman, "This Napalm Business," p. 150.
86. Richard Fernandez, one of the national organizers of the protests against Dow, reports that an executive at Dow privately informed him that the protests had been responsible for the cessation of Dow's napalm production. According to Friedman, Dow was informed that the American Electric Company of Los Angeles was planning to submit a bid to produce napalm, thus giving them a way out. Their bid was identical to the one they had offered the previous year—about twelve cents a pound. Friedman also concludes that Dow deliberately did not submit a competitive bid.
87. Sethi, "Dow Shalt Not Kill," p. 21. Both Gerstacker and Dow identified themselves as personally opposed to the war.
88. Ibid., p. 8.
89. Lasser, "Dow Chemical Company," p. 16.
90. Sethi, "Dow Shalt Not Kill," p. 21.
91. Sethi, "Dow Shalt Not Kill," p. 24 and Lasser, "Dow Chemical Company," p. 16.
92. Sethi, "Dow Shalt Not Kill," p. 24.
93. Medical Committee v. SEC, p. 16. For an extended discussion of the significance of the ruling that focuses on the relationship between corporate law and corporate social responsibility, see Marvin A. Chirelstein, "Corporate Law Reform," in *Social Responsibility and the Business Predicament,* ed. James W. McKie (Washington, D.C.: The Brookings Institution, 1974), pp. 41–78. Chirelstein suggests that even if Dow's managers had been more circumspect in their public utterances, the company's shareholders might still be entitled to vote on their own ideas of what constitutes social responsibility and what are the conditions for long run economic survival. This is the case, for example, when shareholders propose resolutions condemning the use of corporate assets for philanthropic purposes (pp. 62–63).
94. Brandt, "NAPALM," p. 15.
95. "Activists Lay Plans for War on Gulf," *Business Week,* April 11, 1970, p. 23.
96. Quoted in Henry C. Egerton, "Handling Protests at Annual Meetings" (New York: Conference Board, 1971), pp. 5, 7.
97. This paragraph is based on "1970 Annual Meetings: Corporate Policies Challenged," *Economic Priorities Report* 1, no. 2 (Summer 1970): 1–13; and Gene Maeroff, "Stinging the Corporations," *Nation,* June 22, 1970, pp. 753–56; see also "An Activist Agenda for Annual Meetings," *Business Week,* March 28, 1970, pp. 45–6.
98. Egerton, "Handling Protests," pp. 58–9.
99. Maeroff, "Stinging the Corporations," p. 754.
100. See Phillip I. Blumberg, "The Politicization of the Corporation," *Business Lawyer* 26 (1971): 1552; and "The Corporation Becomes a Target," *Time,* May 11, 1970, pp. 94–5.
An executive from Gulf remarked:
   . . . From another direction we were suddenly beleaguered by a more radical group of critics who had decided to shift their focus from the campus and the Pentagon to the board room or to the stockholders meeting. [Quoted in Charles W. Powers, ed., *People/Profits* (New York: Council on Religious Affairs, 1972), p. 174.]
101. "Violence in America: One Company's Position," reprinted by the Bank of America. For a fuller statement of the position of the bank's management, see Louis B. Lundborg, "The Lessons of the Isla Vista," *Business Lawyer* 26 (1971): 943–52.
102. *Ramparts,* Cover, May 1970.
103. "IBM, Chase Manhattan and Bank of America Criticized for Fueling the War," *Economic Priorities Report* 1, no. 2 (Summer 1970): 8.
104. "Bank of America Annual Meeting Protest," *Economic Priorities Report* 2, no. 1 (April–May, 1971): 9.
105. "The Antiwar Bank," *New Republic,* April 10, 1971, pp. 12–13.
106. Egerton, "Handling Protests," p. vii; see also Michael Traynor, "Protest Demonstrations," *Business Lawyer,* April 1971, pp. 1329–43. Traynor offered a guideline for the managements of companies preparing for a demonstration.
107. Egerton, "Handling Protests," pp. 14–15.

108. This section is based primarily on the following sources: the publications, pamphlets, and memos of Clergy and Laymen Concerned; "Antipersonnel Weapons: Honeywell," *Analysis*, no. 2 (April 2, 1973), Investor Responsibility Research Center (hereafter cited as IRRC); "Reports on Military Production Activities," *Analysis*, no. 11 (April 16, 1974), IRRC; Jesse E. Christman and Hugh C. White, Jr., "Honeywell, Inc. and the Bomb," distributed by Institute of the Church in Urban-Industrial Society, no. 1045; James Munves, *Minding the Corporate Conscience* (New York: Julian Messner, 1974), pp. 83–96; interview with Richard Fernandez; interview with Trudi Schutz, née Young.

109. "Honeywell Meeting Adjourned to Avoid Protest Activities," *Economic Priorities Report* 1, no. 2 (Summer 1970): 13.

110. Munves, *Minding*, p. 85.

111. Christman and White, "Honeywell, Inc.," app. 1, p. 1.

112. "Interview with Marv Davidov," pamphlet published by NARMIC, 1970, pp. 2–3.

113. Christman and White, "Honeywell, Inc.," p. 9.

114. Ibid., p. 1.

115. Ibid., p. 8.

116. "CALC Joins Corporate Struggle," *American Report*, March 3, 1972, p. 3.

117. Ibid.

118. Interview with Richard Fernandez.

119. Interview with Trudi Schutz.

120. "Church Investments, Technological Warfare and the Military-Industrial Complex," New York Corporate Information Center, 1972.

121. "CALC Corporate Campaign Aimed at Major Military Contractors," *American Report*, April 14, 1972, p. 3.

122. Dick Usher, "Honeywell Campaign Meets the Press," *American Report*, May 5, 1972, p. 8.

123. "CALC Corporate Campaign," p. 12.

124. Ibid.

125. "An Occasional Memo," *Clergy and Laity Concerned*, May 10, 1972, p. 2.

126. Ibid.

127. Reported in Munves, *Minding*, pp. 93–4.

128. The above statements are drawn from Schomer's presentation at the 1973 and 1974 annual meetings; press release, Minnesota Conference, United Church of Christ, April 25, 1973; press release, Office of Community, United Church of Christ, May 8, 1974.

129. "CALC vs. Honeywell," *American Report*, March 24, 1972, p. 2.

130. Richard A. Falk, "The Basis of Moral and Legal Responsibility for Corporations in Relation to the Indo-China War," unpublished mimeo, pp. 5–6. A similar argument was made by Harvard Nobel Laureate George Wald about the responsibilities of Dow Chemical's management. See Wald, "Corporate Responsibility," p. 6, where he argued that the "civilian sector [was] . . . where much of the special interest and political powers are based."

131. "An Occasional Memo," *Clergy and Laity Concerned*, February 22, 1973, pp. 2–3.

132. Interview with Trudi Schutz.

133. Honeywell press release, April 18, 1972, quoted in "Honeywell Responds," *American Report*, May 5, 1972, p. 9.

134. "Reports on Military Production Activities," IRRC, p. 9.

135. Honeywell press release, April 18, 1972, quoted in "Honeywell Responds."

136. Michael C. Jensen, "ACLU Suit Says Honeywell Conspired with F.B.I.," *New York Times*, April 21, 1977, pp. 1, 51. According to the ACLU statement:
> The FBI engaged "paid informants" to infiltrate, surveil and report on our clients' activities. . . . The information collected by the FBI . . . was indiscriminately disseminated to Honeywell officials, . . . the "White House," "the Department of Justice," "the military services," and the "Defense Contracts Administration Services."

Furthermore, the ACLU statement says:
> Starting in 1969, a Honeywell official ("Robert Roe") acted as "a confidential

# References

(FBI) source in the company's management." . . . The evidence suggests that Honeywell asked for and encouraged all of the illegal and unconstitutional conduct of the FBI. In addition, Honeywell participated in and cooperated with the FBI in planning, arranging, and carrying out these illegal and unconstitutional activities. The suit filed by the ACLU charges Honeywell with:

. . . failing to disclose the Honeywell/FBI conspiracy to its shareholders in the corporation's annual proxy solicitation materials for the years 1970–1974. . . . Honeywell's failure to reveal all material information was a violation of the Securities Act of 1934 and SEC regulations.

See ACLU press conference release, April 21, 1977, at the Minnesota Press Club, Raddison Hotel, issued by the ACLU, New York.

137. Quoted in "Honeywell Responds," p. 9.

138. Dick Usher, "Honeywell Declines to Turn Swords into Plowshares," *American Report*, May 12, 1972, p. 3.

139. "Antipersonnel Weapons: Honeywell, Inc.," IRRC, p. 8.

140. Usher, "Honeywell Declines," p. 3.

141. Honeywell press release, "Honeywell Responds," p. 9.

142. "The B–1 Bomber and Corporate Defense Contracts," *Analysis*, no. 9 (March 27, 1975), IRRC, p. 1.

143. Kay Halvorson, "To Build the Future: A Look at the Past," pamphlet produced by Minnesota CALC (n.d.), p. 2.

144. Byron E. Calame, "Rockwell Listens to Roar of Holders Over Its B1 Bomber," *Wall Street Journal*, February 13, 1976, p. 6.

145. Paul Fitzgerald, et al., "Rockwell International," Pacific Northwest Research Center, 1975; James Conroy and Paul d'Eustachio, "Boom and Bust," Environmental Action Foundation, 1975; Gordon Adams, "The B–1 Bomber," Report by Council on Economic Priorities, 1974.

146. Interview with Gordon Adams.

147. "The B–1 Bomber Program: Social and Environmental Issues," *Analysis* A, Supplement, no. 2 (April 2, 1976), IRRC, p. 2.

148. Interview with Gordon Adams.

149. Interview with Trudi Schutz.

150. David Dworsky, "New Annual Meeting Note: Social Protest," *New York Times*, May 28, 1967, Business and Finance Section III, pp. 1, 14.

# CHAPTER 3

1. The discussion of Campaign GM is based on the following sources: the publications of the Project on Corporate Responsibility; Donald E. Schwartz, "Toward New Corporate Goals: Co-Existence with Society," *Georgetown Law Journal* 60 (1971): 57–104; Donald E. Schwartz, "Proxy Power and Social Goals—How Campaign GM Succeeded," *St. Johns Law Review* 45 (1971): 764–71. E. J. Kahn, Jr., "We Look Forward to Seeing You Next Year," *New Yorker*, June 20, 1970, pp. 40–52; "Campaign to Make General Motors Responsible," a case prepared by Professor W. Collins (Boston: Inter-Collegiate Case Clearinghouse, no. 9–371–660); "Corporate Performance and Private Criticism—Campaign GM: Rounds I and II," a case prepared by Mrs. A. T. Sproat under the direction of Professor C. Roland Christensen (Boston: Inter-Collegiate Case Clearinghouse, Harvard University, no. 9–372–026, revised September 1971); Norman Pearlstine, "Activist Shareholders Provoke GM Offensive at Its Annual Meeting," *Wall Street Journal*, May 21, 1970, pp. 1, 8; Norman Pearlstine, "GM Management Wins Smashing Victories Over Social Critics at Its Annual Meeting," *Wall Street Journal*, May 24, 1971, p. 10; Philip W. Moore, "What's Good for the Country is Good for GM," *Washington Monthly* 2 (December 1970): 10–18; interviews with Susan Gross, Donald E. Schwartz, Philip Moore, Joseph Onek, and George Coombe; Jesse E. Christman and Hugh C. White, Jr., "Campaign GM—Round II and General Motors—November 1970–May 1971," distributed by the Institute on the Church in Urban-Industrial Society, no. 1049; Donald E. Schwartz, "Corporate Responsibility in the Age of

Aquarius," *The Business Lawyer* (November 1970): 513–31, and "The Public Interest Proxy Contest: Reflections on Campaign GM," *Michigan Law Review* 69 (January 1971): 421–45; Chris Welles, "The Greening of James Roche," *New York Magazine*, December 21, 1970, pp. 35–8.

2. Peter Drucker, *Concept of the Corporation* (New York: John Day Co., 1946).
3. Blumberg, "Politicization of the Corporation," p. 1564.
4. Robert Dahl, *After the Revolution* (New Haven: Yale University Press, 1970), p. 120.
5. Interview with Joseph Onek.
6. For a detailed description of this incident, see Sethi, "General Motors' Nadir, Ralph Nader," *Up Against the Corporate Wall*, pp. 189–214.
7. Interview with Joseph Onek.
8. Moore, "What's Good for the Country," pp. 10–11.
9. Schwartz, "Public Interest Proxy Contest," p. 422.
10. The full statement reads: "For in the last analysis, no court decision, no new law, no public sentiment is meaningfully implemented without the full commitment of corporations to the decision, or to the law, or to the public sentiment," Philip Moore, Campaign GM press conference, Philadelphia, April 1, 1971.
11. Project on Corporate Responsibility, "Proposal for Support," March 1972, p. 2.
12. Collins, "Campaign to Make General Motors Responsible," p. 3.
13. "Project on Corporate Responsibility," *News and Thoughts*, Summer 1971, p. 1.
14. Schwartz, "Public Interest Proxy Contest," pp. 485, 487.
15. Moore, "What's Good for the Country," p. 15; and Moore, Campaign GM press conference, Philadelphia, April 1, 1971.
16. Project on Corporate Responsibility Inc., "Proposal for Support," September 1972, p. 5.
17. Abram Chayes, "The Modern Corporation and the Role of Law," in *The Corporation in Modern Society*, ed. Edward S. Mason (New York: Atheneum, 1966), p. 39.
18. Ibid.
19. See James Willard Hurst, *The Legitimacy of the Business Corporation* (Charlottesville: University Press of Virginia, 1970), for a discussion of this development, especially chap. 11.
20. David P. Riley, "Taming GM, Ford, Union Carbide, U.S. Steel, and Dow Chemical," in *With Justice for Some*, ed. Mark Green and Bruce Warrenstein (Boston: Beacon Press, 1970), p. 257.
21. Quoted in Collins, "Campaign to Make General Motors Responsible," p. 2.
22. Schwartz, "Corporate Responsibility," p. 520.
23. Quoted in Collins, "Campaign to Make General Motors Responsible," p. 2.
24. Blumberg, "Politicization of the Corporation," p. 1563.
25. Schwartz, "Public Interest Proxy Contest," pp. 485, 530.
26. Luther J. Carter, "Campaign GM: Corporation Critics Seek Support of Universities," *Science* 168 (April 24, 1970): 152.
27. Quoted in Schwartz, "Public Interest Proxy Contest," p. 438. This was the section of the act to which the business community was most opposed.
28. "Proxy Rule 14a–8: Omission of Shareholder Proposals," *Harvard Law Review* 84 (1971): 700–28.
29. Ibid., pp. 707–8.
30. Ibid., p. 708. The principle underlying the commission's ruling, however, remained uncertain, in part because of the ambiguity of the proposal itself: did it refer to Greyhound's practices or the entire system of segregated bus seating in the South? Moreover, the proposal might also have been inappropriate on the ground that it conflicted with state laws that made integrated seating illegal.
31. Ibid.
32. Schwartz, "Public Interest Proxy Contest," p. 452.
33. Ibid., pp. 452–53.
34. Interview with James Needham.
35. Ibid.
36. For a more extended discussion of the legal aspects of the Dow case and the commission's ruling on Campaign GM, see: "Comment: SEC Shareholder Proposal

# References

Rule 14a–8: Impact of the 1972 Amendments," *Georgetown Law Journal* 61 (1973): 781; Henry G. Manne, "Shareholder Social Proposals Viewed by an Opponent," *Stanford Law Review* 24 (1972): 481–506; Charles A. Bane, "Shareholder Proposals on Public Issues," *Business Lawyer* 26 (1971): 1017–26; "Liberalizing SEC Rule 14a–8 Through the Use of Advisory Proposals," *Yale Law Journal* 80 (1971): 845–64; Patrick H. Allen, "The Proxy System and Promotion of Social Goals," *Business Lawyer* 26 (1970): 481–95.

37. Schwartz, "Corporate Responsibility," p. 523.
38. Pearlstine, "Activist Shareholders Provoke," p. 1.
39. Schwartz, "Corporate Responsibility," p. 523.
40. All quotes in this paragraph are from Pearlstine, "Activist Shareholders Provoke," pp. 1, 8.
41. Schwartz, "Public Interest Proxy Contest," p. 506.
42. "Businessmen in the News: James Roche," *Fortune*, June 1970, p. 31.
43. Quoted in Collins, "Campaign to Make General Motors Responsible," p. 4.
44. Quoted in Kahn, "We Look Forward," p. 50.
45. Ibid., p. 51.
46. Ibid.
47. "GM's Ordeal May Set the Fashion," *Business Week*, May 30, 1970, p. 84.
48. Quoted in Schwartz, "Public Interest Proxy Contest," p. 478.
49. "GM Makes Criticism a Family Affair," *Business Week*, September 5, 1970, p. 17.
50. Ibid.
51. "A Black Director Pushes Reforms at GM," *Business Week*, April 10, 1971, p. 100.
52. Welles, "Greening of James Roche," pp. 36–37.
53. Christman and White, "Campaign GM—Round II," p. 22.
54. Welles, "Greening of James Roche," p. 35.
55. Pearlstine, "GM Management Wins," p. 10; also see, "Dissent Knocks at the Corporate Walls," *Business and Society Review* 3, no. 22 (May 13, 1971): 1. For a discussion of the reaction of the universities to the issue, see Marilyn Bender, "Universities' Corporate Voice," *New York Times*, April 4, 1971, section 3, p. 1.
56. Pearlstine, "GM Management Wins," p. 10.
57. Ibid.
58. This section is based primarily on the following material: Alma Smaby, "The CAPUR Crusade," *Progressive*, July 1974, pp. 19–23; "Fall Corporate Challenge," brief of Corporate Information Center (hereafter cited as CIC), August 1973; publications of the Council for Corporate Review and the Coalition to Advocate Public Utility Responsibility (CAPUR); issues of *Taking Stock*.
59. CAPUR pamphlet, p. 1.
60. Letter to author from Frederick Smith, September 12, 1975.
61. Quoted in CAPUR public statement.
62. "Little Guys Want Public Advocate," *Taking Stock*, n. 1, p. 1.
63. Quoted in Smaby, "The CAPUR Crusade," p. 21.
64. Ibid.
65. Quoted in "Fall Corporate Challenge," p. 3B.
66. CIC editorial, "Northern States Power: Beating the Challenge by Changing the Rules?" *Corporate Examiner* 2, no. 5 (May 1973), p. 2.
67. Smaby, "The CAPUR Crusade," p. 21.
68. Ibid.
69. Ibid., p. 22.
70. Ibid.
71. Ibid.
72. Blumberg, "Politicization of the Corporation," p. 1561.
73. See Robert J. Larner, *Management Control and the Large Corporation* (New York: Dunellon Publishing Co., 1970). The statistics in this and the following paragraph are from Phillip I. Blumberg, *The Mega Corporation in American Society* (Englewood Cliffs, N.J.: Prentice-Hall, 1975), especially chap. 5, pp. 84–144.
74. Adolf A. Berle, Jr., and Gardiner C. Means, *The Modern Corporation and*

*Private Property* (New York: Macmillan Co., 1932); see also Peter F. Drucker, *America's Next Twenty Years* (New York: Harper & Row, 1957).

75. Adolf A. Berle, Jr., *Power Without Property* (New York: Harcourt Brace & World, 1959), p. 50.

76. James Willard Hurst, *The Legitimacy of the Business Corporation in the Law of the United States, 1780–1970* (Charlottesville: University Press of Virginia, 1970), p. 87.

77. Bevis Longstreth and H. David Rosenbloom, *Corporate Social Responsibility and the Institutional Investor* (New York: Praeger Publishers, 1973), pp. 42–43.

78. Ibid., p. 81.

79. Ibid., pp. 82–83.

80. Ibid., p. 83.

81. John G. Simon, Charles W. Powers, and Jon P. Gunnemann, *The Ethical Investor—Universities and Corporate Responsibility* (New Haven: Yale University Press, 1970), p. 7.

82. Ibid.

83. Ibid., p. 17.

84. Ibid., p. 65.

85. Quoted in Longstreth and Rosenbloom, *Corporate Social Responsibility*, p. 79.

86. Marilyn Bender, "Investment Return vs. Social Role," *New York Times*, April 4, 1971, section 3, p. 1.

87. Note, for example, the contrast between Harvard's involvement and that of Yale's. See Keith Roberts, "Shareholder Votes: Has Business Won Harvard's Heart?" *Business and Society Review* no. 20 (Winter 1976–77), pp. 65–67; and Charles W. Powers, "Ethical Inventory: Yale's Third Year as a Responsible Investor," *Yale Alumni Magazine*, January 1976, pp. 43–44.

88. See Ann Crittenden, "Teachers Wield Their Proxies," *New York Times*, March 19, 1978, section 3, pp. 1, 13.

89. See "What One Foundation Does About Corporate Responsibility," *Business and Social Review/Innovation* no. 6 (Summer 1973), pp. 56–7.

90. Longstreth and Rosenbloom, *Corporate Social Responsibility*, p. 2.

91. Interview with Roger Kennedy. See also, Roger G. Kennedy, "Portfolio Decisions and Social Responsibility," in *Social Responsibility and Accountability*, ed. Jules Backman (New York: New York University Press, 1975), pp. 137–45.

92. See "Utility Challenges," *Corporate Examiner* 3, no. 10 (October 1974): 1.

93. Letter from Wade Rathke to author, December 12, 1974.

94. Quoted in Terry Robards, "Organization Created to Assess Corporate Role in Social Issues," *New York Times*, December 14, 1972, pp. 71, 78.

95. For a discussion of IRRC's subsequent history, see Robert J. McCartney, "Research Firm Finds a Booming Business for its Impartial Studies of Public Issue," *Wall Street Journal*, September 4, 1974, p. 20.

96. Quoted in "Research," *Economic Priorities Report* 4, no. 1 (January/February/March 1973): 48.

97. See CIC editorial, "A New Center for Corporate Responsibility," *Economic Priorities Report* 4, no. 1 (January/February/March 1973): 49.

98. Interview with Elliott Weiss.

99. Hugh Jeffery Leonard, "Institutional Investors and Corporate Governance: Transcending the Wall Street Rule," (senior thesis, Department of Government, Harvard College, March 25, 1968) p. 4. The basic arguments in both this section and the following one on "The Corporate Watergate" owe much to Leonard's detailed and thorough analysis. Leonard also served as an intern with IRRC.

For additional discussion of the changes in the role of institutional investors, particularly in the profit sector, see "How Institutions Voted on Shareholder Resolutions, 1974," *IRRC Special Reports*, December 1974; Jeffery Leonard and Jamie Heard, "How Institutions Voted in 1975 on Shareholder Resolutions and Management Proposals," *IRRC Special Report* 1975–C, September 1975; Elliott J. Weiss, "How Institutions Voted in 1976 on Shareholder Resolutions and Management Proposals," *IRRC Special Report* 1976–B, August 1976; "Investor Responsibility: Problems and Prospects," *IRRC Special Report* A, January 18, 1974; Peter Landau, "Do Institutional Investors Have a

# References

Social Responsibility?" *Institutional Investor*, July 1970, pp. 25–33, 81–88; Elliott Weiss, "Proxy Voting On Social Issues: A Growth Industry," *Business and Society Review*, no. 17 (Autumn 1974), pp. 16–22; Phillip I. Blumberg, Eli Goldston, and George D. Gibson, "Corporate Social Responsibility Panel: The Constituencies of the Corporation and the Role of the Institutional Investors," *Business Lawyer* 28 (1973): 177–213; Marilyn Bender, "Stockholder Dissent: Activists Win Support of Institutions," *New York Times*, July 8, 1973, section 4, p. 3.

100. Leonard and Heard, "How Institutions Voted, 1975."

101. Quoted in "Investor Responsibility: Problems and Prospects," pp. 3, 4.

102. "Institutions that Balk at Anti-Social Management," *Business Week*, January 19, 1974, p. 67.

103. Interview with institutional investment manager, quoted in Leonard, "Institutional Investors and Corporate Governance," p. 128.

104. For example, in 1977 the Bank of America disclosed that it had voted against the recommendation of management on a total of 164 shareholders resolutions affecting 122 companies.

105. Emma Latham, *A Place for Murder* (New York: New York Pocket Books, 1963, 1972), p. 66. Latham's account appears remarkably prescient.

106. Telephone conversation between Leonard and a pension fund manager, quoted in Leonard, "Institutional Investors and Corporate Governance," p. 135.

107. Kenneth Bacon and Mitchell Lynch, "Firms That Have Illegal Campaign Gifts Now Encounter SEC, IRS, Shareholders," *Wall Street Journal*, April 8, 1975, p. 34; "Proxy Statements Feel the Watergate Ripples," *Business Week*, April 13, 1974, p. 89. The most comprehensive discussion of shareholder activism and illegal domestic corporate political activity is Elliott Weiss, "The Corporate Watergate," *IRRC Special Report 1975–D*, October 1975; see also Henry Weinstein, "Stockholders versus Payoffs," *New York Times*, March 14, 1976, section 2, pp. 1, 7.

108. Quoted in Leonard, "Institutional Investors and Corporate Governance," p. 104.

109. Weiss, "Corporate Watergate," p. 73. The proceedings of the conference are reported in "Panelists Urge Institutional Investors to Push Corporations on Ethical Standards," *News for Investors* 3, no. 1 (January 1976): 13–18.

110. Quoted in Leonard, "Institutional Investors and Corporate Governance," p. 87.

111. Leonard and Heard, "How Institutions Voted, 1975."

112. "Panelists Urge Institutional Investors," p. 16.

113. Ibid., pp. 16–17.

114. Ibid., p. 18.

115. See Thomas Jones, "Shareholder Suits: A Contemporary Survey of Their Utilization" (Ph.D. diss., School of Business Administration, University of California, Berkeley, 1977).

116. "Corporate Democracy and the Corporate Political Contribution," *Iowa Law Review* 61, no. 2 (December 1975): 545–79.

117. The Project on Corporate Responsibility also filed proxy resolutions to five corporations concerning corporate political activity in 1974. In an interview with the author, Susan Gross, who worked with the project, recalled, "Once we learned of all those campaign funds, we knew business had to be involved. Where else could Nixon have secured such large sums?"

118. For a detailed discussion of the Northrop case, see Sethi, "Northrop Corporation, Los Angeles," *Up Against the Corporate Wall*, pp. 179–93; and "Silver Cloud, Dark Lining," *Forbes*, December 15, 1974, p. 40. The settlement of the Phillips case is discussed in Henry Weinstein, "Phillips Petroleum Agrees to Change in Reply to Suit," *New York Times*, February 19, 1976, pp. 1, 55.

119. Weinstein, "Stockholders versus Payoffs," p. 7.

120. Robert Lindsey, "Northrop Shareholders Focus on Rising Profit, Not on Bribes," *New York Times*, May 12, 1976, p. 57.

121. Ibid.

122. Ibid., p. 69.

123. Weinstein, "Phillips Petroleum Agrees," p. 55.

124. Ibid.

125. Ibid.

126. Detailed accounts of the Gulf case can be found in Byron E. Calame, "Mellon Interests Are Likely to Force Gulf to Shift Management in Wake of Scandals," *Wall Street Journal*, January 13, 1976, p. 38; and Wyndham Robertson, "The Directors Woke Up Too Late at Gulf," *Fortune*, June 1976, pp. 121–25, 206–10.

127. In an interview in *Industry Week*, Scully stated:

I think [shareholder activists] are very important. The better able they are to formulate proposals and resolutions with sufficient documentation and careful thought, the more helpful it is to the corporation. Businesses tend to be insulated from the normal public opinion and some of the views held by the social and religious groups of this country. Proposals that are presented at the shareholders' meeting are very beneficial in helping the corporation to know where people's thoughts and views are.

Quoted in Vivian C. Pospisil, "Shareholder Activists File More and More Resolutions," *Industry Week*, February 23, 1976, pp. 15–16.

128. John C. Perham, "Annual Meetings—Dissidents on the Attack," *Dun's Review*, April 1976, p. 55.

129. Ibid., p. 58.

130. Quoted in John C. Perham, "Stockholder Showdown—1974," *Dun's Review*, April 1974, p. 55.

131. Quoted in Donald E. Schwartz and Elliott J. Weiss, "An Assessment of the SEC Shareholder Proposal Rule," *Georgetown Law Journal* 65, no. 3 (February 1977): 638–39.

132. "SEC Shareholder Proposal Rule 14a–8," p. 793.

133. Ibid., p. 784.

134. Ibid., p. 795.

135. Carol H. Falk, "SEC Is Rewriting Its Rules on Screening Holders' Bids for Annual Meeting Votes," *Wall Street Journal*, April 19, 1976, p. 3.

136. See Schwartz and Weiss, "An Assessment," for a detailed legal summary and analysis of the SEC's revisions. The account that follows is drawn from "SEC Announces Revisions of Rule 14a–8," *News for Investors* 3, no. 11 (December 1976): 229–36.

137. Falk, "SEC Is Rewriting," p. 3.

138. "SEC Announces Revisions," p. 232.

139. Ibid.

140. Ibid., p. 233.

141. Ibid.

142. "SEC Asks for Comments by September 7 on Proposals to Change Proxy Rules," *News for Investors* 3, no. 7 (July/August 1976): 153.

143. For a yearly chronicle, see, for example, "Social Activists Switch to Proxy Power," *Business Week*, February 13, 1971, pp. 38–39; "The Moral Power of Shareholders," *Business Week*, May 1, 1971, pp. 76–8; "Campaign GM Was Just for Starters," *Business Week*, February 12, 1972, pp. 21–22; "Social Activists Stir Up the Annual Meeting," *Business Week*, April 1, 1972, pp. 48–49; "Activists Step Up Annual Attacks," *Business Week*, March 31, 1973, pp. 76–7; Marilyn Bender, "Stockholder Dissent," *New York Times*, July 8, 1973, section 3, p. 3; "Proxy Statements Feel the Watergate Ripples," *Business Week*, April 13, 1974, p. 89; John C. Perham, "Stockholder Showdown—1974," *Dun's Review* 103 (April 1974): 54–8; Steven Greenhouse "Activists Take Aim at Industry," *New York Times*, January 4, 1976, pp. 47, 49; V. C. Pospisil, "Shareholder Activists File More and More Resolutions," *Industry Week*, February 23, 1976, pp. 15–16; John C. Perham, "Annual Meetings—Dissidents on the Attack," *Dun's Review*, April 1976, pp. 53–57; Peter B. Roche, "Activist Shareholders Are Pushing Drive for More Disclosure About Firm's Ethics," *Wall Street Journal*, April 5, 1976, p. 26, and "Ethics, Social Responsibility Resolutions Lost Again in '76, But Activists Did Score," *Wall Street Journal*, May 25, 1976, p. 7; John C. Perham, "Shareholder Proposals Multiply," *New York Times*, April 12, 1976, pp. 45–6; H. J. Aidenberg, "As Meeting Season Nears, Issue-Minded Shareholders Regroup," *New York Times*, March 6, 1977, section 2, p. 13; Michael C. Jensen, "Dissident Stockholders Begin to Get Somewhere at Last," *New York Times*, May 16, 1977, pp. 43, 46.

144. The following statistics on public interest proxy resolutions are compiled from

# References

two sources: "Minding the Corporate Conscience," an annual survey of the movement for corporate responsibility published by the Council on Economic Priorities since 1970; "Annual Reports on the Voting of Institutional Investors," published by IRRC, 1973 to the present.

145. Roger G. Kennedy, "Portfolio Decisions—Social Responsibility," *Vital Speeches* 41 (January 15, 1975): 213.

146. See, for example, Marilyn Bender, "The Celanese Corporation's 60% Loan Proposal for Officers Makes Shareholders Angry," *New York Times*, April 10, 1975, pp. 57, 62; see also Michael Jensen, "Norton Simon Shareholders' Suit on Chairman's Pay to be Settled," *New York Times*, June 29, 1977, pp. 49, 51.

147. Milton Moskowitz, "The Stockholders Are Up in Arms," *San Francisco Chronicle*, June 11, 1977, p. 35.

148. The Gilbert brothers' activities are reported in their annual report. See Lewis D. Gilbert and John J. Gilbert, *35th Annual Report of Stockholder Activities at Corporation Meetings During 1974; 36th Annual Report of Stockholder Activities at Corporation Meetings During 1975;* and *37th Annual Report of Stockholder Activities at Corporation Meetings During 1976* (New York: Corporate Democracy, Inc., 1977). One public relations director noted in 1976:

> We used to regard Gilbert as something of a squirrel, but if you look back at the things he has been pushing you'll find that some of them are now common practice. For example, I'd guess that 40% of the NYSE listed companies now have cumulative voting, which is one of Gilbert's favorite causes. ("Annual Meeting Time," *Forbes*, April 15, 1976, p. 40.)

149. See, for example, Michael C. Jensen, "Shareholders Chop Away at Mahoney's Salary," *New York Times*, July 3, 1971, section 3, p. 13.

150. See "The Board: Its Obsolete Values Overhauled," *Business Week*, May 22, 1971, pp. 50–58.

151. See, for example: "Mattel's Successful Retreat," *Business Week*, May 16, 1977, p. 43; "Federal Judge Approved $30 Million Settlement of Class-Action Lawsuits Against Mattel that Charged Securities Laws Violations," *Wall Street Journal*, March 16, 1976, p. 14; "Mattel, Inc." *Forbes*, March 1, 1976, pp. 27–8; "Study of Firms' Last Financial Affairs Begun by U.S. Attorney's Office in Los Angeles," *Wall Street Journal*, November 14, 1975, p. 16.

152. B. E. Calame and Eric Morgenthaler, "Outside Directors Get More Careful, Tougher After Payoff Scandals," *Wall Street Journal*, March 24, 1976, p. 14.

153. The most comprehensive discussion of the contemporary corporate board of directors is "Changes in the Corporate Board Room: What Should Be Done?" *IRRC Special Report B*, March 18, 1974; see also Myles C. Mace, *Directors: Myth and Reality* (Boston: Division of Research, Graduate School of Business Administration, Harvard University, 1971); Peter Drucker, "The Bored Board," *Wharton Magazine* 1:1 (Fall 1976): 19–25; Courtney C. Brown, *Putting the Corporate Board to Work* (New York: Macmillan Co., 1976); B. E. Calame and Eric Morgenthaler, "Outside Directors Get More Careful, Tougher After Payoff Scandals," *Wall Street Journal*, March 24, 1976, pp. 1, 14.

154. See, for example, Harold Koontz, "The Corporate Board and Special Interests," *Business Horizons*, October 1971, pp. 75–83.

155. "Commission Authorizes Board Re-examination of Proxy Rules," Security and Exchange Commission press release (No. 34–13482, 35–20008, IC–9740) April 26, 1977, p. 1.

156. Ibid., pp. 9–17.

157. See, for example, "Shareholders, the Board of Directors and Corporate Governance," *Analysis* I, (March 15, 1976), IRRC and "Shareholder Nomination of Candidates for Director," *Analysis* no. 7 (April 6, 1973), IRRC.

158. See, for example, the testimony of Ralph Nader and Tim Smith, U.S. Senate Ninety-fifth Congress, First Session, Hearings before the Subcommittee on Citizens, and Shareholders' Rights and Remedies of the Committee on the Judiciary, "The Role of the Shareholder in the Corporate World," Part I (Washington, D.C.: U.S. Government Printing Office, 1977), pp. 32–47, 156–63.

# CHAPTER 4

1. Albert O. Hirschman, *Exit, Voice, and Loyalty* (Cambridge, Mass.: Harvard University Press, 1970).

2. Alice Tepper Marlin was Alice Tepper during the council's first years; she is referred to solely by her married name to avoid confusion. This analysis of the Council on Economic Priorities is based on the following sources: interviews and correspondence with Alice Tepper Marlin; publications, press releases, and press clippings of the council; "Social Dividends—A New Corporate Responsibility," *Trends in Management/Investor Relations* no. 210, October 1970; "The Council on Economic Priorities (A) and (B)," two cases prepared by Michael R. Pearce under the supervision of Raymond A. Bauer (Boston: Inter-Collegiate Case Clearinghouse, Harvard University, No. 9–373–275 and No. 9–373–276).

3. Pearce, "Council on Economic Priorities (A)," p. 1.

4. Quoted in "Investors' Guide to Social Concern," *Business Week*, June 20, 1970, p. 85.

5. Marlin quoted in "Social Dividends," p. 2.

6. Ibid., p. 1.

7. Constance Holden, "Corporate Responsibility: Group Rates Company Social Performance," *Science*, February 5, 1971, pp. 463–66.

8. Leslie Allan, et al., *Paper Profits: Pollution in the Pulp and Paper Industry* (Cambridge, Mass.: MIT Press, 1970); Joseph H. Bragdon and John Marlin, "Is Pollution Profitable," *Risk Management*, April 1972, pp. 9–18.

9. See, for example, "Investors' Guide to Social Concern," p. 85; "Report on Paper," *Time*, December 28, 1970.

10. See, for example, "Alice Tepper—She Rates," *Playboy*, September 1970 p. 195; "One Crusading Citizen Can Become a Power," *Vogue*, August 1971, p. 115; "Alice in Businessland," *Business and Society Review* 2 (Summer 1972): 28.

11. See, for example, David Bird, "Paper Industry Gains in Cleanup," *New York Times*, August 28, 1972, p. 1, and "Study Finds Utilities Lag in Curbing Air Pollution," *New York Times*, April 16, 1972, p. 1; John V. Conti, "Steel Firms Lag Badly in Curbing Pollution, Says A Private Study That Rates 47 Mills," *Wall Street Journal*, May 22, 1973, p. 14; "Pollution: Pointing the Finger," *Newsweek*, June 4, 1973, pp. 76, 80; "Drug Firms Are Rapped by Consumer Group in Study Based Partly on Rate of Recalls," *Wall Street Journal*, October 30, 1973, p. 8; Henry Weinstein, "Abuse Is Charged in Defense Hiring," *New York Times*, August 19, 1975, p. 45.

12. Quoted in Pearce, "Council on Economic Priorities (A)," p. 5.

13. Interview with Marlin.

14. The report was subsequently published as a book, Leslie Allan, et al., *Efficiency in Death* (New York: Harper & Row, 1970).

15. Quoted in "Report on Paper."

16. In 1972, the Council on Economic Priorities (CEP) released an update of *Paper Profits* which reported a significant increase in the industry's pollution control efforts. The council did not publicly take responsibility for the change in the industry's policies, but attributed it largely to improvements in technology and effective government regulatory efforts. See David Bird, "Paper Industry Gains in Cleanup," *New York Times*, August 28, 1972, pp. 4, 12. A study of the industry's changes concluded that CEP's role was not critical. Eileen Kohl Naufman, "Why the Paper Companies Cleaned Up," *Business and Society Review/Innovation* 6 (Summer 1973): 51–5.

17. "Corporate Advertising and the Environment," *Economic Priorities Report* 2, no. 3 (September/October 1971); see also "Pollution: Puffery or Progress?" *Newsweek*, December 28, 1970, pp. 49–51.

18. Quoted in "Pollution," *Newsweek*, p. 50.

19. Quoted in Pearce, "Council on Economic Priorities (A)," p. 8.

20. Six of CEP's studies have been published in book form: James Cannon, *Environmental Steel: Pollution in the Iron and Steel Industry* (New York: Council on Economic Priorities, 1973); Tina L. Simcich, et al., *Shortchanged: Minorities and*

# References

*Women in Banking* (New York: Council on Economic Priorities, 1976); J. Zalkind et al., *Guide to Corporations: A Social Perspective* (Chicago: Swallow Press, 1974); Charles Komanoff et al., *The Price of Power: Elective Utilities and the Environment* (New York: Council on Economic Priorities, 1972); Allan et al., *Paper Profits.*

21. Quoted from a CEP pamphlet, "The Pollution Audit," 1977.

22. Interview with Marlin.

23. Council on Economic Priorities, "Power Plant Performance," 1976; other CEP studies in this vein include: Adams, "The B-1 Bomber," 1976; Gordon Adams and Sherri Zann Rosenthal, "The Invisible Hand: Questionable Corporate Payments Overseas"; and "An Analysis of the Interchange of Personnel Between Defense Contractors and the Department of Defense."

24. Interview with Marlin.

25. See "A Guide to Corporations." The report is summarized in Lee Stephenson, "Prying Open Corporations: Tighter than Clams," *Business and Society Review/Innovation* 8 (Winter 1973–74): pp. 42–9.

26. It has also published a research methodology guide in order to help individuals research corporations on their own. Approximately 50,000 copies of the guide have been distributed since 1970.

27. See *Inform News* 1, no. 1 (Spring 1974).

28. There have also been some detailed studies of particular corporations by various organizations, but their quality is uneven. For example, see John Woodman, et al., *The World of a Giant Corporation: A Report from the GE Project* (Seattle, Wash.: North County Press, 1976); and Pacific Studies Center, ed., *Strike at GM: Articles on General Motors Corporation and Its Adversaries* (East Palo Alto, Ca.: Pacific Studies Center, 1970).

29. Interview with Michael Locker.

30. See "Stock Ownership and Control in U.S. Corporations," CIC brief, July 1976.

31. "Campaign for Corporate Responsibility," *Economic Priorities Report* 1, no. 1, April 1970, pp. 13–17.

32. "1970 Annual Meetings: Corporate Policies Challenged," *Economic Priorities Report* 1, no. 2 (Summer 1970) pp. 1, 3–14.

33. Interview with Marlin.

34. The most widely circulated publication is Jeb Mays, Mike Riesch, Gretzel Stansbury, Phil Wheaton, and Mollie Babize, *Corporate Action Guide* (Washington, D.C.: Corporate Action Project, 1974). This collection of studies includes cases on such issues as corporate power, multinational corporations, political activities of corporations, and ways in which citizens can influence corporate activities. It is largely critical of citizen challenges on the grounds that they have not proven a serious threat to corporate power.

35. Interview with Mike Phillips.

36. "SEC May Ask Investors for View on Corporate Disclosure of Data," *News For Investors* 11, no. 1 (January 1975): 2.

37. Ibid., p. 5.

38. Letter to "Friends" by Glenn Stover, Project Director, National Resources Defense Council, Inc., March 1, 1975.

39. Ibid.

40. For a summary of the testimony see, "SEC Due to Act This Month on Guidelines for New Corporate Disclosure," *News For Investors* 11, no. 8 (August 1975): 145–53. See also, "Disclosing Social Data," *Business Week*, April 4, 1975, pp. 76–7.

41. "SEC Due to Act This Month," p. 153.

42. "Disclosing Social Data," p. 76.

43. "SEC Due to Act This Month," p. 150.

44. Quoted in "Disclosing Social Data," p. 77.

45. For a summary of the commission's ruling see, "SEC Rejects Move for Broad New Corporate Disclosure of Social Matters," *News For Investors* 11, no. 11 (November 1975): 205–9. The commission's official decision is contained in Release no. 5627 and no. 11733, October 14, 1975.

46. SEC Release no. 5627 and no. 11733, p. 35.

47. Ibid., p. 37.
48. Ibid., p. 46.
49. Ibid., p. 40.
50. Ibid.
51. "Social Dividends," p. 2.
52. "Stick and Carrot," *Nation*, January 4, 1971, p. 4.
53. Ibid.
54. The volume of literature on this subject is out of proportion to the topic's importance—presumably reflecting its superficial popular appeal; see, for example, Walter Goodman, "Stocks Without Sin," *Harpers*, August 1971, pp. 61–7; Les Gapay, "Mutual Funds and Social Conscience," *Progressive* 37 (March 1973): 40–3; Harry Shapiro, "Social Responsibility Mutual Funds: Down the Down Staircase," *Business and Society Review*, no. 12 (Winter 1974–75), pp. 90–3, and "Social Responsibility Funds Get Off to a Bad Start," *Business and Society Review/Innovation*, no. 5 (Spring 1973), pp. 81–7; Robert Schwartz, "A Cold Eye on Guilt-Edged Investing," *Business and Society Review*, no. 3 (Autumn 1972), pp. 81–4; "The Funds," *Forbes*, July 1, 1971, pp. 55–62; "Doing Well by Doing Good: What's Happened to Ethical Investing," *Harper's Weekly*, May 23, 1975, p. 6; "The Dreyfus Fund: Experience With Investing in the Public Interest," *Business and Society Review*, Spring 1976, pp. 57–61.
55. "The Funds," p. 55.
56. Gapay, "Mutual Funds," p. 42.
57. Ibid.
58. Goodman, "Stocks Without Sin," p. 66.
59. Burton G. Malkiel and Richard E. Quandt, "Moral Issues in Investment Policy," *Harvard Business Review*, March–April 1971, p. 42.
60. Milton Moskowitz, "Profiles in Corporate Responsibility," *Business and Society Review*, Spring 1975, pp. 28–42.
61. U.S. Congress Hearings before the House Subcommittee on Africa of the Committee on Foreign Affairs, "U.S. Business Involvement in Southern Africa," Part I, 92nd Congress, 1st Session (Washington, D.C.: U.S. Government Printing Office, 1972), pp. 206–7.
62. The initial draft of this section was written by Stephanie Lenway. It is based primarily on the following material: "AT&T Agrees to Massive Wage Boosts and Back Pay for Women, Minorities in Settling U.S. Job-Bias Case," *Wall Street Journal*, January 19, 1973, p. 3. "EEO Stockholder Actions: A Progress Report," *Corporate Examiner*, December 1974, pp. 3A–3D, "Equal Employment Opportunity: Toward Corporate Accountability," *Corporate Examiner*, December 1973, pp. 3A–3D, and "Images of Women in Advertising," *Corporate Examiner*, July 1975, pp. 3A–3D, including an extensive bibliography of relevant articles on the subject; "Equal Employment—What's the Big Secret?" *Corporate Examiner*, June 1973, p. 2; Jamie Heard, "Availability and Use of Information on Corporate Equal Employment Programs," *IRRC Special Report 1975–B* (Washington, D.C.: Investor Responsibility Research Center, July 1975); Judy Klemesrud, "Feminist Shareholders Challenge the Corporate Structure," *New York Times*, May 15, 1975, p. 52; Lisa C. Wohl, "Liberating Ma Bell," *Ms. Magazine*, November 1973, pp. 52–4, 93–7.
63. Egerton, "Handling Protests," pp. 59–60.
64. Wohl, "Liberating Ma Bell," p. 54.
65. "AT&T Agrees to Massive Wage Boosts," p. 3.
66. Wohl, "Liberating Ma Bell," p. 93.
67. National Organization for Women, "Ask for a Woman: Handbook for a Corporate Suffragette" (Chicago: N.O.W., 1971), pp. 1–2.
68. Ibid., p. 2.
69. Ibid., p. 9.
70. This quote is from a memo written by Fred Curtis, researcher in corporate responsibility for the Interfaith Committee on Social Responsibility in Investments, to Mike Phillips of the Glide Foundation, San Francisco, dated September 4, 1973, p. 2.
71. Ibid.
72. Judy Klemesrud, "Feminist Shareholders," p. 52. Hull claims credit for the

# References

subsequent appointment of a woman to the board of directors of Celanese: "It would not have happened without the shareholder resolution." The company denies the connection. (Klemesrud, p. 52.)

73. "Disclosure of Information on Equal Employment Programs," *Analysis* E (March 5, 1976), Investors Responsibility Research Center.

74. Heard, "Availability and Use of Information."

75. Klemesrud, "Feminist Shareholders," p. 52.

76. See, for example, Thomas De Baggio, "Issue for the Seventies," *Nation*, February 28, 1972, p. 265. Willard F. Mueller, "Corporate Secrecy vs. Corporate Disclosure," in Nader and Green, *Corporate Power in America*, pp. 111–27.

77. Gordon Adams, "Corporate Social Issues," unpublished memo, February 16, 1977. See also Phillip Blumberg, "Disclosure of Matters of Social or Environmental Concern in the Major American Corporation (Washington, D.C.: Investors Responsibility Research Center, n.d.).

78. Adams, "Corporate Social Issues."

79. Donald E. Schwartz, "A Case for Federal Chartering," *The Business Lawyer* 31 (February 1976): 1149.

80. Thomas Schoenbaum, "The Relationship Between Corporate Disclosure and Corporate Responsibility," *Fordham Law Review* 40 (1972): 588.

81. Ibid.

82. For a recent and comprehensive summary of what corporate reformers would like corporations to disclose see, Ralph Nader, Mark Green, and Joel Seligman, *Taming the Giant Corporation* (New York: W. W. Norton & Co., 1976), especially chap. 5, "Corporate Secrecy vs. Corporate Disclosure," pp. 132–79.

83. See Donald K. White, "Pre-Meeting Media Hype," *San Francisco Chronicle*, April 22, 1977, p. 2.

84. See, for example, "Corporate Information," *Analysis*, no. 2 (March 5, 1974).

## CHAPTER 5

1. Corporate Information Center, Agenda Item no. 13 for Presentation to General Board, February 11–15, 1972, p. 1.

2. Ibid., p. 6.

3. Ibid., p. 3.

4. Ibid.; also see, Doris Grumbach, "Whose Business Is Business?" *Commonweal*, June 6, 1972, pp. 333–4.

5. Corporate Information Center, p. 3.

6. As of 1972, the nation's 360,000 Protestant churches held approximately 22 billion in securities. See "Companies Feel the Wrath of Clergy," *Business Week*, March 18, 1972, p. 84; see also Frank White, "The Church and Corporate Responsibility—Three Tasks," *Corporate Responsibility and Religious Institutions* (New York: Corporate Information Center, 1971), p. 22.

7. Horace E. Gale, "Why Are the Churches Getting Involved in Investments?" *Corporate Responsibility and Religious Institutions*, p. 34.

8. "Interview with Frank White," *JSAC Grapevine* 8 (March 1973): 2; also see, Marilyn Bender, "Investment Missionary," *New York Times*, April 15, 1973, section 3, p. 7.

9. See "Churches and Corporate Responsibility: International," CIC brief, May 1973; also see "Statement by the Greater London Council and Certain Other Shareholders Opposing Loans to the South African Government, March 1977," *Corporate Examiner* 6, no. 6 (June 1977). While the tactics of shareholder activists in Europe—the proposal of shareholder resolutions, attendance at annual meetings, and private discussions with management—appear to parallel those initiated in the U.S., they are much more feeble, in part due to the relative lack of shareholder rights in European corporate law.

10. For accounts of the history of the church's role as a shareholder activist, see

Corporate Information Center, Agenda no. 13, "Discovering Proxy Power," *Together*, July 1973; and "Companies Feel Wrath" pp. 84–6.

11. "Fifth Anniversary Issue," *Corporate Examiner* 5, no. 8–9 (September 1976): 1.

12. The best single document on the ethical and economic implications of the church's socially oriented investment policies is *Corporate Responsibility and Religious Institutions.* Also see, Howard Schomer, "The Church and the Transnational Corporation," A.D. 1975 4, no. 2, pp. 15–25; and "A New Area for Mission-Investment Policies," *JSAC Grapevine* 2 (February 1971): 7.

13. CIC pamphlet, p. 1.

14. See "Investing in Peace," *Progressive* 36 (March 1972): 7–8.

15. "Companies Feel Wrath," p. 84.

16. Horace Gale, "Why Are the Churches Getting Involved in Investments?" *Corporate Responsibility and Religious Institutions*, p. 35. See also "We've Prohibited Investments in Tobacco and Liquor. Why Should We Help Pollute the Air?" A.D. 1975 4, no. 2, p. 25

17. Quoted in "Companies Feel Wrath," p. 86.

18. "Corporate Responsibility: Introduction," p. 1, and Robert S. Potter, "The Investment Responsibilities of Boards Concerned About Human Welfare: A Response to the Threshold Objections to the Notion of Social Investment," in *Corporate Responsibility and Religious Institutions*, p. 7.

19. Letter to author, May 30, 1977.

20. Peter B. Roche, "Activist Shareholders Are Pushing Drive for More Disclosure About Firm's Ethics," *Wall Street Journal*, April 5, 1976, p. 26.

21. For a discussion of the role of Catholic institutions, see Michael H. Crosby, *Catholic Church Investments for Corporate Social Responsibility* (Milwaukee, Wisc.: Justice and Peace Center, 1973).

22. See "Revolution by Proxy? The Church vs. the Corporation," *San Francisco Bay Guardian*, February 17, 1977; see also Carl Irving, "Business Is Getting Religion," *San Francisco Examiner*, February 13, 1977, section C, p. 11; Philip Greer and Myron Kandel, "Collar Power Growing," *San Francisco Chronicle-Examiner*, March 6, 1977, section 3, p. 11.

23. "Comments on the 'Corporate Advisory Panel' Proposal," in Richard A. Jackson, ed., *The Multinational Corporation and Social Policy: Special Reference to General Motors in South Africa* (New York: Praeger Publishers, 1974).

24. This paragraph is based primarily on items appearing in the "Corporate Action News" section of various issues of *The Corporate Examiner*. For a background, see CIC brief, "The Frankfurt Documents," July 1973; see in particular *The Corporate Examiner* 3, no. 1 (January 1974): 4; also see Richard Fernandez, "Making Global Consciousness Work—How Local Churches in One State Talked a Bank Out of Granting a Loan to the Government of South Africa," *New World Outlook* (October 1974).

25. "Corporate Action News," *Corporate Examiner* 3, no. 6 (June 1974): 5.

26. See the CIC brief, "Banking on Apartheid," *Corporate Examiner* (October 1976): 3A; also see Reed Kramer, "In Hock to U.S. Banks," *Nation*, December 11, 1976, pp. 624–6.

27. This is from the testimony of Timothy Smith, Director of ICCR, at a congressional hearing in 1976 on bank loans to South Africa. It is taken from the CIC brief, "Banking on Apartheid," p. 3D.

28. Quoted in *Corporate Examiner* 6, no. 6 (June 1977): p. 4; also see *Corporate Examiner* 6, no. 1 (January 1977).

29. Michael C. Jensen, "The American Corporate Presence in South Africa," *New York Times*, December 4, 1977, p. 9.

30. Quoted in "The Controversy Over Computers," *Business and Society Review*, no. 15 (Fall 1975), p. 58.

31. For material on the controversy of IBM's role in South Africa, see "The Controversy Over Computers," pp. 58–9; also see "The Role of IBM in South Africa," a transcript of hearings sponsored by the National Council of Churches (New York: Investor Responsibility Research Center, November 20–21, 1974).

32. Quoted in "The Controversy Over Computers," p. 59.

33. "The Role of IBM," p. 3.

# References

34. Quoted in "Corporate Activity in South Africa: IBM Corporation," *Analysis* F, Supplement no. 2 (April 1, 1976) IRRC, p. 40.

35. "The Role of IBM," p. 134.

36. For the controversy over Polaroid's role in South Africa, see "The Polaroid Case," in *Multinational Corporations and the Third World*, ed. Louis Turner (New York: Hill and Wang, 1973), pp. 233–6; also see "Polaroid in South Africa (A)," a case prepared by Dr. Dharmendrat Verma (Boston: Inter-Collegiate Clearinghouse, Northeastern University, 1971, no. 9–372–604). See also Dr. Dharmendrat Verma, "Polaroid in South Africa (B)," Case No. 9–372–625 (Boston: Inter-Collegiate Case Clearinghouse). For a more critical review of this issue, see George M. Houser, "The Polaroid Approach to South Africa," *Christian Century*, February 24, 1971.

37. Quoted in "The Controversy Over Computers," p. 59.

38. "500 Miners Greet the Southern Co." See also, "Power Politics: The Georgia Power Project Newsletter," June–July 1974, p. 2.

39. *Analysis* (May 5, 1975) IRRC: 2–47.

40. *Analysis* (May 3, 1976) IRRC: F–76.

41. Ibid., p. F–78.

42. Interview with Robert Potter.

43. "General Motors and South Africa," a case prepared by Jesse E. Christman and Hugh C. White, Jr. (Detroit, Michigan: National Industrial Ministry).

44. Ibid., p. 15.

45. "Corporate Responsibility," *Corporate Examiner* 1, no. 1 (November 1971): 1.

46. Pearlstine, "GM Management Wins," p. 10.

47. *Church Investments, Corporations and Southern Africa* (New York: Friendship Press, 1973).

48. Quoted in "Churchmen Report on U.S. Businesses in Southern Africa," *Congressional Record*, March 22, 1972, p. 5.

49. Ibid., pp. 4–5.

50. See William Cotter, Nancy McKeon, and Robert Denerstein, "The Proxy Contests Over South Africa," *Business and Society Review*, no. 5 (Spring 1973): 61–9; also see "Corporate Activities in South Africa," *Analysis*, no. 6 (April 2, 1974); *Analysis*, no. 2 (March 14, 1975); and *Analysis* F (March 1976) IRRC.

51. This quote is from a speech by Tim Smith, Executive Secretary of the Interfaith Committee on Social Responsibility in Investments, entitled "Strategy Options for the Church in the Area of Corporate Responsibility," presented on October 19, 1972, to the Urban Industrial Mission Consultation (no location given).

52. *Corporate Examiner* 1, no. 2 (August 1972): 4.

53. *Corporate Examiner* 1, no. 10 (November 1972): 36.

54. "Mobil in the Republic of South Africa: An Analysis of Mobil's Report on Operations in South Africa," Corporate Information Center, p. 36.

55. Quoted in "The Withdrawal Debate: U.S. Corporations in South Africa," CIC brief, June 1973, p. 36.

56. "U.S. Companies Feel Pressure for Change," *Business Week*, February 14, 1977, p. 68; also see Richard R. Leger, "U.S. Firms' Operations in South Africa Cope with Varied Pressures," *Wall Street Journal*, March 16, 1977, pp. 1, 17.

57. "Labor Practices of U.S. Corporations in South Africa," *Special Report* 1976–A (April 1, 1976), IRRC, p. 98. Donald McHenry, now U.S. Ambassador to the Security Council, wrote in 1974 that as a result of proxy campaigns, "Major corporations have been forced to inform themselves and, in order to avoid criticism, to make or plan improvements prior to release of information." Gillette, for example, has indicated that the "timing and size of its wage increases for black workers were influenced by conversations with shareholders." (Martha Cooper and Jamie Heard, "The 1977 Proxy Season: How Institutions Voted on Shareholder Resolutions and Management Proposals," IRRC, pp. 64–5.)

58. See "U.S. Corporate Expansion in South Africa," CIC brief, April 1976; and "U.S. Firms Doing Business in South Africa Face Mounting Pressures from Students, Churches, Institutional Investors, Activist Groups," *News For Investors* 4, no. 7 (July/August 1977): 125–9.

59. See, for example, John C. Harrington, *The State of California and Southern*

*African Racism: California's Economic Involvement with Firms Operating in Southern Africa* (Sacramento: California Legislature, Assembly Office of Research, 1972).

60. H. J. Maidenberg, "As Meeting Seasons Nears, Issue-Minded Shareholders Regroup," *New York Times*, March 6, 1977, section 3, p. 13.

61. "People and Business," *New York Times*, June 21, 1977, p. 45.

62. Timothy Smith, "A Response to the Statement of Principles by Twelve U.S. Firms Operating in South Africa—Too Little, Too Late," *Corporate Examiner* 6, no. 5 (May 1977): 4.

63. "The Oil Conspiracy," Center for Social Action of the United Church of Christ, 1976, p. 31.

64. Michael C. Jensen, "U.S. Checking Mobil's Role in Rhodesia," *New York Times*, August 2, 1975, p. 1.

65. "Mobil Oil Says Study of Sales to Rhodesia by South African Unit Is Blocked by Laws," *Wall Street Journal*, August 30, 1976, p. 5.

66. U.S. Senate, Stenographic Transcript of Hearings Before the Subcommittee on African Affairs of the Committee on Foreign Relations, "United States Policy Toward the Horn of Africa" (Washington, D.C.: Reynolds Reporting Associates, September 17, 1976).

67. "Church Group Files First Shareholder Resolution for 1977; Seeks to Ensure that Mobil Affiliates Supply No Oil to Rhodesia," *News For Investors* 3, no. 8 (September 1976): 170.

68. For background on the American economic presence in Namibia, see Reed Kramer and Tami Hultman, "TSUMEB," Corporate Information Center, National Council of Churches, 1973; see also, Winifried Courtney and Jennifer Davis, "Namibia: U.S. Corporate Involvement," The Africa Fund, 1972.

69. Quoted in "Plaintiffs' Complaint," in Schott et al. v. American Metal Climax, Inc. et al., p. 8.

70. Ibid., pp. 9–10.

71. Quoted in "TSUMEB," p. 13; see also, Barry Newman, "Newmont, Amax Face Mounting Pressure to Take Stand in Namibia Political Hassle," *Wall Street Journal*, February 7, 1972, p. 8.

72. Schott et al. v. American Metal Climax et al., Complaint for Injunction and Damages, Stockholders' Derivative Suit, Superior Court of California, City and County of San Francisco, August 21, 1973.

73. See "Statement at Annual Stockholders Meeting of Newmont Mining Corporation (Wilmington, Delaware, 3 May 1977)" (New York: Office of Communication, United Church of Christ); and Laurence G. O'Donnell, "Churchmen's Efforts to Get Data From GM Points Up a New Force on Corporations," *Wall Street Journal*, May 19, 1972, p. 26.

74. Timothy Smith, "South Africa: The Churches vs. the Corporations," *Business and Society Review* no. 15 (Fall 1975), p. 80.

75. Quoted in Everett C. Parker, "CONOCO Withdraws from Namibia Explorations," *A.D.* 1975 2, no. 2, p. 21.

76. Smith, "Churches vs. Corporations," p. 61; see also, Marilyn Bender, "U.S. Oil Concerns Quit African Nation," *New York Times*, January 29, 1975, p. 47. An official from Conoco stated that the churches' role had been "one of many factors" in its decision to withdraw.

77. For a discussion of the controversy surrounding Gulf's investment in Angola, see James Munves, "Should a Corporation Have a Conscience About Colonists Seeking Freedom," *Minding*, pp. 113–27; "Gulf Oil and Portugal: Partners in Colonialism," CIC brief, April 1974; "Gulf Oil: Portuguese Ally in Angola," CIC brief, March 1972, updated December 1972; newsletters of the Gulf Boycott Coalition; Richard L. Righter and Patricia M. Roach, "A Response to Exploitation—The Gulf Oil Boycott," pamphlet; "Gulf Oil," CIC brief, March 1972; "Activists Lay Plans for War on Gulf," *Business Week*, April 11, 1970, p. 23.

78. Quoted in Righter and Roach, "A Response to Exploitation," p. 2.

79. Ibid., pp. 2–3.

80. "Gulf Oil," p. 11.

81. Quoted in Righter and Roach, "A Response to Exploitation," pp. 29–30.

# References

82. Quoted in Robert Engler, *The Brotherhood of Oil* (Chicago: University of Chicago Press, 1977), p. 109.

83. "Repression in Southern Africa," pamphlet prepared by the Pan-African Liberation Committee, September 1971, p. 14; see also "Harvard's Investments in Southern Africa," *Upstart* 4 (April 1972): 21–8.

84. Righter and Roach, "A Response to Exploitation," p. 48.

85. Quoted in Engler, *The Brotherhood of Oil*, p. 109.

86. Ibid.

87. Ibid.

88. See Engler, *The Brotherhood of Oil*, p. 115; and Leslie H. Gelb, "U.S. Backing Gulf's Ties with Victorious Angolans," *New York Times*, February 27, 1976, pp. 1, 8.

89. Phone interview with Marshall Robinson.

90. This section is based primarily on the following material: "Formula for Malnutrition," CIC brief, April 1975; "Infant Nutrition, Breast Feeding, Formula Promotion Practices," *Analysis* K, March 18, 1976, *Analysis* K, no. 2, March 23, 1976; and *Analysis No. 5*, March 14, 1975, IRRC; "Bottle Baby Lawsuit," CIC brief, April 1977; Ann Crittenden, "Infant Formula at Issue," *New York Times*, April 3, 1977, section 2, p. 15; "INFACT: Infant Formula Action Coalition," newsletter.

91. Quoted in *Analysis* K (March 18, 1976), IRRC: 6.

92. Quoted in *Analysis* K (March 23, 1976), IRRC: 2.

93. See Jeffery Leonard and Jamie Heard, "How Institutions Voted in 1975 on Shareholder Resolutions and Management Proposals," IRRC Special Report 1975-C, September 1975.

94. *Analysis* K (March 18, 1976), IRRC: 3.

95. Ibid., p. 11.

96. *Analysis* K (March 23, 1976), IRRC: 32.

97. Ibid.

98. Quoted in "Bottle Baby Lawsuit," p. 3A.

99. Quoted in Vernon A. Guidry, Jr., "Catholic Order Sues Over Baby Formula Sales," *Washington Star*, April 19, 1976, p. A–7.

100. "INFACT Newsletter," p. 1.

101. This section is based primarily on the following sources: Will Maslow, "How You Can Fight the Boycott," a pamphlet distributed by the American Jewish Congress; "Boycott Report," issued by the American Jewish Congress, 1, no. 1 (March 1977); 1, no. 2 (May 1977); 1, no. 3 (June 1977); American Jewish Congress, press release, March 16, 1976, and May 30, 1977; "The Arab Boycott of Israel," *Analysis* D (February 26, 1976) IRRC; interview with Edwin Epstein.

102. Letter by Will Maslow to the Secretary, United States Securities and Exchange Commission, regarding the Proposed Amendment to Proxy Rules, File no. 57–643, August 10, 1976, p. 1.

103. Ibid., p. 2.

104. Interview with Edwin Epstein.

105. Maslow, "How You Can Fight the Boycott," p. 2.

106. Ibid., p. 3.

107. Ibid.

108. John C. Perham, "Annual Meetings—Dissidents on the Attack," *Dun's Review*, April 1976, p. 56.

109. Maslow, "How You Can Fight the Boycott," p. 4.

110. Ibid.

111. Quoted in "Resolutions Withdrawn," *News For Investors* 3, no. 3 (March 1977): 47.

112. Ibid., p. 54.

113. American Jewish Congress, press release, May 30, 1977.

114. Quoted in Albert O. Hirschman, *The Passion and the Interests* (Princeton: University Press, 1977), p. 58.

## CHAPTER 6

1. For a summary of the speech and public reaction to it, see "Corporate Performance and Private Criticism, Campaign GM: Rounds I and II," a case prepared by Mrs. A. J. Sproat under the direction of C. Roland Christensen (Boston: Harvard University, Inter-Collegiate Case Clearinghouse, no. 9-370-026), pp. 16-17.

2. Quoted in Timothy H. Ingram, "The Corporate Underground," *Nation*, September 13, 1971, p. 212.

3. Earl A. Molander, "Ethics and Responsibility in Business Organizations: Internal Reform vs. External Controls," paper presented at Business Ethics Workshop, Graduate Theological Union, Berkeley, California, February 18, 1977. According to the Opinion Research Corporation, "Most businessmen and financial editors . . . believe that stockholder activism will be beneficial to publically owned companies." Kenneth Schwartz, "How Social Activists See Business," *Business and Society Review*, no. 4 (Summer 1975), p. 73.

4. Carl Irving, "Business Is Getting Religion," *San Francisco Chronicle*, February 3, 1977, p. 11.

5. "Annual Meeting Time," *Forbes*, April 15, 1976, p. 40.

6. Ibid., p. 42. Mary Gardiner Jones, a former member of the FTC who serves on three corporate boards, notes:
   I know from my own experience that corporate managements . . . pay close attention to the views expressed by their institutional nonprofit investors on the issues raised by their stockholders' proxy resolutions as well as to the number of votes which these resolutions receive. [Testimony before Subcommittee on Citizens' and Shareholders' Rights and Remedies, "The Role of the Shareholder in the Corporate World," Committee on the Judiciary, U.S. Senate, Ninety-fifth Congress, First Session, part I, June 27, 28, 1977.]

7. Roger G. Kennedy, "Portfolio Decisions," *Vital Speeches* 41 (January 15, 1975): 213.

8. Peter B. Roche, "Activist Shareholders Are Pushing Drive for More Disclosure About Firms' Ethics," *Wall Street Journal*, April 5, 1976, p. 26.

9. Will Maslow, "How You Can Fight the Boycott," reprinted from *Moment* by the American Jewish Congress, New York, p. 2. Exxon reportedly was anxious to seek a compromise with the American Jewish Congress because, "it could not afford to offend Jewish customers and investors," "Annual Meeting Time," p. 40.

10. William D. Hartley, "More Concerns Willing to Enter Negotiations on Shareholder Resolutions," *Wall Street Journal*, March 23, 1977, p. 17.

11. John C. Perham, "Annual Meetings: Back to Basics," *Dun's Review*, (April 1975): 106.

12. Vartanig G. Vartan, "AT&T Finds Annual Meeting Needs Careful Staging," *New York Times*, August 18, 1977, p. 52. Its chairman had previously instructed his staff: "This year find something we can recommend a vote in favor of."

13. *Preparing for the Annual Meeting and Stockholder Proposals*, Proceedings of a Conference sponsored by the New York Law Journal, 1976, p. 16.

14. See David Vogel, "The Corporate Board: Membership and Public Pressure," *Executive* 3, no. 3 (Spring 1977): 8-11, for a more detailed discussion of the impact of social pressures on the composition of the corporate board; see also "The Corporate Machinery for Hearing and Heeding New Voices: A Panel Discussion," *Business Lawyer* 26 (1971): 195-222. A poll of corporate activists on the effectiveness of "public interest" directors found that 5 percent regard them as "very effective," and 32 percent see them as "only somewhat effective," while 28 percent view them as "very ineffective." Kenneth Schwartz, "How Social Activists See Business," p. 72.

15. "A Big Jump in the Ranks of Female Directors," *Business Week*, January 10, 1977, p. 50.

16. Peter Vanderwicken, "Change Invades the Boardroom," *Fortune*, May 1972, pp. 157, 290. For more on the role and presence of blacks on the corporate board, see Jonathan Kwitny, "Firms Find Integration in Their Boardroom Is Working Quite Well," *Wall Street Journal*, October 5, 1972, p. 1; and Milton Moskowitz, "The

# References

Black Directors: Tokenism or a Big Leap Forward," *Business and Society Review,* no. 3 (Autumn 1972), pp. 73–80.

17. "A Big Jump in the Ranks of Female Directors," p. 50.

18. Kwitny, "Firms Find Integration," p. 1. For a discussion of Sullivan's impact on GM during the first five years of his tenure, see "The Black on GM's Board," *Time,* September 6, 1976, pp. 54–5.

19. Interview with James Langton.

20. See William L. Cary, "Greening of the Board Room," *New York Times,* August 4, 1971, section 3, p. 33; and "The Greening of the Board Room: Reflections on Corporate Responsibility—A Panel Discussion," *Columbia Journal of Law and Social Problems* 10, no. 1 (Fall 1973): 15–46.

21. Richard H. Holton, "Management Responses to Shareholders' Proposals," prepared for a Union Bank Seminar, May 29, 1974, pp. 12–3.

22. John C. Perham, "Annual Meetings—Dissidents on the Attack," *Dun's Review,* April 1976, p. 57.

23. Roger E. Celler, "The Challengers," Public Affairs Council, 1971.

24. Judith Cole, "The Challengers," Public Affairs Council, 1975, p. 3. For other efforts to inform the business community about the tactics of the public interest movement, see "Managing Business' Social Concerns, I—Expectations and Pressures," Stanford Research Institute, 1972; and "Principal Activist Tactics," *Corporate Responsibility Planning Service,* Human Resources Network, September 9, 1977, no. 417. The latter report explicitly deals with shareholder activism.

25. An interview with John Holcomb of the Public Affairs Council helped clarify the difficulties corporations experienced in trying to respond to demands raised by citizen challenges.

26. Stephen Mahoney, "Will the Annual Meeting *Please* Come to Order," *Fortune,* May 1965, p. 141; see also "Shushing the Annual Heckler," *Business Week,* May 22, 1965, pp. 118–23.

27. Mahoney, "Will the Annual Meeting," p. 142.

28. Henry C. Egerton, "Shareholder Proposals as a Vehicle of Protest," *Conference Board Record,* April 1971, p. 51.

29. Bryon E. Calane, "Rockwell Listens to Roar of Holders Over Its B1 Bomber," *Wall Street Journal,* February 13, 1976, p. 6.

30. Mimi Conway, "Confrontation with Stevens' Board," *In These Times,* March 16–22, 1977, p. 8.

31. "Annual Meeting Time," p. 40.

32. For the argument that the annual meeting should be abolished, see J. B. Fugua, "End Annual Meetings," *New York Times,* November 3, 1973, section 3, p. 36.

33. Hazel Henderson, "Politics by Other Means," *Nation,* December 14, 1970, pp. 617–8.

34. Ibid., p. 618.

35. Quoted in "Campaign to Make General Motors Responsible," a case prepared by John W. Collins (Boston: Inter-Collegiate Case Clearinghouse, No. 9–371–660), p. 1; see also, Blumberg, "Politicization of the Corporation," p. 1561.

36. "Project on Corporate Responsibility," *News and Thought,* Summer 1972, p. 6.

37. Saul D. Alinsky, *Rules for Radicals,* p. 175.

38. "Proxies for People—A Vehicle for Involvement," *Yale Review of Law and Social Action* 1 (Spring 1971): 68.

39. Alinsky, *Rules for Radicals,* pp. 178–9.

40. "Proxies for People," p. 66.

41. Strikingly, a poll of 3,500 Presbyterians by the Church's Committee on Mission Responsibility Through Investments taken in 1976 revealed that only 16 percent were aware that the church had filed public interest proxy resolutions.

42. See Sethi, "La Huelga Y La Causa (A) and (B)," *Up Against the Corporate Wall,* pp. 160–8, 340–55. For a discussion of the labor-management conflict at Farah, see "A Boycott Begins to Hurt at Farah," *Business Week,* June 2, 1973, p. 56; and "A Texas Pants Maker Loses to a Boycott," *Business Week,* March 2, 1974.

43. See Peter Drucker, *The Unseen Revolution: How Pension Fund Socialism Came to America* (New York: Harper & Row, 1976).

44. For the labor dispute involving J. P. Stevens, see Damon Stetson, "Church Groups Support Union Drive at J. P. Stevens," *New York Times*, February 15, 1977, p. 12; Mimi Conway, "Confrontation with Stevens' Board," *In These Times*, March 16–22, 1977, p. 8.

45. Quoted in Robert Friedman, "For J. P. Stevens It's Cheaper to Violate the Law than Recognize It," *Seven Days*, April 11, 1977, p. 11.

46. Quoted in Michael Jensen, "Union Strategist on Wall Street," *New York Times*, March 26, 1978, section 3, p. 5.

47. Donald Schwartz, "Federal Chartering of Corporations: An Introduction," *Georgetown Law Journal* 67 (1972): 71–121; Robert N. Shwartz, "A Proposal for the Designation of Shareholder Nominees for Director in the Corporate Proxy Statement," *Columbia Law Review* 74 (1974): 1139–74; Stephen Schulman, "Shareholder Cause Proposals: A Technique to Catch the Conscience of the Corporation," *George Washington Law Review* 40, no. 1 (1971): 1–75; Howard M. Friedman, "The Public Interest Derivative Suit: A Proposal for Enforcing Corporate Responsibility," *Case Western Reserve Law Review* 24 (1973): 294–329; Thomas J. Schoenbaum, "The Relationship Between Corporate Disclosure and Corporate Responsibility," *Fordham Law Review* 40, no. 3 (1972): 565–94; Melvin Aaron Eisenberg, "Access to the Corporate Proxy Machinery," *Harvard Law Review* 83 (1970): 1489–1526; William J. Feis, "Is Shareholder Democracy Attainable," *Business Lawyer* 31 (1976): 621–43; David L. Ratner, "The Government of Business Corporations: Critical Reflections on the Rule of One Shareholder, One Vote," *Cornell Law Review* 56 (1970): 1–56.

48. See Ralph Nader, Mark Green, and Joel Seligman, *Taming the Giant Corporation* (New York: W. W. Norton, 1976); and Schwartz, "Federal Chartering."

49. Robert Townsend, "Let's Install Public Directors," *Business and Society Review*, no. 1 (Spring 1972), pp. 69–70; John Kenneth Galbraith, "What Comes After General Motors," *New Republic*, November 2, 1974, pp. 13–17; Christopher D. Stone, *Where the Law Ends* (New York: Harper & Row, 1976), and "Public Directors Merit a Try," *Harvard Business Review*, March/April 1976, pp. 20–42; Nader, Green, and Seligman, *Taming the Giant Corporation*, pp. 115–39, especially 118–31; for an additional discussion of proposed reforms of the corporate board, see Phillip I. Blumberg, Eli Goldston, and George Gibson, "Corporate Social Responsibility Panel: The Constituencies of the Corporation and the Role of the Institutional Investor," *Business Lawyer*, March 1973, pp. 177–213; Melvin Aaron Eisenberg, "Legal Models of Management Structure on the Modern Corporation: Officers, Directors and Accountants," *California Law Review* 63 (1975): 373–439; Detlev Vagts, "The Governance of the Corporation: The Options Available and the Power to Prescribe," *Business Lawyer*, February 1976, pp. 929–38; Phillip I. Blumberg, "Reflection on Proposals for Corporate Reform Through Change in the Composition of the Board of Directors: 'Special Interest' or 'Public Directors,' " in *The Unstable Ground: Corporate Social Policy in a Dynamic Society*, ed. S. Prakash Sethi (Los Angeles: Melville Publishing Co., 1974), pp. 112–34. No one has seriously proposed that directors be chosen by any group other than shareholders, the government, or employees. The issue of worker participation in corporate governance is beyond the scope of this study.

50. Eileen Shanahan, "Reformers: Urging Business Change," *New York Times*, January 24, 1971, section 3, p. 1.

51. Schwartz, "How Social Activists," p. 73.

52. Donald Schwartz, "The Federal Chartering of Corporations: A Modest Proposal," in *The Unstable Ground*, ed. Sethi, p. 158.

53. Philip W. Moore, "Corporate Social Reform: An Activist's Viewpoint," in *The Unstable Ground*, ed. Sethi, p. 55.

54. With the exception of the issues of corporate military production and American corporate investments in South Africa, groups and individuals explicitly opposed to capitalism have tended not to participate in direct challenges to business. One of the few accounts of the movement for corporate accountability to appear in a radical publication was published by the North American Congress for Latin America in 1972 en-

# References

titled, "Moving Against the Corporations," *NACLA's Latin America and Empire Report*, VI:9 (November 1972), pp. 20–5. For discussions of the relationship between radicals and counter-corporate politics, see "Why Your Radicals Zero in on Business," *Nation's Business*, July 1967, pp. 31–4; and David Vogel, "Corporations and the Left," *Socialist Review* 20 no. 2 (October 1974), pp. 45–66. For a highly exaggerated view of the role of the left in citizen pressures on business—which fails to distinguish between those who propose proxy resolutions and the Weathermen—see William Braznell, Jr., "The Radicals Are Coming—Are You Ready?" *Public Relations Journal*, December 1976, pp. 12–15.

55. Interview with Ralph Nader.

56. Neil Chamberlain, *The Limits of Corporate Responsibility* (New York: Basic Books, 1973), pp. 199–200.

57. Berle, *Twentieth-Century Capitalist Revolution*, p. 62.

# Index

# Index

# Index

# Index

Firestone Tire and Rubber Company, 151
First Chicago Bank, 170
First National City Bank, 36–37, 68, 105, 170, 171
First Pennsylvania Bank, 88, 136, 170, 206
First Spectrum Fund, 148–149
Florence, Reverend Franklin, 32, 33, 35
Florida, 25, 174, 216
FMC Corporation, 90
*Forbes* (magazine), 212
Ford, Henry, 203
Ford Foundation, 112, 184, 208; citizen challenges and, 99; infant formula protests and, 190, 191, 192; institutional investor survey of, 97, 98
Ford Motor Company, 154, 161, 177, 178, 179, 180
Foreign policy, 8, 42
Foreign Relations Committee, 53
Foreign trade, 120, 159–200
Forman, James, 163
*Fortune* (magazine), 18, 210
Fossil fuel plants, 136
Foundations: Campaign GM and, 83; as institutional investors, 87–88, 97–100, 102, 144; Investor Responsibility Research Center (IRRC) and, 101–102; proxy mechanism and, 97–100
Frank and Hirsch Company, 173
"Frankfurt Documents, The," 169
Freedom of Information Act, 18, 157
Freedom Rides, 25
Friedmann, Wolfgang, 5
Furness, Betty, 78

Galbraith, John Kenneth, 10, 68, 220
Gale, Horace, 165
General Dynamics Corporation, 31
General Electric Company, 41, 51, 58, 67, 154, 179
General Foods, 40, 195
General Motors (GM), 31, 68, 210; Arab boycott and, 195; black employment in, 9; board of directors of, 94; Campaign GM against, 71–89; choice of, 72, 209; church groups and, 164; divestment and, 151; employment practices of, 154; impact of protests against, 12; long-range goal of campaign against, 75; 1970 annual meeting of, 84–86; objectives in protest against, 72–73; Project on Corporate Responsibility and, 4; public debate over protests against, 82–83; as public corporation, 10; Reverend Sullivan's role in, 91; Round II of campaign

against, 86–89; SEC and, 79–82; South African protests and, 174–176, 177, 179, 180, 183; tactics used against, 75–79
General Public Utilities, 109, 122
General Telephone and Electronics, 116
Geneva Protocol, 62
Georgeson and Company, 92, 131
Gerstacker, Carl, 47, 48, 49, 54, 65
Gerstenberg, Richard, 207
Getty Oil Company, 184
Ghetto riots, 30
Gilbert brothers, 4, 122
Gillette Company, 155, 177
Gillford, Bernard, 31
Gitlin, Todd, 41
Glide Foundation, 141, 155
Goheen, Robert, 37
Goodman, Walter, 149
Goodyear Tire and Rubber Company, 110, 154, 177, 178
Gordon, Robert, 5
Government: antiwar movement and, 43; business interdependence with, 48–49; citizen protests in anticipation of changes in, 14; civil rights movement and, 40–41; corporation viewed as, 6–9, 219; decline of public authority and, 9–11; government contracts and, 157; military and business interdependence with, 66
Greater Metropolitan Foundation, 57
Greenough, William C., 99
Greensboro, North Carolina, 24
*Guardian* (newsweekly), 51
Gulf Action Project, 185
Gulf Boycott Coalition, 187
Gulf Oil Company: Angola and, 185–189; church groups and, 150, 160; divestment of, 151; impact of protests against, 12; political participation by, 110, 111–112, 114–115; proxy resolutions and, 120; South African investments of, 175, 177, 197; student protests against, 100; women in, 155

Hague Convention of 1907, 62
Hamilton, Walton, 5
Hampshire College, 151
"Handbook for the Corporate Suffragette" (NOW), 153
Handi Wrap, 45
"Handling Protest at Annual Meetings" (Conference Board), 54
Harris, Elizabeth Forsling, 156

# Index

# Index

# Index

# Index

Woolworth sit-ins, 24
World Council of Churches, 186
World Health Organization, 189
World War I, 47–48, 49, 65

Xerox Corporation, 31, 35, 68, 150, 155,
177, 195, 206

Yale University, 83, 97, 98, 184
Young, Reverend Andrew, 186
Young, Dr. Quentin, 45–46
Young, Russell, 110

Zenith Radio Corporation, 134